FROM GOD'S HOUSE
TO A CRACKHOUSE

FROM GOD'S HOUSE TO A CRACKHOUSE

◆

A Recovering Addict's Journey

David G. O'Donnell

iUniverse, Inc.
New York Lincoln Shanghai

FROM GOD'S HOUSE TO A CRACKHOUSE
A Recovering Addict's Journey

iUniverse books may be ordered through booksellers or by contacting:

iUniverse
2021 Pine Lake Road, Suite 100
Lincoln, NE 68512
www.iuniverse.com
1-800-Authors (1-800-288-4677)

The views expressed in this work are solely those of the author and do not necessarily reflect the views of the publisher, and the publisher hereby disclaims any responsibility for them.

ISBN-13: 978-0-595-40769-9 (pbk)
ISBN-13: 978-0-595-85133-1 (ebk)
ISBN-10: 0-595-40769-2 (pbk)
ISBN-10: 0-595-85133-9 (ebk)

Printed in the United States of America

This book is dedicated to the memory of all those addicts who didn't make it. May God rest your souls.

Contents

Pipe Dreams

What happened to my dreams? They went up in crack smoke. I'm not supposed to be where I am at this point in my life. Fifty-three years old, I live in a studio apartment on South Main Street in Worcester, Massachusetts. I live near the PIP Shelter (People In Peril, homeless shelter). My apartment is clean and I have nice things in it. Most of my neighbors are decent and the building management and maintenance men do a terrific job running it. I have thirty-nine months of clean and sober time going for me. But, I'm suppose to be somewhere else at this stage of my life. Why me; why not me? I guess it could be worse. It could be better, too.

When I was twelve years old, I had a paper route. While delivering papers in my hometown neighborhood of Braintree, Massachusetts, not far from Boston, I use to look up at the jet planes that were flying overhead on their way to or from Logan Airport. I told myself that one day I would be flying one of those planes. That was my first dream. A couple years later I had my second dream. To play football in the NFL. Pipe dreams, no, not really. God gave me a special gift, something I was born with. The extraordinary ability to catch a football, any and every pass thrown at me. Couple that with the gift of not allowing any defensive back to cover me, build and bulk up my size a bit, a little luck and I was on my way to the NFL, via high school and college football.

The first thing I had to do was apply to Archbishop Williams High School in Braintree, Massachusetts. At that time, the caliber of football was better in the Catholic Football Conference then it was in my public high school, and many other public high schools. I took the entrance examination, was accepted and was now ready to enter Archie's for my first year of high school, ninth grade.

Enter nephritis with nephrotic syndrome, a chronic kidney disease. One dream down the tubes. My kidney doctor would not allow me to play contact sports. I was not going to allow him to stop me though, I had way too much talent to let someone do that to me. I decided to let it go freshman year. No big deal, it wasn't that important to play freshman football. I had a simple plan for sophomore year. All I had to do was forge my parent's signature on the permission to play football form. They gave us a physical exam, but it was easy to pass.

The only way to detect my kidney disease was through a urine specimen. My urine protein and creatine counts would have given me away. The football physical exam at that time (1966) did not require a urine test. I was on my way to the NFL, so I thought.

Enter one of my brothers, Gene (one year older than me, first born of seven kids; four boys and three girls). We started football training camp somewhere around the middle of August, a few weeks before the school year began. My dream was turning into reality. I was going to impress people, and I did. For about a week in a half, I got to show off my skills, I was turning heads. Nothing I had to work at, a gift from God. My size and build needed improvement. After one of our practices, the coach (Arnie Columbo, great guy, ended up leaving Archies for Brockton High School, Brockton, Massachusetts, where he had a brilliant coaching career) called me over. He said, starting Monday you're going into the weight room and we're going to put you on a special diet to bulk you up a bit (I was 6 ft, 140 lbs. at the time). That was a Thursday afternoon. It was the last time I put on my practice uniform. I never got to put on a game uniform.

We use to practice one-half mile from the school, same field they played their home games at. We would suit up in the locker room at Archies, walk to the field, and then walk back to the locker room after practice. While walking back to the locker room that afternoon in my practice uniform, my brother Gene saw me. He did what he had to do. He told my parents. They called the schools principal, she called the coach. When I showed up for practice Friday morning, the coach called me into his office. I did not like the look on his face. He said, "I understand you have a kidney disease?" I said to myself, oh no, I got caught and the coach is going to start blasting the crap out of me for forging my parents signature. He didn't, instead he said, "What can we do about this?" He knew he had lost a very talented skinny kid from his squad. He was feeling bad for him and he was feeling bad for me. I suggested he call my doctor and talk him into letting me play. He said he couldn't do that, it would be a violation of the rules. He said, "I'm very sorry Dave, you have to turn in your uniform."

My heart sank. My life was over. If someone had offered me a deal where I could play three years of football, and then die, I would have taken it. What was I going to do? Classes started and I lasted about six weeks into my sophomore year at Archies. One morning, I got up from my desk in class, walked out of the classroom without saying anything. Did not even answer the teacher when she asked me what I was doing. I walked into the principals office, and said to her, "I'm out of here, I'm going to Braintree High School." She said, "You can't leave here just like that." I said, "Watch me."

I walked into the office at Braintree High and said, "I just left Archies, how do I sign up for Braintree High?" That was the first major bad decision I had made. There were many more bad decisions to come, many more.

The Former Reverend Paul Shanley Encourages Me To Enter A Seminary

My three years at Braintree High School did not go well. While at Archies in my ninth grade, I made honor roll two out of the four terms. C's, D's and F's were common grades for me at BHS. I consider myself average intelligent, a C student with the ability to get B's if I worked hard at it. One exception was math. I like math, I'm good in math. My father taught math at South Boston High School for thirty years until he was sixty-five. He retired from Southie High, then went to the University of Massachusetts, Boston campus, where he taught math for thirteen more years until he finally retired at age seventy-eight. I inherited some of his math genes.

Speaking of my father, here's a guy who went to work in the coal mines in Lansford, Pennsylvania, after he graduated from high school. In 1935, the year he graduated, his parents had no money to send him or any of his five brothers and five sisters to college. There were no student loans back then like there are today. He did what his father, his uncles, cousins and brothers did. He was a coal miner for six years until WW II broke out. Then he joined the army. During the invasion of Normandy, his right wrist was hit by a mortar shell fragment on Omaha beach. His hand was almost completely blown off. He credits the medics and his other army buddies with saving his hand because of their quick actions taken immediately after he was hit, risking their own lives to save his hand.

But they did save his hand. He can't use it, there is no feeling in his hand, but at least he has it. He spent the next year at the San Diego Veterans Hospital. They grafted skin from his stomach to replace the section of wrist he lost. There is a bulge of skin around his wrist that is noticeable. That doesn't matter to him. He is extremely grateful to his army pals for saving his hand.

He use to be a righty, he is now a lefty. At the Vets hospital, they taught him how to do everything with his left hand. Brush his teeth, shave, the rest of his hygiene and everything else. He does all right for himself. Even his writing isn't too bad. He has had to do a lot of writing on chalkboards throughout his teaching career. It's not the neatest, but it's OK. I kidded him one time about his sloppy hand printing. He told me that before his injury he use to print like me. I have neat hand printing. I guess that's another thing I inherited from him.

He ended up going to college through the G.I. bill. He received his undergraduate, two masters, and forty-five credits towards a Ph.D. at Boston College. He never finished up his doctor of philosophy because he and my mother were having too many kids. He told me that B.C. use to have army barracks on campus. That's where he lived while going to school there.

Getting back to my three years at Braintree High. Sad, sad and sad. My two dreams were shot to crap. I wasn't going to play in the NFL. I wasn't going to fly jet planes. You have to be in almost perfect health to become a jet test/fighter pilot. My kidney disease would exclude me from that. Now what? How about if I start hanging around with the guys who smoke cigarettes, drink beer, and pretty much have a good time? I like that idea. Bob C., God rest his soul, died at forty-one, heroin overdose. Jerry E. blew his brains out at twenty-eight. Johnny M. has been in jail for a long time.

Some of them straightened out. Steve N. became a nurse. Richie V. worked as a ships carpenter at General Dynamics for fifteen years before they shut down. Patrick M. started driving a truck after graduating from high school and thirty-seven years later he is still doing it. Patrick is just about the nicest man I have ever known in my life. Patrick and Beaker (Richie V.) were best buddies. Beaker passed away on March 8, 2003. Patrick did an incredible amount of things for Beaker. He was glad to do so. Beaker was a great guy, one of the best (why do the good always die young?).

Patrick had a lot of talent in gymnastics. I think he could have gone somewhere with that talent. He hated school, could not wait to graduate and was definitely not going to college. He has done all right for himself. He owns a nice home in Whitman, Ma. He is divorced and has two daughters, Andrea and Stephanie. His ex-wife, Cheryl (I set them up) lives with her boyfriend in Pembroke, Ma.

Phil G. was beaten up one night after getting drunk. Doctors performed major plastic surgery to repair his face. He almost died. He does not drink or drug today. He is married and living with his wife, Cheryl, in Hopkinton, Ma.

I have lost track of some of the others.

I hung around with two different groups of guys in high school. Those guys that I just mentioned and another group of guys. Guys who were interested in working hard to get good grades so that they could get into good colleges and try to make good lives for themselves, which they did. I'll talk more about those guys later.

I was arrested twice in my junior year of high school and twice in my senior year, I believe, (not while in school) for being a drunk and disorderly person. I was suspended from school several times. I missed an awful lot of my senior year. Towards the end of senior year my high school principal called my mother. It was around 10:00 a.m. I was sleeping. He told her if I showed up for the last twelve days of the school year he would graduate me. So I did and I got my high school diploma. I know my principal did not want me to repeat my senior year. He did not want to put up with my crap for another year.

Some of my buddies and I pretty much screwed up our three years of high school. With the exception of math, all my other grades were C or lower. We drank a lot of beer, some liquor, and smoked a lot of cigarettes. We drank Romilar CF cough syrup once in a while to get high. We smoked weed (Idid not like it, it made me paranoid) and on occasion tried a couple other things, speed and hashish. A couple of the guys took acid. Acid scared me.

So what now? I'm of average intelligence. I didn't do too bad on my scholastic aptitude tests. I scored around 600 in math and I think about a 450 in English. Should I go to college, get a college degree and try to turn my life around?

Why not, I can do it. Even though my Scholastic Aptitude Tests weren't bad, my high school grades were poor for the most part. I thought it might be best for me to apply to a community college. They were easier to get into and less expensive. After two years at a C.C. I could transfer to a four year school and get my bachelor's degree. Sounds good to me. Easier said than done.

I was accepted to a community college, but continued to be a screw up, even without the help of my high school buddies. Drinking was a regular part of my life. An important part of my life. I looked at my drinking as the glue that held me together. Looking back at it now, I believe I was an alcoholic the very first time I picked up a drink, around age fourteen. It made me feel like the person I could never seem to be. I felt taller, stronger, better looking, more popular and less inhibited. Those feelings never lasted very long. Soon after starting to drink, I would get drunk. But that didn't stop me from doing it again, and again and again.

I signed up for five courses my first semester of college, a full load. By the end of the semester I had either withdrawn, did not complete, or failed three of those courses. I got an A in College Math 101, and a B in Intro to Psychology. An A, a B, an F, an Inc., and a WD. Well, at least I have two successful college courses under my belt. Not bad for a guy who drank almost every Thursday, Friday and

Saturday nights during the semester. Some weeks I drank on Sunday, Monday, Tuesday and Wednesday nights as well. I guess I was already settling for less.

Nobody told me I had to leave school, so I signed up for five more courses at the beginning of second semester. This time I passed three of them, failed one and with drew from one. It appeared that my drinking was having an effect on my college studies. The school I went to, Massasoit Community College, located in Abington, Massachusetts at that time, did not tell me I couldn't come back sophomore year, so I went back. I pretty much did the same thing sophomore year.

Two wasted years at Massasoit Community College, for the most part. I did manage to get ten or eleven college courses under my belt. It took me two years to do one years worth of work? I guess nobody can take those courses away from me.

So, what should I do now? Enter the former Rev. Paul Shanley. I'm not exactly sure when Paul arrived at St. Francis of Assisi church in Braintree, Massachusetts. It was sometime when I was in high school, maybe sophomore year, 1966? He was different from all the priests that I had known up until then. He had long hair and smoked Kool cigarettes. He wore his street clothes when he came to French's Common to talk to us, hang out with us. French's Common was a recreation area, baseball field, basketball court, tennis court, some picnic tables. We use to drink beer and play basketball and cards there at night. It was one of our hang outs.

I got to know Paul pretty good. We got along well. There were suspicions among us that Paul might be gay. None of us had any idea that he might also be a pedophile. The one time that Paul brought up the subject of homosexuality while I was alone with him, I told him I hated gays (not the word I used). He never brought it up again and we got along fine. One of my brothers is gay and at the time I hated him for it. Today, I love him. He is a kind, good, hard working man. He owns a nice home in Plymouth, Ma. Alcoholics Anonymous tells me to live and let live, and I do these days, to the best of my ability.

One day, Paul said, "What are you going to do now that community college didn't work out for you?" I said, "I'm going to join the marines." He said, good for you. One of the guys in my neighborhood, Gerry Bradley, had joined the marines. He was a couple of years older than me, but he took me under his wing. He saved me from Kevin C. one day. A huge guy who I got wise with, being the punk that I could be at times. Kevin was walking down the street with a big smile on his face. He had just bought a brand new pair of bright white sneakers. Kev had a huge stomach. As he got closer to us, he said, "What do you think of my new sneakers?" I said, "How can you see them?" I think Kevin was really going to kill me until Gerry stepped in and saved my butt. Kevin never did say much of anything to me after that. He couldn't stand me. And visa versa. Gerry was the captain of the Braintree High hockey team his senior year. I didn't get to hang around with him much because he was three years older than me. I think that if we were the same age we would have been best buddies. He was a beautiful person. He was killed in Vietnam (why do the good always die young?). I still have his marine corps picture in my wallet, one of the few things I have not lost throughout my years of addictions.

My cousin, Billy DiNatale (Italian side of the family) was a marine. I looked up to Billy. I admired him. I still do even though I have not seen or heard from him in ten years. He is a Massachusetts State Police Officer.

Now it was my turn to be a marine. Not quite, I forgot about my kidney disease. I failed the physical exam; they 4F'd me. Physically unfit for all branches of the United States Armed Forces. How about that!!! Now what the hell am I going to do?

While attending community college for those two years, I had been hanging around with my other group of high school buddies. Guys who had a lot of ambition. Tyracks (Tom Rowan), a successful salesman who has been in all fifty states through his sales jobs. Tyracks is a nickname. Tom and I gave all our buddies nicknames. Tyracks went to the same community college I went to. He did a good job there. He transferred to Bentley College where he received his undergraduate degree. He is quite a character, more so than myself. He is a good, kind, compassionate guy who would give you the shirt off his back and buy you a new one if it didn't fit. He is a witty, funny, humorous, sharp man. Very sharp man. We voted him class clown our senior year of high school. His wife, Terry, a Braintree girl, is just about the prettiest girl to ever come from the town, a real knockout and a sweetheart of a person. She graduated from Bridgewater State College and got a job with the phone company where she had been for many years. She is now a school teacher. They moved to Broomfield, Colorado a long time ago and fell in love with that part of the country. Terry took a transfer to the phone company out there. They're still there raising their two gorgeous daughters, Katie, a freshman at the University of Wyoming and Tracy, a junior in high school.

Tyracks has always tracked me down over the years. He has called my folks just about every year to find out where I was (sometimes my folks didn't know). He would try calling me if I had a phone, and ask me how I was doing? I was never doing good. I remember Tyracks calling me one time when I lived in

Brockton, Massachusetts. It was the only time I ever had a phone during my five years in Brockton. He said, "Chelcherooni (or Chelch, my nickname), it's Tyracks." I was sick from drinking and drugging. I said, "Chelcherooni just left", and I hung up and unplugged the phone. Before I hung up I could hear Tyracks saying, "Dave, don't hang up, talk to me."

Tyracks has always told me to never give up on myself, to hang in there no matter what. His Mother, God rest her soul, would tell me the same thing. Mrs. Rowan (Tyracks called his mother Bigsy. I use to call Mrs. Rowan, Mrs. Bigsy) told me on several occasions, in a kind way, to straighten out and do something positive with my life. She was a beautiful lady (why do the good always die young?).

I don't know if Mrs. Rowan and Tom know how much their encouragement meant to me. It meant a lot. Sometimes, a little encouragement can make all the difference in the world. In their case, it was a lot of encouragement.

One time, I was building a shed in the back yard for my father. I was trying to cut an opening in the plywood for a window. The saber saw blades kept breaking on me as I was trying to make the corner cuts. I forgot to drill holes first in the corners. Tyracks and one of his younger brothers, Soupy (Paul), stopped by. I was down to my last saber saw blade. Tyracks said, "Chelch, you're not doing it right, let me show you how." He tried rounding the corner with the saber saw and broke my last blade. Tyracks said, "Chelch, you shouldn't be wasting your money on cheap blades. I'd like to stay longer but I have to get Soupy to soccer practice." I said, "Thanks for stopping by guys." Soupy said, "Ya, I'll bet you're real happy we stopped by."

Kennard (Rick Kennedy), great guy, one of my closest friends. Rick is a very intelligent man. After graduating from Braintree High School somewhere near the top of our class, he went to the Naval Academy in Annapolis, Maryland. His plebe (freshman) year went well. The summer after plebe year, they went on a training cruise. Something happened on that cruise. I'm not sure exactly what happened, but Rick didn't feel the same about the Naval Academy any more. It might have had something to do with his father being lost at sea. His father was a navigator for a major airlines. His plane went down in the ocean, no survivors.

Rick finished his second year at the academy and then resigned. He finished up his undergraduate work at Boston University. He went on to get an M.B.A. He has held some great jobs with some great outfits., One of those jobs he held was Human Resources Manager for the Boston Gas Company (currently Key-span). Rick got me a job working for the gas company. It was the best job I ever had. I lasted twenty-six months before they fired me.

I was a full blown crack head, had been faithfully smoking crack for about three years when they hired me. Rick knew I liked to drink. He knew nothing about my crack habit.

I remember one time when we were in high school, I came up with the bright idea to paint Mrs. Kennedy's hall way. Rick bought the paint and I started painting. We forgot to ask Mrs. Kennedy if it would be OK. She was at work. Her garage was attached to her house. The inside garage door opened into the kitchen. When she pulled into the garage, she noticed the inside door was wide open. I opened it to let the paint fumes escape. She entered the house cautiously, looked down the hallway and saw me painting. I said, "Hi Mrs. K. I hope you like the color." She shook her head in disbelief and said, "Where's Ricky?" I said, "He's in the recreation room studying." The recreation room use to be the cellar until we remodeled it. Wall paneling, dropped ceiling, carpeting. We wired it, built a bar with padded arm rests (thanks to Rick's sister Corinne, who knew how to do that). Mrs. Kennedy bought pool and ping pong tables, and some sofas. It really came out nice. I played a lot of chess games down there with Rick and his older brother Bill. I could never beat either one of them and I'm a decent chess player. Bill is as sharp as his brother, Rick, a very successful attorney who went to my fathers alma mater, B.C. to get his law degree.

He did his undergraduate work at Duke University. Bill was the captain of his Braintree High School chess team.

Mrs. Kennedy yelled downstairs to Rick, "Why is Dave painting the hallway?" Rick said, "Because he likes to paint, it keeps him out of trouble." Mrs. Kennedy said, "Do you think one of you guys could have asked me if it would be all right?" Rick said, "We forgot." I said, "You didn't tell me if you like the color?" She turned around and went into the kitchen to make herself a cup of coffee … or was it a drink?

I set Rick up with his first wife, Susan. She was from Medford, Massachusetts, the sister of one of the upper classmen at St. Johns Seminary, where I ended up going to school for two years. She was a beauty queen, a real pleasure to the eyes.

Kennard, like Tyracks, has stayed in touch with me over the years, or has at least tried. It was not easy to keep track of me. I let him down when I was fired from the Boston Gas Company. He went to a lot of trouble to get that job for me. An awful lot of people would like to work for Boston Gas, or any utility. He was working somewhere else at the time that he got me into the gas company. He had to call in some favors.

The first time I saw him after I had been fired, I said, "I blew it Rick, Boston Gas fired me for unreliability due to drinking and drugging." Rick said, "Have you drank or drugged today?" I said, "Not yet." He said, "Try not to for the rest of today. Give me a call tomorrow and let's go out for a coffee and a sandwich on me (it was always on Rick, I never had any money)."

They had sent me away to three different rehabilitation centers in twenty-six months. Boston Gas was unbelievably good to me. Some of my co-workers could not believe how many chances I was getting, considering how new I was. I got along well with Stu Hemingway. He was in charge of all gas servicemen, my boss' boss (my boss was Coley Joyce, the best boss I ever had in my life. Another man I let down).

Stu grabbed me one day and said, "What is your problem? You have a great job with a great company. You're a nice guy, you're good with your hands, you know what you're doing when it comes to your job, but you haven't got a clue when it comes to what you're doing to yourself with that crack shit. We're going to end up firing you. That's not the bad news. The bad news is that you're going to die! Or maybe for you, that would be good news. It would get you out of the hell you're living in right now."

I mentioned that conversation to Jack Keefe, my shop steward and my best friend at the gas company. I would have to write a book to tell you all the things Jack did for me while I was there. What a great guy, what a great friend, still is. Jack and his son, Matt, visited me at a rehab one time, a few years after I had been fired.

Jack asked me if I had learned anything from what Stu said to me. I said, "Of course I did," but I hadn't.

I really miss some of those guys at the gas company. They bent over backwards to try to talk some sense into me. Paul Richardson, Paul Hannon (former president of our union), Pat O'Donnell (no relation to me), Mike Griffin, Vinnie S., Hermon Wilkinson, Marty Coyne, Danny Picard, Bill Ahearn, Mucker, George Manet and Vinnie the Best, and some others. It would be nice to see them again sometime.

Jack Keefe recently lost his nephew, Johnny Mullin. Johnny and I had not hung around together a lot up until we both ended up in Naukeg Rehabilitation Center in Ashburnham, Massachusetts, in November, 2001. For the three weeks that I was there and I believe the two weeks Johnny was there, we did many things together. We became friends. We talked about Jack a lot, just the good stuff, we left out the bad stuff. I was sad when Jack told me that Johnny had passed away (why do the good always die young?).

Kennard and Tyracks were big influences on my life. But I guess the biggest influence on my life at that time was Plank (Steve Burke). What a heck of a guy.

What an athlete. He played basketball and baseball all three years at Braintree High School. We use to play tag football at Thayer Academy in Braintree. Tyracks had a great arm, a good quarterback. Plank was a good wide receiver and he had good size, 6 ft, 2inches, 185 lbs. Neither one of them wanted to play football for the high school team. I never could figure that one out. Had Tyracks quarterbacked the team and Plank played wide receiver, Braintree High would have had a good football team instead of the lousy team they had during our years there.

Plank came from a family of thirteen, six boys, five girls and their parents. I got along with all thirteen of them. Why they all accepted me into their lives is beyond me. I know that my true nature is to be a kind, generous, compassionate, caring human being. But back then, there were way too many times when I was a punk, a troublemaker, an instigator. I will be forever grateful to the Burke family for seeing something in me at that time that a lot of other people could not see. Plank's older brother, Big Al (oldest boy), is an author. He has written four books. "Firewatch", "Dead Wrong", "Driven" and "Getting Away With Murder" (Alan Dennis Burke). I read "Firewatch". It was a decent book. Newsweek magazine gave his book a nice review. Al is also a reporter for a Salem, Massachusetts newspaper.

Plank ended up going to Suffolk University on an athletic scholarship. He played baseball and basketball all four years there. He was the captain of the baseball team in his senior year. He received his undergraduate degree in journalism. I remember a year or so after he graduated he had put on a few pounds. I changed his nickname to Tank. He lives with his wife, Sandra and their two children, Matthew (Plank, Jr.), and their daughter (I think her name is Sarah) on Cape Cod. Plank Jr. recently graduated from the University of Massachusetts, Amherst campus. Sarah is a senior there.

I dated one of Plank's younger sisters, Mary Ellen, a couple of times. I ended up messing up that relationship. I pulled into the Burke family driveway one evening to pick Mary Ellen up for a date. One of Plank's younger brothers, Albie, was looking out the living room window. He saw me open my car door and then stumble out of my car and almost fall onto the driveway. Mary Ellen did not go out with me that night or any other night after that …

Mr. and Mrs. Burke, God rest their souls, have both passed away. Mrs. Burke was one of the kindest, nicest ladies I have ever known in my life.

Cookie Man (Gerry Cook), or Gigatini, Walker, Cookie, Gig or the Gig Man. We gave Gerry several nicknames. Gig is my favorite. He went to Eastern Nazarene College in Quincy, Massachusetts. He landed a job with Hewlett Packard after graduating, where he has been his whole career. If there ever was a guy who had that certain competitiveness to play in the NFL, besides myself, it was Gigatini. He's another one, besides Tyracks and Plank, who, had he decided to play football for our high school team, would have made Braintree High a much better football team. No one could cover me better on a pass play than the Gig Man.

Not even the defensive backs who tried to cover me in the Boston Park Football League where I played for the South Boston Chiefs for one season. There was some talent in that league. Most of those guys played high school football, some played college football and a few had played some semi-pro football. Without sounding too cocky, oh what the hell, with sounding too cocky, I turned some heads in that league. The big problem with that league was that a lot of things that should have been called for penalties, weren't. Guys knew that they could get away with some dirty stuff. We all had full time jobs. We played football in our spare time. One dirty hit and we were out of work. We were out of a pay check.

Had Gerry played high school football, he probably would have received a full, four year football scholarship to a Division II college football team. He didn't have to go that route. He has done well for himself. He married Tom's wife Terry's sister, Patty. A beautiful lady just like her sister, Terry. Patty is a school teacher. They live in Braintree, Massachusetts. Their son, Kevin, is a sophomore at Providence College. Their daughter, Molly, I believe is a college freshman.

My man, Don O'Leary. I could always count on Don, or the Duck, to cheer me up no matter what. He was always in a good mood, great disposition, fanatical sports nut and another good athlete who played on his college baseball team.

Don did his undergraduate work at Bridgewater State College. He has been a science teacher his whole career.

Tyracks put together a softball team for us one time. We had a pretty good team. I remember one game when Don was on second base, I was on first base. Cookie Man was up at the plate. Cookie lined a single to center. Don scored from second, but it was a close play at the plate. I ended up on third base.

The catcher was arguing the call at the plate with the umpire and he did not call time out. The catchers back was to me so I decided to sneak home. By the time the catcher saw me coming, it was too late, another close play at the plate. I slid head first stretching my arms and fingers out as far as I could. I was barely safe. Don got a huge kick out of that one.

Don dated and ended up marrying a real sweetheart from Braintree, Patti. Not only a good looking lady, but, also a gorgeous personality. She is a Special Education Assistant. I remember the time when I asked Patti to go to the prom with me. I almost had a heart attack when she said yes. I took her to a Red Sox game another time. Patti said, "All the umpires names are Al." I said, "A.L. is not their name, Patti. It stands for American League."

I remind her of that every now and then. If I hadn't been such a screw up, who knows, maybe Patti and me instead of Patti and the 'Duck'. From one D. O. to another D. O., you're a lucky guy, Don. And Patti is a lucky lady, too. They have three kids, Kerry Ann, Shaun and Kevin. They have a nice home in Pembroke, Massachusetts.

Patti recently lost one of her older brothers, Bobby. Bobby and my older brother, Gene, were friends. Because of my smartass mouth, Bobby bailed me out of trouble one time. I will never forget him for that. He was always kind and nice to me (why do the good always die young?).

Rich Pompeo or 'The Arm' was another talented athlete. He had good size, 6', 2", around 190 lbs. He too, would have made a difference had he played for the high school football team. I remember one time we were warming up before a tag football game at Thayer Academy. Tyracks and I were talking. Rich was a few yards away from us when he threw a pass that must have traveled fifty yards in the air, almost a perfect spiral. Tyracks and me looked at each other and T said, "Did you see that pass?" I said, "Ya, but I don't believe it." Rich looked at us, winked and said, "Don't worry, T, I'll leave the quarterbacking to you."

'The Arm' landed a good job with the Sears company after he graduated from high school. He still works there today as a supervisor. He has a nice personality. He is a pleasure to hang around with. He lives with his wife, Ellie (they have been married for about thirty years) and their kids in Plymouth, Massachusetts.

John Cumming (J. C. Nickel) is a very nice guy. He never bothered anyone. He hardly ever gave anyone a hard time. He did his own thing and was happy doing it. He decided to go to college in the southwest, the University of Houston. I'm pretty sure he spent one or two years there before coming back east. He had some nice stories to tell us about the experiences that he had with folks in that different part of the country. I use to enjoy hearing about people, stuff, things in different parts of this country. He enjoyed the time he spent out there. I know that they enjoyed him.

One of the guys was kidding around with J. C. one night. We were in Rick's recreation hall. I think that it was Duck (Don O'Leary). Don said, "You know something, J. C.? Not only are you dull, but, you are the cause of dullness in others!" Not one to get flustered too often, J. C. said, "Let me tell you something, Duck. Some people cause happiness when they arrive. Others, like yourself, when you leave!!!"

Three of the ladies, Patti O'Leary, Carolyn Royce and Pat O'Connor along with J. C. and Rick (Kennedy) went on a cross country trip one summer. The five of them drove to California, in one car … Once they got to California, Patti flew back home. She missed Don. All five of them got together for a reunion not too long ago. Both Rick and Carolyn told me that they had a pretty good time talking about the cross country trip that they had taken many years ago.

JC. lives with his wife, Ellen, in Hull, Massachusetts. They have been married for a long time.

Those seven guys and I made up the eight ball.

So anyway, I'm not going to be a marine. I stopped by the rectory one day to tell Paul the bad news. He made what I thought to be at that time a nutty suggestion. He said, "Why don't you take a ride out to St. John's Seminary in Brighton (Massachusetts). Drive around the grounds and then park your car somewhere and walk around for awhile.

Spend some quiet time there with yourself. You're going to love the scenery. The buildings and the grounds are gorgeous." I said, "OK, you want me to try to figure out what I'm going to do with the next part of my life in a peaceful, quiet surrounding?" Then, he really hit me with a lulu. He said, "I would like to see you apply for admission to St. John's Seminary." I was staring at him. I don't know why, but I still remember what he was wearing. He was wearing sneakers, dungarees and a navy blue polo shirt. He had his legs crossed on top of his desk. He was leaning back in his chair smoking a Kool cigarette. His hair was down to his shoulders. He wasn't a bad looking guy.

I remember that a lady friend of mine told me that she thought Fr. Shanley looked like Gregory Peck. I said, "What are you nuts! I meant to say, what are you nuttier than usual!" I use to joke around with him a lot, and visa versa. He said, "No, I'm no more nuttier than usual. If you go to St. John's, you are going to turn your life around." I said, "That statement alone is nuttier than usual because both you and me know that St. John's would not accept me." He said, "How do you know until you try?" I said, "I don't want to be a priest anyway, nothing personal." He said, "You don't have to go there with the intention of positively wanting to become a priest. The first four years are college, same as any other college. Your major area of concentration will be philosophy." I chuckled a little bit to myself when he said that. One of my younger brothers, Billy, use to say, "Dave the Philosopher" once in awhile. I guess I could go off on a tangent trying to explain certain things sometimes.

Paul went on to say, "You will get a good education in a great environment. There will be some restrictions there that you didn't encounter at Massasoit

Community College. They will be to your benefit. You need some rules in your life right now. After four years at St. Clement's Hall (the college), then, if you want to, you can go across the ball field to Bishop Peterson Hall for four more years of theology, leading to ordination." I said, "So, if I apply to St. John's Seminary, I tell them that I don't want to become a priest. I just want a good education?" He said, "Not exactly. You might want to mention that you're considering the priesthood." I said, "It doesn't matter anyway, Paul. They would never accept me." He lit up a Kool and blew out his smoke. He said, "Don't be so sure about that." I lit up a Marlboro, blew out my smoke and said nothing.

Paul Shanley, a former Roman Catholic priest, was defrocked by the Archdiocese of Boston after being indicted for child molestation. In February, 2005, he was convicted of child molestation. He was sentenced to twelve to fifteen years in prison.

Two Years At St. John's Seminary

I wrote to St. John's Seminary requesting an admissions application. That was in the spring of 1971. I had been out of high school for two years. The application arrived, I filled it out and sent it back. I received a letter from the Dean of Admissions, Fr. Author Driscoll (Dribsey-good basketball player). I thought that the letter would say, thanks but no thanks. It didn't. Instead, Fr. Driscoll, who became my freshman year biology teacher, gave me a date and time for an entrance interview. At first, I thought maybe he had made a mistake and he did not look close enough at my application. Especially the part where I had been arrested four times (I believe-three or four times), during my high school years for being a drunk and disorderly person (twice junior and senior years). But what the heck, I use to be a decent catholic, I have a lot of respect for the church and most of the folks involved with it. I was curious about what I would be asked in the interview and what St. John's looked like. I wondered if it was as nice a place as Paul Shanley said it was.

I still hadn't said anything to my family about St. John's. I wasn't sure if I should since St. John's wasn't going to accept me anyway. Might be a good time to say something now. I was working in the IF's (Iron Fist-my father's nickname) back yard one day. The IF was on his way to Richardi's, a local sub shop. Richardi's and Double GG's had the best grinders in Braintree. He said, "Do you want me to pick you up a grinder?" I said, "Get me a steak bomb, Dad, and I've got an interview for admission at St. John's Seminary next week." I was a joker much of the time with a lot of people. The IF chuckled at that one not believing me for a second.

He said, "Large steak bomb and a 2 liter jug of Coke." He didn't have to ask me what size grinder or what flavor drink. Even though I was a string bean, my appetite was huge. I was blessed with an over active metabolism and I was always doing something to burn off calories. The only thing I drank was Coca-Cola, when I wasn't drinking beer. I said, "And tell them that I want extra steak, and did you hear what I said about St. John's Seminary?" He said, "That's right, Dave, that's right ..."

My friend, Bob C., God rest his soul, gave my father his nickname. Bob and I were walking down one of the high school corridors one day. As we walked by Ron S. (Snitchel) and Greg D. (aren't I gorgeous looking), Snitchel stuck out his leg and tripped me. I stumbled a little bit and would have turned to him and said, good one Snitch, I'll get you back later and then kept walking.

But, I was with Bob, I couldn't let it go. I had an image to keep up. Snitch was a small guy, good kid, clowned around a lot. We always got along OK. I slept over his house a couple times when we were younger. I walked up to him, grabbed him by his collar, half serious, half kidding around, and shook him a little bit … just as one of the teachers was coming down the hall. Mr. Reynolds, my math teacher of all subjects. I was a good student in his class. Mr. Reynolds walked up to me as I was brushing off Snitch and telling him what a good kid he was, and said, "You know where you have to go, O'Donnell, don't you? I said, "I'm on my way, Mr. Reynolds." I went to the Vice-Principal's office, Mr. Palsits. I had been there before.

I was suspended from school for three days for initiating physical contact on another student. I left Mr. Palsits' office and headed for Richardi's to get a grinder and think of a good story to tell the IF. I had my grinder, went home and told my mother what happened. She wasn't happy. She said, "You better stay here until your father gets home." He usually got home from Southie High around 3:00. He came home and my mother told him what happened. He came out to the back yard where I was working. He said, "Your mother told me you were suspended from school for fighting." I said, "That's true Dad, but …" before I could say anything else he said, "That's too bad", and he walked away. I wasted time thinking up a good story to tell him. I saw Bob that evening at the Braintree Five Corners Mister Donut store, one of our hang outs. He said, "How come you're not grounded?" I told him about my father's response to my suspension. Bob said, "The Iron Fist." I said, "What?" He said, "That's your father's nickname from now on. The Iron Fist."

That incident along with one other contributed to his nickname. The IF taught CCD (Catholic Christian Doctrine) at St. Francis of Assisi Parish in Braintree for several years. He taught eighth graders. I wasn't looking forward to being in his class with all my buddies, some of them being the clowns that they could be at times. I knew I would behave myself and surprisingly enough, Tyracks behaved himself in my father's class, too. I guess out of respect for my father and me.

Tyracks and my father got along well, as I did with Tyrack's father, Chico. Kennard always behaved himself, when appropriate to do so. He is a gentleman, knew when and when not to goof around. Plank, same as Kennard. Gig, 'The Arm', Duck and J.C. Nickel were from different religions and/or parishes. But there were still plenty of others there to take up the slack.

One evening in CCD class, the IF gave us a lesson to read. The IF looked tired. I think he had had a long day. It looked like he was falling asleep behind his desk. My buddy Steve N., sitting to my right, turned to me and said, "Dave, watch this." I said, "Oh God" to myself.

Steve got down on his hands and knees and started crawling towards the IF's desk. The desk was open in the middle, you could see the IF's legs and feet. Steve took out his pen and started writing something on the IF's shoes, then crawled back to his chair undetected by the IF.

I said, "What did you write on my father's shoes?" He said, "F___ you." I said, "Come on Steve, you can tell me what you wrote on his shoes." He said, "F___ you." I said, "You're not going to tell me?" He said, "I told you, Dave. I wrote f___ on one shoe and you on the other shoe." I said, "I'll be a son of a guy who has f___ you written on his shoes."

I don't remember the exact date that I had my interview at St. John's, but, I think that it was toward the end of June. I was going to drive there by myself until my father offered to take me, once he realized that I wasn't kidding about my interview. I asked him if he knew anything about Brighton. He said, "What are you looking for?" I said, "St. John's Seminary." He said, "You were serious about your interview?" I said, "Ya, hard to believe isn't it?" He said, "No it isn't hard to believe. I hope they accept you and let me take you in, I know where it is." I said, "They told me to prepare myself for at least a one hour interview, maybe longer." He said, "My school year is over. I don't start my summer job (he always had a summer job after his school year ended-not easy raising seven kids) until next week. What else do I have to do?" I said, "Thanks a lot, Dad, I appreciate it."

It was a nice day. It was a nice ride out there. I had been smoking cigarettes since I was fourteen. My father would not allow me to smoke in his car, or around him for that matter. He said, "Go ahead and light up if you want to." I said, "I quit." I had not had a cigarette in a couple of weeks. He said, "Good for you." I said, "I doubt it if anyone smokes in a seminary." He said, "No, that's not going to be the case. You will see some priests and some students who are smokers. But, try to stay off them if you can, for your own good and the good of others around you who would be affected by your second hand smoke." I stayed away from cigarettes for twelve years before picking up the habit again when I was going through a divorce.

We arrived at St. John's. Paul Shanley was right. We had time to drive through the campus before my interview. The grounds and buildings were absolutely gorgeous, a different world. The Cardinal's residence was on the grounds. Humberto Medieros, at that time. I couldn't get over how pretty everything was. My father had seen the campus from Commonwealth Avenue, but had never driven through it. He was impressed. He said, "What a nice place for a new beginning." I said, "I don't think they're going to take me, Dad." He said, "Try not to go into the interview with that attitude. Be honest with them, and be positive with them. Let them know you want to be a student here. Think of yourself as an asset for St. John's Seminary." That was going to be hard for me to do, but I was going to give it a heck of a shot. I really liked the campus, a lot.

I'm sure that my father's encouraging words and our drive through the campus changed my attitude for my interview. Instead of going to an interview because I was curious, now I was going to an interview because I wanted to be a student at St. John's Seminary. I had nothing against living at home with my folks, my brothers and sisters. It was a good environment. We were middle class. We didn't have any fancy possessions, but we had everything we needed.

I had good friends in the town. I know that at times, I had been a disappointment to some of them. I had been a disappointment to some of them not because I hadn't lived up to their standards. I am who I am. I was not a people pleaser, most of the time, then and now. But, I was a disappointment to them because they were on my side. They wanted to see me do well. I was young and I was making some bad decisions. I was confused. I can remember wondering why anyone would want to have anything to do with me. Not because I thought of myself as a bad guy. I didn't. I thought of myself as someone who didn't have anything to offer to anyone. I had nothing to bring to the table. I might as well hang around with myself and not bother with anyone else. My self-confidence and self-esteem were not there like they were when I had dreams.

Here was an opportunity for me to start fresh, living away from home (I think almost every young person who wants to go to college looks forward to living there, if it is financially possible) in a good environment. The tuition at St. John's at the time was $1,000.00 for the year. Not a lot of money for an education, room and board. Nothing compared to other schools. Some parishes would pick up the tab if one of their parishioners was going there and the family didn't have the money. I hadn't been to church in years so I couldn't ask my parish to do that for me. One thousand dollars is one thousand dollars that I didn't have. My father told me not to worry about the tuition, he and my mother would take care of it. Thank God for my parents. Even though lack of funds would not prevent a student from being accepted at St. John's, I knew that it had to be paid eventually and I felt a lot better when my father told me that it would be taken care of.

We drove through the campus twice. That gave me a chance to get a good look at the grounds and buildings (I'm of average intelligence, a little better than average in math, and for me to be able to absorb things, it usually takes 2 times). Bishop Peterson Hall, the School of Theology (where the guys go after four years of undergraduate studies at St. Clement's Hall, for four more years of theological studies)—holy mackerel. How do I describe it. It looks like something that was built a long time ago, and is going to be around for a longer time. Granite block construction, corner towers with cones on top, ivy, fancy front doors. I remember saying to my father, "Hey Dad, want me to install a set of front doors like those for you and Ma?" He said, "I'd have to get a second mortgage on the house, Dave, to pay for them."

There were four entrances into St. John's. Bishop Peterson Hall's address was 127 Lake Street. Lake Street came into the seminary grounds from off of Washington Street near downtown Brighton, not too far from St. Elizabeth's Hospital. We did most of our shopping at the businesses on Washington and Market Streets in downtown Brighton.

Coming in from Washington Street, Lake Street went for maybe an eighth of a mile. It was lined with one beautiful tree after another. Then, you came across two tennis courts on the left and Bishop Peterson Hall on the right. A little further down on the right was the new (at that time) library. It was a nice looking building. Set back from Lake Street a little bit and tough to see in the daylight with all the trees around it. You couldn't miss seeing it at night when it was all lit up.

It was a two story, concrete design, rectangular structure. The first story was smaller than the second with a a lot of large windows. The second story had windows around the entire perimeter that were twice as high as they were wide. Because of those style windows and the way the second story extended out over the first story, it looked to me like a rectangular space ship at night when it was lit up.

I ended up spending many hours at that library during my two years at St. John's. I think it had a name, but I can't remember who or what it was. The windows on the second floor were private study rooms and some music rooms. You could reserve a room for yourself for a period of time if you wanted to leave all your paperwork, books, notes, etc. there while you were working on a project. I enjoyed the time I spent at that library. I had been to the Braintree Public Library a few times when I was a student at Archbishop Williams High School in my ninth grade and about six weeks into my tenth grade. I do not remember going to the library during my tenth through twelfth grades, when I was a student at Braintree High School. If Braintree High School had a library, I didn't know where it was.

Let me think … a little further down Lake Street, on the left was the gymnasium (thank you, God). It was an older building, but the full size basketball court was in medium condition. I had a lot of enjoyable times there. I'm an OK b-ball player. I use to love the game, love the running up and down the court, the competitiveness, the working up a good sweat, having a great time with the guys. There is a lot to be said for playing sports. There were two handball/racquetball courts downstairs in that building, as well. There were some priests who played handball on a regular basis and had been playing handball for many years. I played against a few of them and I always lost to them (handball is a tremendous workout). I learned two things when playing a priest in handball. In the handball court, a priest is no longer a priest. And … a game is a game, no hard feelings afterward.

I would say more, but, you know how they say what happens in Vegas stays in Vegas … I'm just kidding. The games were rough. Pushing, shoving, blocking, swearing. Doing whatever it took to win. A great outlet for stress, a great game … would have been nice if I won a game once in awhile. I would lose in handball on a regular basis to Fr. Gerry Dorgan. He was my professor for Ancient Literature, Freshman Composition, English Poetry, Shakespeare and Modern American Novel my freshman and sophomore years (I'm looking at my transcript. I had Fr. Dorgan for at least one subject each of my four semesters at St. John's). I also played against Fr. Ray Devitere, my Theology of Roman Realism professor and Fr. Bernie McGlaughlin, who taught us The Church As A Faith Community.

There was one guy who I could beat in handball toward the end of my sophomore year. Fr. Ron Coyne, a third year Theology student when I was a freshman. Ron had the least amount of handball experience under his belt out of the guys that I played against. I have always been competitive. Even though Ron beat me in most of our games, we had some great battles. I tried doing different things to psych Ron out. I think that he got a kick out of some of the things that I use to pull, sometimes, not all the time.

Like the time I took a black magic marker and wrote on the back of my white T-shirt, "Ron Sucks In Handball", and wore it during one of our games. That plan back fired on me. He gave me a hell of a whooping that game and told me to retire the T-shirt. I think what got him more upset than me wearing the T-shirt during our game, was the fact that I wore the T-shirt on my walk from St. Clement's Hall to the gym. I walked by the faculty garage, the ball fields, the tennis courts, Bishop Peterson Hall and the Library. St. John's Seminary was a small community. Everyone knew everyone. We knew a lot about each other. Who hung around with who, what we did. Some of the folks I walked past on my way to the gym got a kick out of my T-shirt. Can't say the same for Ron.

He's a darn good guy. I know he had been an asset to his church in Weymouth, St. Albert The Great. The Archdiocese of Boston closed it down. I saw the story on TV recently. I saw Ron on TV. It was the first time that I had seen him since I left St. John's. Because of the hard work of Fr. Coyne and St. Albert The Great's parishioners, the church was re-opened. I think about good guys like Ron. There are a lot of guys like Ron who are good priests. What a shame that there are also some sick guys who became priests. Pedophiles who have cast a dark shadow on all clergy. What an awful shame …

Further down Lake Street on the right was Williams Hall. A place to hold meetings, conferences and retreats. Fr. James Haddad use to be in charge of Williams Hall. I got along well with him. My father met him one time when he came to visit me.

My father and Fr. Haddad hit it off pretty good. They had something in common. If I'm not mistaken, Fr. Haddad was a BC alumnus, same as the IF.

Across Lake Street from Williams Hall is the Cardinal's residence, or the Archbishop's residence, depending on his status, whoever is the leader of the Archdiocese of Boston. I was never inside, but I did make it to the back door one time. I hand delivered a letter from one of the St. Clement's Hall faculty members to Cardinal Medieros's assistant, Fr. Tom Daily (there were two Fr. Tom Daily's at St. John's; Cardinal Medieros's assistant, Big T, and Little T, a resident faculty professor at St. Clement's Hall, who taught French and who, along with Fr. Arthur Driscoll, hardly ever missed being at a Boston Bruins home game. You may have seen the two of them on TV during a Bruins telecast; they were the two priests who sat behind the Bruins bench).

I heard on the news that the church either sold or was thinking about selling the cardinal's residence for fifty million dollars. I know that there is a small TV studio inside. I wonder if there's an in-floor swimming pool inside as well.

The Lake Street entrance to the Cardinal's residence leads to the back and side doors, if my memory serves me correctly. The front door driveway entrance comes in off of Commonwealth Avenue. That is the last building on the left. I'm trying to think … Across from the Cardinal's residence on Lake Street, the second to the last building on the right is the Chancellory building where they conduct church business for the Archdiocese of Boston. I think there might be a

Catholic Charities office in there, a terrific outfit. They do a lot of things for the less fortunate. I have been in one of their detoxes on Main Street in Brockton. I think that I've been in that detox about four or five times. There is one more building on Lake Street on the right after the Chancellory, that I had never been in. I forget what it was and I think it may have been vacant.

Right after that building Lake Street exits to a residential side street, fifty feet before Commonwealth Avenue and the Boston College trolley car station. I remember that there were a few stores across from the the Boston College trolley station. There was a Brigham's store there and a grinder shop. We were fed a lot better than medium at St. John's. Very nice meals. But, I had nothing against getting a grinder once in a while. Those stores were on the St. John's side of the trolley car tracks. On the other side of the tracks was Boston College. Another beautiful campus on a much, much larger scale. There is a big Catholic church there before you enter B. C.'s campus. I can't remember the name of it. Boston College, one of the schools where I dreamed about playing football.

My father would take Gene (oldest kid in our family, one year older than me) and me to at least one football game a season starting when we were around ten and eleven. Every now and then my mother would come with us. She loves football and most other sports. Crazy Esther (my mothers nickname) would always wear one of her goofy hats. She loves goofy hats. Once in awhile my sister Sheila (one year younger than me, she did what I didn't do; she graduated from Archbishop Williams High School with honors) would come with us.

My other two sisters, Barbara (three years younger than me) wasn't interested and Mary (baby in the family, I think around eleven years younger than me) was too young at the time. I can't remember if my brother Kevin (two years younger than me) ever came to a game with us. My brother Billy (youngest boy in the family, I think he's six or seven years younger than me) was too young at the time.

I use to love going to Alumni Stadium, or the 'Heights'. I loved everything about it. I would always go down to where the players entered the stadium to watch them run onto the field. I would stick my arm out over the fence to try to get a few hand slaps as the players were yelling, screaming, getting themselves psyched up for their opponent. I started calling them the 'screaming eagles' instead of just the B.C. Eagles.

I would go back to my seat in the stands afterward and my father would say, "Did the 'screaming eagles' scream loud enough for you, Dave?" I'll never forget going to B.C. football games.

This past November, Rick (Kennedy) took me to a B.C.-Rutgers game. I can't remember how long it had been since my last trip to the 'Heights'. There had been some major changes. There had been a lot of new construction since my days at St. John's. One being a beautiful hockey arena, Conte Forum. Every seat in the house was B. C. maroon (B. C.'s colors are maroon and gold) and fully cushioned. What a great time it was going back there. I ran into one of my brothers-in-law at the game, Bob Foy, my sister Sheila's husband.

I know I got off track a little bit, but before I finish describing the St. John's campus I'd like to tell you about the time I had my big time college football interview with coach Joe Yukica of the B.C. Eagles. Well … it wasn't a scheduled one on one interview in his office, but none-the-less, I like to think of it as a big time college football interview.

It was in the spring of 1973. I was a second semester sophomore at St. John's. I had made a decision to leave St. John's at the end of the school year (it was a tougher decision to leave then it was to enter) and transfer to Boston College for my junior and senior years of college. I walked over to the B.C. campus one week day afternoon, to Alumni Stadium where the football team was working out, in full pads (complete uniform).

Spring work outs help to get the guys focused and in shape for the fall season. They give the coaches a chance to see how each player is doing, improving or not, etc. Walk-ons (guys who want to play college football, but were not recruited by any college to play) can show the coaches what they have to offer, that they belong on the team. I had heard that with big time football schools, you could not just apply to their school, get accepted, and then show up for football practice and tell the coaches you were there to try out for the football team. You had to be invited to try out if you had not been recruited by the school. That's partly because of the numbers involved, because of the college having already looked at your high school football career (video tapes, college scouts watching you play, your statistics, etc.). I didn't play high school football. I wasn't allowed to play high school football. What the heck was I going to say to coach Yukica, if he would even talk to me, if he had the time to talk to me.

But … there he was on the sideline. The football field had an artificial turf, with Eagles painted in both end zones and the B.C. Eagle with his/her wings spread painted in the middle of the 50 yard line. A football field is 120 yards long (each end zone is 10 yards long, 2 end zones, 100 yards of playing field). It is almost 55 yards wide. The rectangular perimeter is painted white, every 10 yards is painted white the width of the field, and every yard is painted white (called a hash mark, I don't know maybe 6 inches by 12 inches). The hash marks run the length of the playing field, distanced 1/3 of the width of the field from each sideline.

On each 3 yard line there is a hash mark in the middle, probably 6 inches by a yard. The football is spotted there after a touchdown is scored. The team that scored the touchdown will then try to kick an extra point through the 2 goal posts located at the end of the end zone. The distance between the goal posts for college and professional football is eighteen-and-a-half feet. They can go for 2 points if they choose by running or passing the ball. What a beautiful field.

There was a four foot high chain link fence that went around the perimeter of the sideline of the football field, an area for the coaches, players, staff, officials, refs, photographers, cheerleaders, etc. There is a reason for that fence. You are not suppose to go into that area unless you belong there. You could walk into the stadium. The gates were open, it wasn't a closed workout. There were students and other people there watching the team work out. Coach Yukica was too far away from the fence for me to talk to him. I was trying to work up the courage to open the gate, walk in and go up to him. One of BC's wide outs that year was Mel Briggs. If I'm not mistaken, I'm almost positive he wore number 22, a number that became famous at B.C. a few years later thanks to a guy named Doug Flutie.

Briggs was not a big guy. Slightly shorter than me, but broader, much better built than me. He was a decent wide-out. I watched him run a down the field 8 yards and out to the sideline where I was standing. The quarterback threw the ball a little high, and I know it was just a scrimmage, but Briggsy didn't jump for it, the ball went over his hands. I said to myself, I would have caught that pass. I opened the gate and headed for coach Yukica.

A few feet away from him I said, "Coach Yukica." He said, "What can I do for you?" I stuck my hand out and said, "My name is Dave O'Donnell." He shook my hand and said, "Yes, Dave." I said, "I'm a student at St. John's Seminary across the way." He said, "Uhhuh." He was watching his ballplayers as he was talking to me. I said, "I'm going to transfer to B.C. and I want to play football." He looked at me, all 140 lbs. of me, and said, "Where did you play your high school ball." I said, "I didn't. I had a little kidney infection. They wouldn't let me play, but I'm OK to play now."

I know, I know, I know—I would not have passed the B.C. football physical due to high creatine and protein counts in my urine. But, I wasn't thinking about that at the time. He said, "Do you see what's out there," nodding to the football field. I said, "Your team." He said, "There are an awful lot of big boys out there. I would never discourage anyone from playing football or any other sport. But … there is a tremendous chance that you might get hurt."

I said, "I'm a very talented wide receiver." He looked into my eyes for a few seconds and then said, "Listen ... I believe you. Once you transfer here you can try out for the team." I shook his hand extra hard and said, "Thank you coach, you won't regret this." As I was walking away he yelled, "Bulk up and beef up during the summer." I yelled back, "I will Coach."

Foster Street runs off of Washington Street in Brighton center and into Commonwealth Avenue on the other end. St. Clement's Hall's address, the seminary college, is 197 Foster Street. It is two buildings connected together. An older four story building and a fairly new at the time, four story building. The entrance driveway circles around in front of the main door of St. Clement's Hall. To the right of the older building is an outside basketball court. To the left, in front of the newer building is a faculty parking lot. Almost all of the faculty that taught at St. Clement's Hall, lived there. The students had medium sized rooms, a single bed, desk, book case, closet and a sink. The faculty had full sized apartments, living room, office, bedroom, full bathroom. Once in a while a course would be taught by an outside professor (priest or lay person). In my two years there, I don't recall ever seeing a female professor teach a course there ... kind of unusual, maybe a little sexist? I know that I would have appreciated the change in scenery.

Running behind St. Clement's Hall to Bishop Peterson Hall is an unlit, narrow, windy road lined with a lot of trees (there was no shortage of trees on the campus). Going down that road from St. Clement's Hall, on the left is the faculty garage. On the right are the ball fields, and there is a walking path around the fields, and several trees along the walking path. A little further up, that windy road intersects with Lake Street at Bishop Peterson Hall.

Plank (Steve Burke) nearly took out the St. Clement's Hall dishwasher on that windy road one evening. I think I had been there for about a month. Plank, Tyracks (Tom Rowan), Gigatini (Gerry Cook), Kennard (Rick Kennedy) and 'The Arm' (Rich Pompeo) came to visit me. I got in Plank's car in front of St. Clement's Hall. I told him to drive around back, I'd show them the campus. Besides being dark, unlit, surrounded by trees, and windy, it was raining out that night. We could hardly see five feet in front of us. Not a good idea on my part for me to pick that night to show them the grounds. As we were slowly coming around a bend, there, right there, not in front of us but right there along side of us was the dishwasher (I forget his name). There wasn't even time to swerve the car.

I think the car bushed his jacket. No one said anything for a few seconds until Gig said, "That was close." Most people get way out of the way when they're walking on that road and they see headlights coming in their direction. But, the dishwasher was an active alcoholic as was the cook, Aram. I'm sure he was looped at the time, probably never saw us coming. He was about fifty years old, in rough shape. Both him and Aram had their own rooms next to the dining hall. It was on the first floor in the old part of the building. The laundry room was in that area and often when I did my laundry I could hear Aram and the dishwasher arguing, yelling, screaming at each other from one of their rooms. They did their jobs OK They just liked to drink. I thought Aram was a good cook, I liked his food. But I'm not a good yardstick to go by when it comes to rating food. I'm not fussy, I guess I'm grateful for food. I heard that after the Tsunami in Southeast Indonesia, some folks could not even get a clean glass of water.

I was watching the news one evening. It was a few years after I had left St. John's. The dishwasher at St. John's had been murdered. He had been stabbed to death, I believe in his room at St. Clement's Hall. The police had no suspects and I don't know if they ever found out who did it. Aram use to have some big knives in his kitchen. I wonder if Aram and the dishwasher had one argument too many?

My father and I pulled into the faculty and visitors parking lot at St. Clement's Hall. He said, "Good luck, I'm going to stay here and take a little snooze." I said, "Thanks!" and headed for the front door.

The office was just inside the front door to the left. I introduced myself to the secretary. She said, "Sit down, Dave, I'll tell Msgr. Connors that you're here." I'm not positive what the hierarchy and titles were, but, to the best of my recollection, the letter I received from St. John's that I think was signed by Fr. Arthur Driscoll stated that he was the Dean of Admissions. I believe Msgr. Connors was the Dean of Students, I think? He was a big man, at least two of me. He had to be three hundred pounds. I think he was going out of his way to try to make me feel comfortable.

I must have had that 'what the heck am I doing here' look on my face. He was a nice man, pleasant, humorous, personable. Enrollment in seminaries was down at that time, and still is. So, I had that going for me. But that didn't mean that they would take anybody off the street. Msgr. Connors explained that to me. He said, "If we accept you here, you will have to start over as a freshman. None of your credits will be accepted from Massasoit Community College. We have a different curriculum here than you had at M.C.C. Your four year degree here will an Ars Bachelordom in Philosophy."

I had had Latin for four terms in the ninth grade at Archbishop Williams High School. I said, "A Bachelor of Arts?" He said "Yes, the reason we print it in Latin on your diploma is because it indicates you have had four years of college

Latin." I did fine with Latin in high school in the ninth grade. I had trouble learning Spanish in the eleventh and twelfth grades, a lot of trouble. I told Msgr. Connors that. He said, you will also have to take four years of either Spanish or French (I said to myself, why, are they going to start saying masses in Spanish and French?). Msgr. Connors said, "If you find yourself having problems with any subject, there is all kinds of help available here. We all have difficulty in certain areas. If you didn't have the intelligence to make it through college, I wouldn't be interviewing you right now."

That was nice to hear.

Msgr. Connors explained to me that a student doesn't have to enter a seminary college, wanting nothing else in life but to become a priest. There are some who have a strong vocation, and some who don't. It's a college, a place to get a good education and check out the priesthood at the same time. He asked me what other things I've thought about doing with my life.

I said, "I'd like to play in the NFL." He laughed a little bit, looked at me and said, "I'm sorry, you were serious." I said, "I know that I'm not a big guy, Msgr. Connors, but I am very talented!" He said, "What position do you play?" I said, "Wide receiver." He said, "I love football. Mike Holovak is a friend of mine (Mike Holovak was the coach of the Boston Patriots at one time, before they changed their name to the New England Patriots). I still go to a Pats game once in awhile. Fathers Arthur Driscoll and Tom Daily have season tickets to the Bruins games. They also go to Patriots games once in awhile and they go to a lot of B. C. home football games. I use to, but not much anymore. Every time I went there, I would upset two people." I said, "What do you mean?" He said, "Picture yourself in a seat at Alumni Stadium and seeing a guy my size coming to sit next to you!" I laughed.

We talked about some personal things, my three or four arrests in high school for being a drunk and disorderly person. My poor grades, for the most part, after leaving Archies. He explained to me that he thought I had had a traumatic event in my life. He said, "You, not being allowed to play football in high school and you, feeling that you were talented enough to play in the NFL, didn't matter if you were talented enough or not. What mattered was that you felt that way. That is traumatic." I think we spent about an hour together. He said, "Can you come back in a couple of weeks for a second interview with a three priest entrance board." I said, "Three priests?" He said, "They are guys just like you and me, you'll do fine. I'm recommending your acceptance here and I think they will do the same." He shook my hand and said, "I'd like to see you here in September, Dave."

I never got to see Msgr. Connors again. The guys at the seminary affection-ately referred to him as 'Chubby', when they were telling stories about him. He passed away that summer from a heart attack (God rest his soul).

My father said, "How'd it go." I said, "Pretty good, Dad. I think I'm going to be accepted here." He said, "I knew you would be." I said, "I have to come back in a couple of weeks for another interview." He said, "You know how to get here." I said, "It's an interview with three priests." He said, "That's three times as many guys who will get to like you. You'll do fine."

Fr. Bernie McGlaughlin, Fr. Gerry Dorgan and Fr. Frank Murphy (I believe) gave me my second interview. It was in the apartment office of Fr. Gerry Dorgan. I remember that the interview was informal, not what I had expected. I had thought that three priests would be sitting down at a table. I would be sitting in a hard, uncomfortable chair in front of them, maybe with a spotlight shining down on me.

Fr. Dorgan and I became handball combatants. What a game. It is not for the physically unfit. Sometimes the language would get rough in the handball court, ya, even for a priest. It's a rough game. It is a tremendous work out and stress reliever. We all need to eliminate stress. Playing handball is one of the best ways to do that. In the handball court, I would address Fr. Dorgan as Gerry, as he had told me to do. That was only in the handball court. I addressed him as Fr. Dor-gan at all other times. The few other priests that I played handball against did not allow me to do that.

One time, Fr. Dorgan and I had a medium volley. I scored the point. He had some unflattering things to say to me. I said, "Gerry, I've never heard you use those words in class!" He said some more unflattering things and then proceeded to kick my butt … again. Fr. Dorgan was a way better than medium guy. We got along great.

Fr. Dorgan was sitting behind his desk. Fr. Bernie McGlaughlin was sitting on the couch with me, smoking his pipe. I played Fr. McGlaughlin in handball one time only. The first one to score twenty-one points, win by two, wins…. unless, one guy gets eleven points before the other guy gets a point. That's an eleven to nothing shutout win. Fr. McGlaughlin shut me out in all the three games that we played (these guys played to win). When I asked him when was a good time and day for a rematch, he was kind to me. He said, "There is nothing wrong with playing someone better than yourself. That's how you improve. But, I have an awful lot of handball games under my belt and you don't.

You need to play someone closer to your skill level so that not only will you improve your game but you will enjoy yourself as well."

I said, "Thanks Fr. McGlaughlin. That sounded a lot better than telling me I stink." He slapped my shoulder and said, "You'll improve, you're a natural athlete." Fr. Frank Murphy was sitting in a nice comfortable looking chair, to my left. He would become my Latin professor. I think I saw Fr. Murphy on the news not too long ago. I believe he has taken a position at the Holy Cross Cathedral in the South End of Boston.

He was a quiet man. Unassuming, pleasant, sometimes in his own world. I did well in all his classes. Freshman year Fundamental Latin l and ll and sophomore year Christian Latin and Latin Biographical Readings.

I don't recall any of the questions they asked me. I remember I felt comfortable and relaxed. I wasn't feeling too much pressure. I felt medium, not too good, not too bad. I think the interview went well.

My acceptance letter came in the mail a few weeks later. This would be an opportunity for me to get an undergraduate degree in a decent environment. I would not have the usual distractions to deal with that most college freshmen, who are living on campus, have to deal with. Having my own private dormitory room would be a big plus, a huge plus. After lying down to go to sleep for the night, I get back up between five and seven times to go to the bathroom, because of my kidney disease. I have been doing this, have had interrupted sleep, since I was thirteen and a half years old. And I am still doing it. It is something that I will never get use to. Many times it has made for a miserable next day.

Most college freshmen can probably drink alcohol responsibly. Not all of them. Most of the time, I never could drink alcohol responsibly. I could not handle it. I believe that I was an alcoholic from my very first drink. It took thirty-seven years of drinking before I was able to put the drink down, this time, one day at a time for a lot of consecutive one day at a times. I knew that if I went to St. John's Seminary, my chances of drinking while going to school there would be lessened. I had a strong feeling that I would not drink alcohol while I was there. And I was right. I did not drink alcohol during the two years that I spent at St. John's.

The ladies would have been another distraction for me. I think most guys know how to have a responsible relationship with a lady. They understand the give and take involved in a mature relationship and the responsibility. I think they are aware, at that young age, that, ya, it's nice to be involved with a person that they care about, to do the right thing with that person, to enjoy life with that person, but ... for the most part, they still keep themselves number one in the relationship in the event that it may not work out in the long run.

I had a difficult time doing that with the girlfriends I'd had up till then. Whether that had anything to do with me being an alcoholic, I'm not sure. Alcoholics Anonymous talks about 'us' having a tough time dealing with life on life's terms, hence, we drink too much. I have no problem identifying with that. Maybe the traumatic event in my life had something to do with my relationships with my girlfriends. I don't know for sure. What I do know is that I always made my girlfriend number one, myself number two. Whatever it took to make her like me, to make her love me. I needed her affirmation. More than one girlfriend has told me (after the relationship was over) that I should stamp SUCKER on my forehead.

I was going to go to St. John's in the fall, and I was not going to do any drinking while I was there. Although I didn't drink, I did sneak over to the B. C. campus with some others a few times to try to crash a party.

It was easy enough to do. It was just something different to do once in a while. We did it a few times. I remember at one of those parties in somebody's dorm room, I made the mistake of telling a nice lady that I was a student at St. John's. Not because I didn't want her to know that I went to St. John's, but because she gave my buddies from St. John's a little bit of a hard time for drinking beers. I was drinking a coca cola. She asked me what dorm I lived in. I said, "St. Clement's Hall." She said, "Where?" I said, "St. John's Seminary." She said, "Oooooh, that's why you're not drinking a beer." And before I could say no, that's not why I'm not drinking a beer, she said to my buddies, "And you guys are with him, you're seminarians too, aren't you? You better put your beers down."

An unusual thing happened to me a few weeks before I was to leave for St. John's. I walked into an armed robbery in progress at Shaeffer's Pharmacy at Braintree Five Corners.

I was working in the IF's back yard, doing something back there. He and my mother had a nice backyard. It bordered on several acres of woods, and after the woods was the Blue Hill Cemetery. It was a nice place to do anything. I started to get an obsession for a cigarette. I had been off them for awhile. I had made my decision to enter St. John's and wanted to enter as a non-smoker. I sold my car a few days earlier since I didn't need a car at St. John's and I wanted to have a few bucks in my pocket while I was there. In those days, I drove everywhere. I didn't walk anywhere. I would drive to Phil G.'s house (four houses away) or he would drive to my house. Almost everyone drove almost everywhere. Just like they do today, except me. I haven't owned a vehicle in over ten years. I walk almost everywhere today.

I asked my father if I could use his car to pick up a pack of cigars at Shaeffer's Pharmacy. It was a a two minute drive from his house, a fifteen minute walk. He said, "Sure, and get it washed for me while you're out there, it's overdue." I said, "Thanks Dad." He said, "Vacuum the interior, too." It was a tan, Chevy station wagon, fairly new. He took pride in his cars, always stayed on top of the maintenance, liked to keep them clean. He enjoys driving. I said, "You can count on me Dad, she'll be shining when I get her back to you!" I never brought his car back to him. He got it back from the police impound yard with two bullet holes in it.

I pulled up right in front of Shaeffer's Pharmacy, in the no parking zone, parallel to the front door, something I usually don't do. I almost always park where I'm suppose to park. By doing that, it may have saved Braintree Police Office Lenny Torrey's life. I'll explain that in a minute.

I walked through the front door and into an armed robbery in progress. One masked man was pointing his gun at Cathy K. who was working the front cash register. She was crying. The gunman was telling her to shut up. He wasn't interested in the money in her cash register.

His two partners were in the back of the pharmacy. One with his gun pointed at the pharmacist while the other was filling up a bag with drugs. The guy pointed his gun at me when I came in. At the same time he was telling Cathy to quiet down before he did something to her. I said, "You're scaring her with your gun." He said, "Shut up and get down on the floor." I did as he said, quickly. I think I was on the floor for about a minute when I could hear the footsteps of the other two running down the aisle, and then the three of them ran out the front door. What they didn't know was that someone had tripped a silent burglar alarm that went off at the Braintree Police station, while they were robbing the place. The trio walked out the front door of Shaeffer's Pharmacy and into the path of officer Lenny Torrey's police car. His vehicle was parked right out front. He was pointed right at them, at a ninety degree angle to the IF's car. The police vehicles bumper was within inches of the drivers door of my father's car, with Lenny still behind the wheel.

Cathy, Mr. Shaeffer, one other customer and I heard a series of gunshots go off. Four, five, six, I don't know for sure. The four of us slowly went to the front door after it had been silent for awhile. The other customer said, lock the door. Mr. Shaeffer started taking his keys out of his pocket.

That probably wasn't a bad idea, except that, Lenny was slumped over his steering wheel. I'm no hero, and I'm not stupid, but ... I had to get to him to see if there was anything that I could do. Stop his bleeding or anything (there was one other thing going through my mind at the time. Those three punks just used my father's car as a shield against Lenny). I said, "Let me out first. They said, "Be careful." Like I said before, I'm not stupid. Before I went out the door I got down on my knees, stuck my head out the door and looked everywhere. There was no one around that I could see. I got up and ran as fast as I could (I should have been timed by the NFL scouts on that run) to Lenny's cruiser door. It was only a matter of fifteen feet, but that was the longest and the fastest five yards that I have ever run.

As the punks left the pharmacy with their guns still in their hands, they saw Lenny sitting in his cruiser. And that's when Lenny first saw them. He had just pulled up. He didn't even have a chance to pull out his gun. They took aim on him and started firing. One bullet went through the cruiser windshield and struck Lenny in his neck. Two bullets went into the roof of my father's car.

I opened Lenny's door. He was conscious, but bleeding a lot from his neck. He was talking, groggily, trying to get out of his car. I wouldn't let him get out. I took off my T-shirt and pressed it against his neck with one hand while trying to keep him from moving around too much with my other hand. It was only a matter of seconds before more cops showed up. Eventually, they all showed up, even off duty police officers. No one likes to see one of their own get hurt.

Everything turned out OK for Lenny. His windshield deflected and slowed down the bullet keeping his gunshot wound to less than what it could have been. He spent a little time in the hospital and then completely recovered and went back to work. All three punks were caught and convicted. One, within a few hours. He was hiding in the woods in that area. Another one was caught the next day in Brockton, Massachusetts (twenty minutes from Braintree). The third guy was picked up, I believe a few weeks later (I forget where they picked him up). It wasn't easy for the prosecutor to get convictions on these guys because they were wearing ski masks. We (the four of us in the pharmacy) had to testify for the prosecutor.

I knew Lenny a little bit. When I was fifteen years old I got a part-time job at the Carlton House Hotel (currently the Sheraton Hotel) in Braintree. I was a dishwasher in their restaurant. Once in a while, Lenny and other Braintree cops would come into the kitchen for a cup of coffee and sometimes a sandwich. We use to talk and kid around with each other. He use to call me Chief (as in police chief). He used that nickname for several people.

I felt terrible about Lenny getting shot. I felt partly responsible because of where I parked my father's car. But, getting back to the statement that I made earlier about how illegally parking my father's car may have saved Officer Torrey's life. If I hadn't parked there, Lenny would have been five or six feet closer to the front door. When the punks exited the front door, they would have had a direct shot at Lenny. They had to shoot over the roof of my father's car. They had to put their guns up and over the roof and then shoot down. They ended up shooting two bullets into the roof of my father's car. I would like to think that the position of my father's car helped Lenny. Who knows. Maybe it did and maybe it didn't.

I had to buy some new clothes for school. The usual stuff plus a couple of sports coats, dress shirts and ties. We had to wear a sport coat and tie for Sunday mass, daily mass, week night suppers except Thursday evenings, and on special occasions. We had Thursdays off to do our apostolic work. We had classes on Saturday mornings, besides Monday thru Wednesday and Friday.

Our Apostolic work was volunteering our services to an outfit or organization of our choice in the community. It didn't have to be in Brighton. Every Thursday for two years, except during the summer, I would take a couple of buses to get to Emmanuel House in Roxbury. Emmanuel House was a small neighborhood center run by a group of Franciscan nuns. It was a medium size brick building, I believe four stories high. There were plenty of activities there for the kids to do including a small gymnasium on one of the floors (my favorite place), ping pong and pool tables, an arts and crafts room and a snack and reading room.

The Sister's residence was on the top floor. These Sister's were the most devoted group of folks that I have ever met in my life. They were incredible. Sister Philip was the boss and she was not one to try to get over on. She was hip to a lot of things.

I think that the ages of the kids that came to Emmanuel ran from six to about fourteen. There weren't many fourteen year olds that came to Emmanuel House, because by that age, most of the kids were not interested in going to Emmanuel House after school. The few fourteen old kids who did come to Emmanuel House were as tall as me. We had some darn good basketball games. Sister Philip had no problem booting a kid for misbehaving. She had to do it a few times when I was there. It was a rough neighborhood and sometimes the kids could get rough with each other. Not often, but once in awhile. This would only happen to an older kid, not the younger kids.

Sister Mary and Sister Justin were two other nuns there. There were a few more, but, I can't remember their names. They ran a summer camp for the city kids in Hull, Massachusetts. It was called Children's Vacation House. I was a camp counselor there the summer after my freshman year at St. John's. The other counselor's were Franciscan Brothers from New York, with the New York accent and love for the Yankees. Oh boy!

I believe that the camp was funded and operated by Catholic Charities of the Archdiocese of Boston. The Franciscan Sisters did a great job running the camp. They had their own private house across the street from the camp. It was different working with nuns, but, I had been use to working with them from volunteering at Emmanuel House. They did a pretty decent job. Not bad at all. And the Franciscan Brothers, a pretty decent group of guys ... even though they were from New York.

I hadn't worn a coat and tie since I left Archbishop Williams High School six weeks into my sophomore year, with a few exceptions. I would always borrow somebody's coat and tie for those exceptions. I do not like wearing ties. I didn't mind wearing a clergy collar. It was not tight around my neck. Not as confining or restricting as a tie was for me. We had to wear clergy collars and cassocks (ankle-length black garment worn by Roman Catholic clergy and Anglican clergy) when it was our turn to be the acolyte (do the readings and assist the priest) at daily mass.

Besides my clothes, I was going to bring my small tool box (a few hand tools, some hardware, masking and duct tape-yup, I don't go anywhere without my duct tape), baseball glove, a baseball and a softball, a bat, a football, a basketball (Plank gave me one of his b-balls; I saw the gym and ball fields when my father took me out there for my first interview, but I wasn't sure if they had any balls) some music, and a bible I purchased for the occasion. I thought that my suitcase in my right hand and my bible in my left hand would be a nice touch walking up the stairs of St. Clement's Hall.

My dormitory room was on the fourth floor (top floor) of the connector. The connector was part of the new building, the part that connected the new building with the old building. There were six dorm rooms on the fourth floor connector. At the beginning of the fourth floor hall of the new building was Fr. Arthur Driscoll's apartment, Dean of Students and our freshman year biology instructor.

The freshmen were assigned to the dormitory rooms starting next to Fr. Driscoll's apartment. Most of us were assigned rooms alphabetically, but not all of us for some reason. I think that there were twenty dorm rooms on that floor. Jim Lynes had the first dorm room on the connector (my best friend at St. John's). Then Dan Liporto, Bill Walsh, Marc Olivere (Braintree boy, grew up in Braintree and went to Sacred Heart High School on the Braintree/Weymouth line), myself, and I can't remember who was in the room to my right.

The first few dorm rooms of the old building, after the connector, were taken by Bill McKinley, Jonathan Jones and Richard Brown. Twenty-nine freshmen entered St. Clement's Hall in the fall of '71. I remember almost all of their faces and a lot of their names. We spent a good part of the day together doing things as a class of college freshmen, in a seminary. We were all in the same classes, with the exception of foreign language class. We could choose either Spanish or French. Everyone had to take Latin. Electives were available junior and senior years. We ate all our meals together, went on our retreats at St. Williams Hall together, went to daily mass together, went to lauds (morning prayers) and vespers (evening prayers) together. We spent a lot of time together. We got to know each other pretty good. On the whole, I felt, a good group of guys.

I wasn't the senior man of our class, but I was close. Most of the guys were eighteen. I was twenty. I think that one guy was twenty-two, another guy was twenty-one and another guy was my age. We got along better than medium. You would expect seminarians to behave a certain way towards each other and everyone else, and we did, most of the time, not all of the time.

No one is perfect. There were no saints there. There might have been a few who thought that they were saints ... I think as seminarians we understood that we had a responsibility to start demonstrating a certain type of behavior, whether or not we planned on becoming priests. We were seminarians. We were expected to behave a certain way. I wasn't the only guy there who had no plans to become a priest. There were others there who liked the idea of getting a four year undergraduate degree at St. John's Seminary, because of the quality of the education one received there and other reasons. A good environment, limited distractions, professors living there, a beautiful campus. Studying for a college degree with a good group of guys. A lot of good guys. Approximately 150 students living and studying together at St. Clement's Hall. Most of our classrooms were on the first floor of the older building. There were a couple of classrooms on the basement floor of the new building. There were about forty-five seniors, forty juniors, thirty-six sophomores and twenty-nine freshmen. Enrollment was on its way down. There are no students at St. Clement's Hall today. The college closed down. I don't know what year. I was told that from an alcoholic priest in recovery, Fr. Tom. We were members of the same AA group in 1994. The Abington Friday night group.

Fr. Tom graduated from St. John's Seminary. He was the pastor of a church in Brockton at the time that I met him in 1994. He was older than me. We went to St. John's at different times. Jim R., John W., Paul C., Bob T., Donna, Scott and Fr. Tom were good folks with good recovery time under their belts from the Abington Friday night AA group.

After my father helped me bring my stuff to my room, we shook hands. He said, "Good luck, give your mother a call tonight." I walked him to the elevator and was going to walk him to his car, but he told me not to. He said, "Go introduce yourself to some of your classmates."

Just as he said that, the elevator door opened and there was Marc Olivere. My father said, "Here's one guy you won't have to introduce yourself to." The day I arrived and the day I left, two years later, were the only two days that I used the elevator. It was for faculty only. We could use it for moving or for a medical reason or an emergency.

Marc was my age, about my height, maybe an inch shorter than me. He was a little less than medium build, not as thin as me, probably 150 lbs. He had long, shoulder length brown hair, average looking guy, nice personality. He told me, but I forget what he did for two years after high school. He was with one of his brothers, John, who was a senior at B. C., and played football for B. C. (wide receiver, second string). John was not a big guy, about Marc's height, 175 lbs., but he was well built. And he was talented. You have to be talented to play for B. C.

I remember that I was talking to John about B. C.'s schedule that year. Marc was trying to talk to me about when and why I decided to come to St. John's. Marc was spiritual, more so than the average guy/gal. I said, "Hold on a second, Marc. I want to find out from John how the team looks this year." Marc smiled and said, "You still have those football dreams, don't you, Dave?" I said, "No, I'm over that. I just like B. C. football." Marc smiled again and shook his head a little bit.

John and me continued to talk while Marc proceeded to tape a poster of the crucifixion (Jesus Christ nailed to a cross) on one of his walls. That reminded me of the poster I had of Jim Plunkett and Randy Vataha (Boston Patriots quarterback and wide receiver) that I was going to put up on one of my walls.

Marc was an intelligent man. Each year St. John's offered a junior the opportunity to spend his senior year studying in Rome at Catholic University. It usually was offered to the top student in his class. That was Dan Liporto, in our class. Dan turned it down. It was then offered to Marc.

I can't remember if Jim (Lynes) told me whether Marc accepted it or not. I had left St. John's at the end of my sophomore year, but I have been in touch with Jim for many years (with some huge gaps during my active years). Marc did not become a priest, as did not most of the guys in my class or any other seminary class. I don't know what the statistics are but I do know that out of the twenty-nine freshmen who entered St. John's Seminary in the fall of '71, at least four were ordained priests for the Archdiocese of Boston, eight years later. Fr. Tom Domurant, Fr. Joe Driscoll, Fr. Bob Dwyer (God rest his soul), and Fr. Joe

Raeke. Fr. Jim Lynes was ordained a priest by the Archdiocese of San Antonio, Texas. Other guys may have been ordained elsewhere or gone into different religious communities. The last I heard about Marc was that he had bought into a bed and breakfast in one of the New England states.

After leaving Marc's room, I went to my room to do some unpacking. I left my door open hoping to meet some more guys. Bob 'Big Bo' Brazeau came by. A Ron Howard look alike, only better looking. We introduced ourselves and talked a little bit about our backgrounds.

He was a sports fan, and played sports. He was going to be OK in my book. I asked him if his nickname was Red. He said, "Please, don't call me that. You don't know how sick I am of hearing that." I said, "How about 'Big Bo'?" He was average size, but that nickname seemed to fit him. He said, "I like that!" Then he said, "What's your nickname?" I said, "Chelch." He said, "What's a Chelch?" I said, "I don't know. You'll have to ask my friend, Tyracks. But, I'm not going to use that nickname here."

Before he could say, what's a Tyracks, I said, "It's a medium story. I'll tell you later." He said, "OK. I've got a new nickname for you." I said, "I'm listening." He said, "Daze." I said, "You have got to be kidding me … aren't you?" He said, "No, I'm not. When I first came to your door, before I said anything, you were sitting on your bed staring out your window. I don't know what thoughts were going through your mind, but, you were in a daze." I said, "Ya, I tend to do that a lot. I don't care, you can call me Daze if you want."

And he did. And so did everyone else including most of the faculty. What a nickname, Daze … I should have stuck with Chelch.

Well, good. There's at least one sports guy in here. I'll bet that the rest of them play the piano. Just then, Big Bo and me heard a basketball bouncing on the floor coming in our direction. Jim Lynes, from Brockton, Massachusetts, yelled into my room, "Who's up for b-ball?' Jim was a 6', 2", 190 lb., well built. A good looking man. He graduated from Cardinal Spellman High School in Brockton. He played on their basketball team. He spotted Plank's basketball on my floor and said, "Whose basketball?" I said, "Mine." He said, "You're playing. How about you, Red?" Bob stuck out his hand and said, "I'm Big Bo, and this is Daze." Jim said, "Nice to meet you and what's your name?" to me. I said, "It's Dave, but …" Jim interrupted me and said, "Oh Dave, I thought Big Bo said Daze." I said, "He did, but …" Jim interrupted me again and said, "Daze, Daze…. . you look like your a little bit lost right now. Put your sweats on, both of you and meet me outside on the court."

Two out of the first three freshmen I met played sports. I liked those odds. There were a few more guys who played sports from my class, but we were in the minority. Same with the upper classmen.

Big Bo took a rain check. I changed into my gym shorts and my number 88 Pittsburg Steelers football jersey. Eighty-eight is the number worn by one of my favorite wide receivers and one of the best wide receivers to ever receive a football in the NFL. The Patriots had never had a stand out wide receiver at that point in their history. They have a few outstanding wide receivers under their belt now, to go with their three super bowl rings. Speaking of Super Bowl rings, I wonder if Patriots owner Bob Kraft is going to get his 2005 super bowl ring back from Russian President Vladimir Putin. Kraft took off his newest ring to show Putin, and Putin put it in his pocket.

Troy Brown is my favorite, maybe not as talented a wide receiver as the guy the Pats traded, Terry Glenn, but almost. On my walk from the side door of St. Clement's Hall to the b-ball court, I watched Jim sink three eighteen footers in a row, no rim. Swissshhh …

He said, "L.S., he's one of my favorites, too. When are the Pats going to get a decent WR?" I said, "If I didn't have a bum kidney, I'd be there man." He said, "Do I feel a hot breeze coming on?" I said, "A few more pounds of muscle and I'm there. You'll see what I'm talking about. You don't happen to have a good throwing arm, do you?" He paused and looked at me for a few seconds. I held my hands out for the ball. He turned to the hoop and shot a twenty-two footer. Swissshhh … He said, "My passing arm is better than my shooting arm!"

He was almost right. He did have a decent throwing arm. Not as good as Tyracks, but not bad. There were many times in my two years at St. John's when it was just Jim and me on the ball field tossing the football around. He was unwilling to give me my full credit. The best that I could get from him was, "You're not bad." He couldn't say the same about me when it came to basketball. I was medium, sometimes, and less than medium a lot of times. I was not good competition for him. It didn't matter. We had fun and enjoyed ourselves.

We all got to meet each other at supper, about 150 of us. It was a nice meal. I sat next to Jim. He said, "You know something, Daze, my food always tastes better after I kick someone's butt in b-ball." We were going to get along just fine. The seniors had a little tradition at St. John's. After our first supper as a new community, they made it a point to introduce themselves to each freshman, say some nice things to us, try to make us feel comfortable. We were unaware of this tradition. At first, when the seniors were coming up to me one after another, I thought the word had gotten out that I had chosen the seminary over the Patriots ...

Orientation was the next day. The only thing mandatory that first day was community supper. We had the rest of the evening free. A lot of the guys went to the lounge to talk, watch TV, play chess or cards. The lounge was a good size room, but it wouldn't hold 150. You could probably fit fifty guys in there. There were about twenty-five lounge chairs in a semi-circle, three rows deep, in front of a medium sized TV in one corner. Maybe four or five chess or card playing tables with wooden chairs, a few sofas and a few more lounge chairs along the walls.

Some guys walked around the grounds or went back to their rooms to read or went to the chapel to pray. I went to the lounge with a few other freshmen. If I talk too much about this one was a 'nice guy' or that one was a 'pretty decent human being', it's only because they were. There were many, many, 'nice guys' and 'pretty decent human beings' at St. John's Seminary. I had thought that would be the case when I was trying to decide whether or not to go there. And I was right.

Jack Ahearn, Fr. Jack Ahearn. I forgot about Jack. Another man from my class who was ordained a priest. He was average height, larger than average width, shoulder length light brown hair, medium looking, pretty good guy. Jack was from Arlington, Massachusetts. He became good friends with Tony Giodone, who was from Saugus, Massachusetts. Tony was another large man, taller than Jack, maybe my height. He had shoulder length, curly brown hair, average looking guy. Jack, Tony, Jim and me spent some time in the lounge talking with each other and meeting some of the other guys. Jack and Tony didn't play sports, but, they liked to play cards, as did Jim. I had not played a lot of cards in the past.

The four of us ended up playing cards together almost every Wednesday night of the school year for the next two years. Wednesday night was like a Friday night to us since we didn't have classes on Thursdays.

Other freshman that I met that evening were Brian Donovan who played sports. He was a decent athlete, very competitive. I can't remember where he was from. Brian and Big Bo became best buddies at St. John's. Big Bo, I forgot to mention earlier, was from Malden, Massachusetts. Bill Giroux, who was from a small town in Vermont. Don Clinton, I think was from the Ayer, Massachusetts area. Larry Jezewski, from Brockton Massachusetts. Tim Collins, a good athlete, was from out of state, I can't remember which one. He had a little bit of an accent. Bill Iverson, from Littleton, Massachusetts. Bill McKinley, I don't remember where he was from. Jonathan Jones, a very large guy, largest in our class. Richard Brown who was the first casualty from our class. He was a nice guy and very quiet. He couldn't keep up with the academic work, and was asked to leave after the first semester.

Bob Dwyer, from Brighton, Massachusetts. The type of guy who couldn't do enough for you. His uncle, Msgr. Dwyer was one of our professors. Bob was the second largest guy in our class. He was ordained a priest, but died not too long afterward from a heart attack. Joe Raeke, another Brighton boy, and another guy who couldn't seem to do enough for you. Last I heard about Joe, he was a priest in Quincy, Massachusetts.

At about 10:55 PM the lounge started to fill up. Very few guys had TV's in their rooms. They were coming in to watch the 11 o'clock news. Jim had brought a small TV from home with him. Our rooms came with two wooden chairs, one for ourselves and one for a guest. Not a lot of room for entertaining more than one person at a time. Jim said, "Anyone want to watch the news upstairs in my room?" Jack and Tony said they were going to stay there and watch it. I said, "I do, but don't get the wrong idea." He said, "What are you talking about?" I said, "I still don't like you for demolishing me in b-ball today." He laughed and said, "I got lucky."

When we got to Jim's room, I went to sit down on his guest chair. He said, "Don't sit there. Sit on my bed." He took the two wooden chairs and brought them across the room to the wall furthest away from his bed. He balanced one chair on top of the other. He put his wastebasket on top of the highest chair. He tossed me a notebook and said, "Start making basketballs, I'm going to the bathroom." The wastebasket hoop was maybe three feet off the ground, about twelve feet away from his bed. I said, "You call yourself a basketball player? I'll be right back." He went to the bathroom down the hall. I went to my room, fours doors over and grabbed my tool box.

I got back to his room first. I took out my hammer, box of assorted small brass nails (brads and tacks), and my roll of duct tape. He walked into his room. I put the wastebasket on the wall about six feet from the floor. I said, "Hold it here while I duct tape it to the wall." I put three strips of duct tape on the wastebasket; top, middle and bottom. He liked what I was doing but looked a little skeptical. After taping it to the wall, Jim gave it some test tugs.

He said, "It's not going to work. The duct tape is going to pull away from the wall." I said, "You want to make a little bet on that?" (When my younger brother Billy was helping me load up the IF's car with my stuff, he looked at my toolbox and said, "I thought a seminary was for priests, I didn't know it was for carpenters?") I took out some tiny tacks with a little head on them so that the duct tape won't pull over them, and nailed them into strategic areas in the duct tape on the wall.

Eighteen tacks per strip of duct tape. Nine on the left side of the waste basket and nine on the right side. Three tacks next to the waste basket, three tacks in the middle of the strip on that side, and three tacks on the end. They are perfect for securing duct tape to a wall when the tape is being used to hold something to the wall that has some weight to it. We were good to go. Jim said, "I like it, but ..." I interrupted him. I said, "You buy another wastebasket."

He did get another wastebasket. Our first class at St. John's was Freshman Composition at 8 am with Fr. Gerry Dorgan. When Fr. Dorgan went to throw something in the wastebasket, it wasn't there. Fr. Dorgan said, "Does anyone see a wastebasket anywhere? "It's usually right there in the corner." I was sitting next to Jim. I whispered, "It's in Jim's room."

We played WB (Wastebasket Basketball) for the two years that I was there. Jim told me that the wastebasket hoop stayed on his wall for four years. The painters took it down during the summer after his sophomore year, to paint his room. He put it back up in the fall. Only one other time did it come off his wall.

Jim and Brian (Donovan) we're having a close game. We use to play to twenty-one, had to win by two. The score had gotten up to twenty-nine to twenty-eight, Jim's lead and Jim's shot. He made the shot. He did a little too much celebrating for Brian's liking. Jim use to do a play by play while we were playing. After his final shot, he started jumping up and down yelling, "The crowd is going wild, the crowd is going wild!!!" I was the crowd. Brian headed for the door. As he was passing the hoop, he decided to tear it off the wall and throw it to the floor. Jim yelled, "Technical, technical, a technical foul has been called on Donavon. He is ejected and is heading for the showers!"

As freshmen, we were assigned rooms. Upper classmen could choose any room that was available on a seniority basis, with the exception of the fourth floor rooms reserved for the freshman class. Not all of the rooms on the fourth floor were taken by freshmen. There weren't enough entering freshmen to fill all of the rooms up there. At the end of freshman year, Jim requested his same room, and got it, and stayed there for four years.

One morning in Freshman Comp class, Fr. Dorgan was writing on the chalk-board. Jim pulled out a couple of pre-made paper basketballs. He handed me one and pointed towards Big Bo. Big Bo was sitting a couple rows over to the right and up from us. We waited for the right moment and then launched our basket-balls at him. I sent a line drive that hit Bo on his left shoulder. He looked at his shoulder when it struck, and then at us. Jim had launched a high arc moon shot that was coming down on Red's head as he was looking at us. Bo spotted it and swatted it out of the air before it hit him, towards Fr. Dorgan, just as Fr. Dorgan was turning toward us.

Fr. Dorgan watched it bounce off his desk a couple times and onto the floor. He said, "If anyone has a question for me, raise your hand and ask me, do not send it via air mail." Then he looked everyone of us in our eyes, and said, "Is someone going to pick that up?"

I thought to myself, sure, why not, we have a new wastebasket. Jim, Big Bo and me all stood up simultaneously. Jim and Big Bo sat down immediately and I was left standing. I walked up to the front of the class, picked up the basketball and put it in the new wastebasket. I said, "Fr. Dorgan, as one of the older guys in the class, let me offer you my apology for whoever did that." He said, *"Sit down!"* On my way back to my chair he said, "By the way, aren't we playing handball this afternoon?" I said, "Yes Fr. Dorgan, we are." He gave me one of his famous looks where he holds a five second stare with his right eyebrow raised the whole five seconds, and then turned back to the chalkboard. Jim whispered to me, "Now he's going to start shutting you out in handball just like Bernie (Fr. McGlaughlin) did."

That afternoon, I met Fr. Dorgan at the handball court. We warmed up, and played a few points and then in between one of his serves (winning point always served-he served a lot) he paused, looked behind at me and said, "What happened this morning?"

I explained to him what had happened. He said, "I know that you and Jim are never going to clown around in any of my classes in the future, are you?" I said, "You can count on me, Gerry. I'll pass the word along to Jim."

He started to serve and then stopped, turned back to me and said, "You wouldn't happen to have any idea about what happened to my original wastebasket, would you?" I said, "I'm just as confused about the disappearance of your wastebasket as you are." He gave me the five second stare and then handed me up a serve that I could not have returned if I had had twenty years of handball playing time under my belt.

He said to me as I was getting up off the floor after a futile dive for the ball, "The reason I asked you is because I've been hearing in the halls something about a WB league in Jim's room. I understand that he has two wastebaskets in that room?" I said, "You know what, Gerry, I was planning on going to the hardware store in Brighton center this weekend. I think I'll pick up a spare wastebasket for maintenance to put in their supply room." He winked at me and then hit me with another killer serve. He said, "Tell me that it wasn't your idea to hang the wastebasket six feet off the floor?" I shrugged my shoulders. Whammm ... Another killer serve. I wasn't going to tell him that Fr. Arthur Driscoll (Dribsey, who loved basketball) came by Jim's room every once in a while for some WB action. Maybe it was Dribsey who told him.

Some of my other freshmen classmates were Bruce Cwiekowski, Chris Hawley, Dan Bennett, Dan Liporto, Bill Walsh and Richard Ross. Dan Liporto was from Beverly, Massachusetts. I can't remember where the other guys were from. Dan Bennett left after freshman year. I don't know if he was asked to leave or left on his own. He was border line failing academically. He was also involved in a water balloon fight incident in the spring of freshman year.

A few of them were throwing water balloons at each other on the fourth floor corridor one afternoon. I was in my room studying. I could hear some running up and down the hall, some yelling and a lot of laughing. I didn't care, I was getting ready to go to the library anyway. At the end of the corridor, it makes a right and then quick left into the connector and then the old building. From what we understood, if the window at the end of that corridor on the fourth floor had not been down, Dan Bennett may have gone out the window and down four stories.

They said Dan was running down the corridor at full speed trying to hit someone with his water balloon. He was in his bare feet. About ten feet before the window he hit a puddle of water and skidded into the window, crashing into it with his right forearm. It was a mess. There was a lot of blood. There was no time to wait for emergency personnel. They wrapped his arm and one of the upper classmen drove him to the E.R. at St. Elizabeth's Hospital, not far from St. John's. He received a ton of stitches. It was made clear to all students in the college that any future water balloon fights would result in immediate expulsion from St. John's.

I think Richard Ross was my other neighbor on the connector, room 426, to my right but I'm not positive. I'm pretty sure that the room numbers ran 401 thru 420 in the new building. Then 421 thru 426 on the connector (421-Lynes, 422-Liporto, 423-Walsh, 424-Olivere, 425-O'Donnell, 426-Ross). If I'm not mistaken, Richard's family moved to one of the Carolina's just before he came to St. John's.

I became close to Bob Hennessey (Fr. Bob Hennessey), a sophomore. He was from West Roxbury. I went to his house with him one time and met his father. His father was a high ranking Boston Police officer. I asked Bob one time if he ever wanted to be a cop? He gave me this look that said, how could you even ask me that?

He really wasn't the police officer type. More of the priest type. At the end of my freshman year, when we picked our rooms for the next school year, I picked a room on the first floor, new building, next to Bob's room. We played some chess together my first year there. I use to love playing chess, and once again, because of being in recovery, I'm playing chess again. I play on a social intermediate level. I'm not a beginning chess player. I can give guys who have got a few chess games under their belts a decent match. Win some, lose some. When it comes to an intermediate tournament chess level, that's a different chess game. I've tried playing a few intermediate tournament level guys and gals on the internet. I've got a ways to go before I can compete with them.

I think tournament level chess players think about their chess moves when they're taking showers, eating meals, sleeping and probably when their making love, too. I'm not that dedicated to the game or that good in the game. I recently received a nice compliment, though, from Rick (Kennedy). Rick told me that my chess game had improved since we were kids. I would have said, my game has stayed the same, but your game has gone down hill. But I didn't say that because if I had, then Rick wouldn't toss me a sympathy win every once in awhile. That was a great compliment to me. Rick is too busy with his work and family to play in chess tournaments. If he wanted to, he could. He is an exceptional chess player.

We play on the same chess board today that we played on forty years ago. It's a good size wooden board with wooden pieces that were hand carved by Rick's father. Those chess pieces are something else to look at. They are not something that Rick's father could have knocked out in a few days. He must have spent many, many hours hand carving out those chess pieces. He did a beautiful job.

We have gotten together on several occasions over the past, almost two years now, for chess games, Red Sox games, B.C. football games, dinner, pizza, grinders, or just to hang around together for a few hours.

I went to Florida in September of 2004 with Rick for a weekend visit to Rick's girlfriend, Florrie's place. The trip was on Rick. It was business trip for the two of us. We made an attempt to repair Florrie's roof after all the hurricanes that she got hit with that year. But, even if it wasn't business, Rick still would have paid my way. He's like that. He is a very generous man. He has always been generous to me.

We met in the fourth grade. One day shortly after meeting him, I walked to his house to visit him. As I was walking up his driveway, he jumped out of a pile of leaves and beat me up. I went home crying. I think that Rick's generosity to me is partly due to his feeling bad about that incident. He wasn't hurting me when he beat me up. He was just goofing around.

I was crying because he scared the crap out of me when he jumped out of that pile of leaves. He almost didn't even have to beat me up. I nearly died from a heart attack. Rick told me years later that he had pulled the same stunt on Tom (Tyracks) the next day. Only, Tom just stood there for a few seconds and then he punched Rick in his nose. That was the last time that Rick jumped out of a pile of leaves. I have done things for Rick, too. But, if I were to add up the plus's and the minus's, I would be into Rick for some money. I hope that I can make some money on this book so that I can toss Rick a few bucks.

One good thing about living on the first floor was that I didn't have to climb all those stairs several times a day. I'm glad that I was young back then. I tried to talk Jim into moving down stairs, but, he was happy were he was. Bob Hennessey is an above average intelligent man. He speaks French and Spanish. I flunked intermediate Spanish my first semester, freshman year. They didn't make me take Intermediate Spanish II second semester. Instead, they accepted six of my credits from Massasoit Community College to replace the six credits that I would have received for Intermediate Spanish l and ll.

The deal was, I would take Intro to Spanish l and ll sophomore year and then Intermediate Spanish junior year and I'm not sure what after that. I never got that far since I left St. John's after my sophomore year. Bob tutored me in Spanish my sophomore year. I got a B plus both semesters. I have my transcript in front of me.

Flunking Spanish first semester, freshman year was not good for my Q.P.A. (quality point average on my transcript), or C.P.A. (cumulative point average). I got an A, a C plus, two C minus' and an F for a Q.P.A. of 1.96. 1.75 called for academic probation. I was close. As I've said before, I'm average intelligent. To get good grades, I have to work twice as hard as the smart guys. And I did that first semester, I tried my best. It was a lot of hard work for me to get the grades that I got. I didn't do much studying in high school with the exception of my ninth grade, and not much studying at Massasoit Community College. I think I was paying the price for that now. But I kept at it. I knew I could be a B student if I worked hard enough. I improved my Q.P.A. each semester, 1.96, 2.21, 2.26 and 3.0 my second semester, sophomore year. I made the Dean's list. I was proud of myself. It was a lot of hard work, for me.

Following my sophomore year, I worked at St. John's as a painter. I had already made my decision not to come back in the fall. I didn't have a job lined up, so when Bob told me to ask Fr. Lind, who was in charge of hiring summer help, if I could work there along with him and a few other guys. I said, "Sure, why not?" I could paint during the day and work out in the evening.

We could use B. C.'s athletic facilities with our St. John's ID. We lived and worked at Bishop Peterson Hall. We painted all the halls, and there were a lot of them. Bob said to me one time, "I bet you never thought you'd make it to Theology House?"

I tried to teach Bob how to play handball that summer. He was not having an easy time with it. He was more academic than he was athletic. After about a half an hour, he said, "I'll be right back." As he headed out of the court's half door, he said more to himself than to me, "Don't they know how to make a full size door?" A half an hour went by before I realized that he wasn't coming back.

I was going to put my plans for transferring to B. C. on hold, for a couple of reasons, none of which had anything to do with my not being able to pass a B. C. football physical. B. C. was expensive. It's one of the more expensive schools in the country. It was one thing for my mother and father to help me out with my St. John's tuition. B. C.'s tuition was an entirely different ball game. I had gotten the application from B. C. in January of my sophomore year at St. John's, but I didn't fill it out. That spring when I talked to Coach Yukica, I never did mention that I had not applied to B. C. yet. I left him with the impression that my paperwork had been filled out, submitted and I was just waiting to hear from admissions.

I think that they would have accepted me. I had written a nice cover letter trying to explain away my lousy high school grades. My math S.A.T. was OK. My English was a little less than OK. About 600 and 450. I told them in my cover letter that the IF was a B.C. alumnus. Nailing the dean's list second semester, sophomore year at St. John's I think would have nailed down my acceptance at B.C. I'm not sure whether or not the admissions board would have paid any attention to what I stated in my cover letter about how I was going to put B. C. on the football map. I wasn't sure if I wanted to apply for the amount of the student loan that was necessary to attend B.C. It was a lot of money. I started thinking about another Boston school. Boston State College, a huge difference in tuition.

The last I heard about Bob, was that he was a priest in either Hanover or Hanson. Some of the other sophomores at St. John's my freshman year were Bob O'Grady, Roger Jacques (Fr. Roger Jacques), Bob Lally, Norman Grenier, Andy?, Jim O'Brien (Fr. Jim O'Brien), and Mike (Crazy) C. He was a character. He ended up going to Boston State College his senior year, when I was a junior there.

Near the end of my junior year at Boston State College, Mike approached me. He said, "Daze, you have to do me a big favor." I said, "Mike, you have to do me a bigger favor first and don't call me Daze anymore." He said, "I'm sorry. That is kind of a strange nickname, isn't it?" I said, "What do you need Mike?" They weren't going to allow him to graduate from BSC until he took a make-up Statistics exam. He flunked the first one. They were going to let him take another one. He wanted me to take the make-up exam for him. I did well in Statistics at Boston State. I was concerned about getting caught, besides not liking the whole idea anyway.

He assured me that it would be easy to pull off. I forget exactly what the details were. I know that we pulled it off. I took the make-up exam for him and he got his college degree. I never did get my college degree. I remember asking him how I was suppose to tell his instructor that I was him. Whether or not he said the instructor didn't know any of her students by their names or someone else would be giving the make-up exam, I can't remember. I remember walking into a classroom at the designated time and telling a lady that I was Mike C., that I was there to take a make-up statistics exam. She gave me the exam, I did it and I handed it back to her. That was something that I never did before, nor would ever do again.

Some of the juniors at St. John's when I was a freshman were Bob Washabaugh, Ed Kelly, Dan Toomey twice (there were two Dan Toomey's), Jim Burke and Jerry Gillespie (Fr. Jerome Gillespie). Fr. Gillespie was on the news not too long ago. It wasn't good. He was alleged to have made sexual advances to a mother and her daughter from the parish that he was stationed at in Chelsea, I believe. I don't know what the outcome was. I haven't heard anything else about it on the news. He seemed like a decent guy at St. John's. I only knew him to say hi.

Also on the news a few days ago was St. Albert the Great church in Weymouth. Fr. Ron Coyne's parish. Archbishop Sean O'Malley decided to re-open it after he had closed it down not too long ago, I forget exactly when. I bet Fr. Coyne had a lot to do with the re-opening. And the hard work of the parishioners also had a lot to do with the opening of St. Albert The Great church.

I played Bob Washabaugh in handball for two years. Medium looking guy, friendly face, light brown medium length hair, my size but a little heavier. Heck of a decent guy. I'll never forget the evening Bob's father passed away. Bob and I were playing handball together. There was a small viewing area above the court for anyone who wanted to watch a game. After one of our volleys, we saw Mike Tierney (another junior) up there watching us.

Mike said, "I'm sorry to interrupt you Bob, but Fr. Driscoll needs to see you right away." I know Bob's heart dropped, as did mine. I said, "Take your time

Bob, I'll be here when you get back." As Bob was going out the court door, Mike looked at me and shook his head from side to side to let me know that we were through playing handball for the night. He held up one hand and mouthed five minutes, letting me know to wait five minutes before l left.

We met Bob's family when they came to St. John's for a memorial mass for his father. They were a whole family of very nice people. Bob was from Waterbury, Connecticut, as was his classmate, Ed Kelly. I don't remember exactly what Bob told me about how that worked. I think that the Archdiocese of Boston allowed students from other archdiocese's to study at St. John's for all eight years if they wanted to. Then they could return to their archdiocese to be ordained a priest and serve there. And the archdiocese of Waterbury would do the same thing for Boston students, maybe all seminarian students in the country. I'm not sure. Bob was ordained a priest and is stationed in a parish in the Archdiocese of Waterbury, the last I heard.

Ed 'My Man' Kelly from Waterbury Connecticut. What a great guy. My height, 170 lbs., little longer than medium length dark brown wavy hair. He styled it the same way Fonzie styled his hair, but, without the grease and blown dry. Ed was a good looking guy. He was a Boston Red Sox fanatic. He could not get enough of them. I swear that his reason for studying in Boston was so that he could be close to Fenway Park. He had a little pocket radio with ear speakers that he carried with him whenever the Red Sox were playing. Starting from spring training to the middle of May, the end of our school year. Ed often liked to spend some quiet time in the chapel, besides the times that we spent there as a community.

I know that he went there at least three or four evenings a week. Every time that I went there to pray, he was there. I went there three or four evenings a week. I walked into the chapel one night during the baseball season, around 9:00. There were a handful of guys there, including Ed. I sat down, a couple of rows in front of him. After about ten minutes went by, I heard a pssst. I turned behind me and looked at Ed. He said, "Fisk just hit a two run homer." And then he added, "This is the best place in the house to listen to a ball game." Ed thought Ned Martin was the greatest baseball announcer ever, even better than Curt Gowdy. He did a decent impersonation of him. I think Martin was good, but I don't know about him being better than Curt Gowdy. Ed got his four year degree from St. John's and then got a job down the street at St. Elizabeth's Hospital, I believe. I knew that he was going to stay close to the Red Sox.

One of the Dan Toomey's (red head, glasses) was ordained a priest. The other one, 6', 195 lbs. and solid, got his undergraduate degree from St. John's and then he became a Massachusetts State Trooper.

I shook hands with every single senior my first night at St. John's, as did every other freshman. Pretty good group of guys. I think eighteen of them were ordained priests for the Archdiocese of Boston. John Coyne (Ron's brother) was just like his brother, except, more brainy than athletic. The Coyne brothers were from West Roxbury. There were others in their larger family who were priests and possibly a nun.

I remember one time at the end of my freshman year, I asked John to sign my yearbook. All students in the college got a yearbook. I think that we called it 'Agape'. Only the seniors had their individual pictures in the yearbook. Juniors, sophomores and freshmen had class photos taken. John said, "What do you want me to write?" Ten minutes later, as he was still writing he said, "I'm pretty sure that my pen is going to run out of ink soon." I said, "OK, that ought to do it." John was not ordained by the Archdiocese of Boston, I think. I'm pretty sure that he was ordained a priest in a different religious order. I think that he is in a monastery somewhere or possibly overseas doing missionary work.

Fr. Fred Barr, what a character. I forget where he was from, maybe Beverly, Massachusetts. I don't know where he is stationed right now. If I was in his area, I would visit him. I liked Fred, even though he was a goof ball. Some of the seniors took it upon themselves to oversee some of the freshmen. That was not a tradition. Fred picked me. What a lucky guy I was … not. Sometimes he was tough to deal with. He could be way too silly and goofy, way too many times. No one is perfect. He's a good man, very spiritual, kind guy. I was eventually going to tell him to stop coming up to my room so often. I wanted to do it my way, I didn't want to hurt his feelings. Jim took care of it for me. I wasn't happy about the way Jim handled it. But, it was Jim's way of dealing with things. Tell the truth, tell it like it is. Don't mince words. Maybe Jim had the right idea.

Fred came up to visit me one afternoon. I was in Jim's room. Fred walked into Jim's room, which wasn't unusual. If someone's door was open (a lot of us left our doors open a lot of the time), it was considered OK to say hi and walk in at the same time, without waiting to be invited in. Jim said, "Who do you think you are walking into my room like that." Fred said, "I'm here to see Daze, not you." Jim said, "Well you just walked into my room, you knucklebrain, now turn around and walk out." They exchanged some unpleasantness and then Fred said, "Can I talk to you, Daze." I said, "I'll stop by your room later, Fred."

Feelings, words … sometimes it doesn't take much to put a dent in someone's day. A couple of weeks ago on a morning TV talk show, co-host Matt Laurer, a decent talk show host, and actor Tom Cruise, a better than medium actor, had a disagreement. They had a battle of words in front of a national television audience to see who could sound better than who. No one wants to look bad. No one wants to feel bad. Has it ever been OK to stop in the middle of a heated discussion, that is taking place in front of onlookers, let's say, one in front of a national television audience and say, "You know what, I think you may be right, and I think that I may be wrong." Or, "I think that you are partly right, and I think that I am partly right."

It never happens during the heat of the moment. NEVER. During the heat of the moment, it is too difficult to bite our tongues and swallow our pride. We're human. I can't remember ever stopping right in the middle of a good verbal fight and giving my opponent some credit. It's similar to having a verbal chess match. I'm not going to point out a good chess move to the other gal or guy.

Some folks thought that one of Jim's problems was that he was too outspoken. He rarely hesitated to say what was on his mind. He had a good mind. He could read almost anything and pretty much remember all of it. It would take me two reads, sometimes three to accomplish that. He was a B plus student. He gave my ego a boost one time when he was trying to figure out a math problem. It had nothing to do with a course at St. John's.

There were no math classes for freshmen and sophomores at St. John's. We could take math electives or any other electives not offered at St. John's, at B. C., as juniors and seniors. It was a math problem that he was trying to figure out on his own, to satisfy his own curiosity. He said to me, "How's your math ability?" I said, "I'm your man." I figured it out for him and said, "No charge."

I cannot remember what any of the issues were that Jim had a problem with back then. I remember that at that time, they were all legitimate. All of them, and there were a few. Big, medium and small issues.

Jim did not get a kick out of raising legitimate issues and pain in the butt issues. He was genuinely concerned. He was going to do his best to try to help change things that he thought needed changing. The hierarchy (all priests at St. John's have input in whether or not a student is accepted into Bishop Peterson Hall, but that final decision really comes down to being made by only a few of them) at St. John's pay extra close attention to guys like Jim. Ironic isn't it; keeping a close eye on a good man like Jim and look at all of the sicko's they missed.

Are you reading this Fr. Banks down there in Baltimore, Maryland, where I last heard that you were hiding out?. Fr. Robert Banks, Dean of Theology House, took a particular dislike to Jim. Banks was implicated, maybe indicted, I'm not positive, in Cardinal Laws (why isn't this man in jail instead of living the good life in Rome? I should send an e-mail to the new Pope. Maybe he didn't hear about the Archdiocese of Boston's travesty before he hired Law?) brainstorm of moving pedophile priests from parish to parish.

He tried to prevent Jim from entering Bishop Peterson Hall after Jim's graduation from St. Clement's Hall. Banks' vote carried a lot of weight, it was 'the vote'. The fact that Jim was accepted into Bishop Peterson Hall attests to what kind of a guy Jim is. A good man, with genuine concern about things that the seminary and the Catholic church, needed to be concerned with. Jim was not without his allies, thank God for that. They overrode Banks' vote.

But the heat was still on. Now they were going to keep an even closer eye on Jim while he was in Theology House. Especially Banks … which I don't completely understand. Him and Law were busy moving pedophile priests around. Where did he find the time to make life miserable for Jim?

I said earlier in this book that I could be a punk at times and have been. Instead of looking at myself as a punk, these days, I would rather look at myself as someone who demonstrates backbone. One of the few times that I showed any backbone at St. John's was when I was no longer a student there.

It was in the spring of '75. Jim was getting ready to graduate from the college. I took a ride to Brighton to visit him and play some WB. He was not in a good mood. I asked him about it. He said, "It doesn't look like I'm going to Theology House." I said, "You're kidding! What are you talking about?" He said, "They haven't decided on my case, yet." I said, "You mean Banks hasn't decided, yet?" He said, "Oh Banks decided a long time ago. Probably the day after I arrived here."

I said, "What's his biggest complaint against you?" He said, "There is no one big complaint, unless you want to say, complaining." I said, "He thinks you complain too much?" Jim said, "About everything." I said, "If something needs to be complained about, what's the problem with complaining about it?" Jim looked at me and said, "Do I complain too much?" I said, "Why do you think I left after two years?" He laughed, a little bit.

I now remember one of Jim's complaints. I better tell you now, before I tell you about what I did or else I'll forget it again. Two types of guys that the entrance board tries to screen out when interviewing applicants are homosexuals and religious nut cases. Someone who, let's say, said he was struck by lightning and while unconscious was told by Jesus Christ that he has to become a priest.

Somewhere around the middle of our freshman year, Jim said to me, "Do you think Larry B. is gay?" I said, "No doubt about it in my mind." And then he said, "What about Jim M.?" I said, "He's kind of obvious about it, isn't he?" He said, "Just this year. He wasn't that obvious about it his first two years here." Jim M. was a junior at the time that we were freshmen. Jim added, "I did some checking." I said, "Jim, why would you want to nose around about someone when you could be losing in WB to me?" He said, "You don't think this is serious? He doesn't belong here. Why hasn't he been thrown out?"

Jim M. was probably careful about who he made his half joking, half serious passes at. Maybe not as careful with someone who he thought would reciprocate, I don't know for sure. I don't think it would be a good idea to start tossing students out on suspicions, and neither did Jim. But, if someone is making a homosexual pass at someone else, and disguising it as a joke if the other guy doesn't accept, then that's a different ball game.

Shouldn't the hierarchy have special guidelines set up for something that serious. Something like, no joking around about homosexuality, feller's, or pack your bags. We don't want anyone to get away with being gay here at St. John's by pretending that he is only kidding around. And if they did, they did not implement them in Jim M.'s case. Rules are rules. The Catholic church is not suppose to ordain homosexuals. Why would they allow a homosexual to continue to study for the priesthood, once they became aware that the person was gay.

Are you thinking, why would St. John's allow a person who never wanted to become a priest to study there. Because if a guy like myself changed his mind about the priesthood while studying at St. John's, then, the Archdiocese of Boston would end up ordaining a decent priest, not a homosexual or a pedophile.

This is the way that it worked at St. John's. If a homosexual snuck by the entrance board without being detected, he pretty much had a free four year ride, if he followed all the other rules. He would be allowed to get his undergraduate degree. He would not be allowed to enter Bishop Peterson Hall. If a homosexual enters Bishop Peterson Hall, having not been detected while attending St. Clement's Hall, we all know what the results can be. Homosexual priests; homosexual/pedophile priests. It's too bad that the hierarchy at St. John's hadn't paid closer attention to what Fr. Jim Lynes (ordained a Roman Catholic priest by the Archdiocese of San Antonio, Texas, 1979) was telling them.

Jim really was in a bad mood. I couldn't even get him to play one game of WB. I felt bad for him. Jim is a good man. I've met his entire family. His mother was a nurse. His father worked his entire life with the post office. His older brother Tom, graduated from college (I forget where), is married and has kids.

His sisters (I remember there being two) are college graduates. One of the sisters dated a ball player from the New England Patriots for a period of time. There are clergy in his extended family. An awful nice family from a blue collar neighborhood in Brockton, Massachusetts.

We took a ride to Braintree and Brockton one time during our sophomore year to visit our families. I remember Jim said some nice things about my father after he met him. Before they met, Jim asked me what the IF did for a living. I said, "He's a math teacher." I'm pretty sure Jim mumbled, "shit," under his breath. I said, "What do you have against math teachers?" He said, "If I told you, you wouldn't believe me." I said, "Give it a shot." He said, "You know I hate and suck in Math. I hated every math teacher I ever had. One of the stupidest things I ever did in my life, I did to a math teacher." I said to myself, "Oh God, don't tell me that he's going to write on the IF's shoes."

He went on, "It was in the eighth grade. My math teacher, Mr. _ at East Junior High School was giving me a hard time about my exam results. I told him that I was doing the best I could. I thought if he gave me a D, I wasn't going to get accepted into Cardinal Spellman High School. I think it was the third term. He gave me a D, I still got accepted into Cardinal Spellman, but the reason that I was so upset with Mr. _, was because my grade could have gone either way. I was high 60's, low 70's. He could have given me a C minus."

I said, "Jim, don't you think that if you deserved a C minus, you would have got a C minus?" He said, "No, I don't. The guy didn't like me from day one. He thought that I was too ..." I interrupted him and said, "I think I've got a good picture here. So, what did you do to him?" He said, "I slashed one of the tires on his car." I said, "You what?" He said, "Hey ... he was lucky. At first, I was going to do all four tires."

We borrowed a classmates car to make the trip to Brockton and Braintree. We stopped at my folks house first. Jim met my parents and a few of my brothers and sisters.

We didn't stay long. As I was pulling away from my parents' house, I stopped and got out of the car. I took a quick walk around the IF's car. I got back in. Jim was staring at me. I said, "Let's rock 'n roll, baby. All tires are a go ..."

I remember when we crossed the Avon/Brockton line into Brockton, on our way to Jim's house, I said, "Where does Sue live?" Sue M., Jim's ex-girlfriend. He looked at me and asked, "Why?" I said, "She's visited you at St. John's a couple of times. I think that we should visit her." Sue was a pretty lady. Model material. She had long black hair, slightly wavy, some of the prettiest eyes that I've ever seen in my life with the prettiest rest of the face to go along with those eyes. Better than nice figure. Jim said, "You think that we should go visit her, huh?" I said, "Sure, why not, we're in Brockton."

They were classmates at Cardinal Spellman High, and dated the last two years there. Jim said the break up did not go well. He said that Sue was a religious lady and had a lot of respect for the church and for priests, but, not for him becoming a priest. I said, "I can understand her point of view." He said, "What are you talking about, you hardly know her." I said, "I don't have to know her to understand her point of view. You are a good looking guy." He said, "What does that have to do with becoming a priest." I said, "A lot." He said, "You're nuts." I said, "I am nuts, but, you being good looking versus us medium looking guys, has a lot to do with you not becoming a priest." He said, "You're nuttier than usual." I said, "I am nuttier than usual, but let me try to explain it to you."

I said, "Simply put, the percentage of good looking guys who become priests to the percentage of good looking guys who get married is disproportionate to the percentage of medium looking guys who become priests versus the percentage of medium looking guys who get married." He stared at me and said, "You did say simply put, right? And, why are you going math on me? After meeting your father, I was starting to feel like maybe I would have done OK in math if I had had a teacher like the IF."

I said, "Listen, Jim. Not a whole lot of guys as good looking as you become priests. You're ticking off a lot of ladies. When you're delivering your sermons from the pulpit, the ladies aren't going to be paying attention to what you're saying. They will be trying to think up ways to get you in the sack." He laughed, a lot, and then he said, "That's enough, Daze."

We didn't visit Sue …

After my visit with Jim that spring of 1975, I was in a bad mood, for Jim. I could not believe that a man with his religious convictions might not be allowed to enter theology house. The Catholic church needed priests. Their numbers were going down every year. The Archdiocese of Boston had a good one in Jim And they were thinking of letting him go. I didn't think that I could let that go without saying something to Fr. Banks. I wasn't sure how this was going to play out.

I wished Jim good luck and walked down the stairs to the first floor. I started to walk toward the right side front door, which opened to the faculty and visitor parking lot. I changed my mind. I thought it would be better if I walked instead of drove to Bishop Peterson Hall. To give myself a little extra time to think about what I was going to say to Fr. Banks, about Jim. If he was there. I walked down one more flight of stairs to the basement and out the back door. I think that was the last time that I made that trip down those stairs behind St. Clement's Hall. Down the windy road past the ball fields, past the faculty garage, the tennis courts and into the front doors of Bishop Peterson Hall. I use to love that walk. It seemed like I could always do some decent thinking while taking that stroll.

As I was walking toward Bishop Peterson Hall, Fr. Marc Noonan was walking toward St. Clement's Hall. We met in front of the ball fields. Fr. Noonan had been my faculty advisor my two years at St. Clement's Hall. We had to pick two faculty members by our first couple of weeks at the college. One to be our faculty advisor, the other to be our spiritual advisor. I picked Fr. Jack McNally (God rest his soul) to be my spiritual advisor.

We said hi to each other, and he said, "You must be getting ready to graduate from Boston State College?" I said, "No Fr. Noonan, I won't be graduating this spring. I'm doing there what I did at Massasoit Community College. I sign up for a full load, and then I end up dropping a couple of courses before the semester is over." Fr. Noonan looked at me for a few seconds and said, "Did you start drinking again?" I said, "Ya, I did." He said, "You know something, Daze. If you are an alcoholic, it will get worse, not better." I said, "Yup, I know that, Fr. Noonan." But, I really didn't know that, not really. I was starting to feel, again, that my drinking was the glue that was holding me together. Especially, now that I didn't have the seminary for my security blanket.

I thanked him for his warning and told him that it was nice to see him again. It was always nice to see Fr. Noonan. He was a nice guy. I had made two good choices when choosing two faculty members to be a part of my life for two years at St. John's Seminary.

As I walked by the tennis courts I thought about the few times that I played tennis there. I had played tennis a couple times before going to St. John's. I was playing a game of chess with my friend Paul (shoot the gap) Rhinehalter one day when he asked me if I wanted to learn how to play tennis. I said, "No thanks. It's bad enough that you beat me in chess all the time (Paul was another exceptional chess player). I'm not going to let you add tennis to your 'things I kill Dave in' list." He said, "Suit yourself." Just then his sister Alice came into the house and said, "What time are we playing tennis Saturday?" Paul said, "Sometime in the late afternoon, I'll let you know later." Alice was cute. I said, "So Paul, where's a good place for me to pick up a tennis racquet?"

I walked into Bishop Peterson Hall. The receptionist was a St. Clement's Hall student. I asked him if there was any chance that I could talk to Fr. Banks. I told him that I did not have an appointment. He made a call and then told me to sit down. The receptionist and me recognized each other but we didn't know each other that well. We exchanged some small talk. About twenty minutes went by when the receptionist told me to go in to Fr. Banks' office. I said, "Hi Fr. Banks, how are you?" He said, "Daze, it's nice to see you. Are you coming to Theology House?"

I said, "No, no, I'm not going to graduate from Boston State this year." He said, "No, and why is that?" I said, "I didn't matriculate. I ended up dropping courses each of my four semesters there. I started spending more time drinking than studying." He said, "You have a drinking problem?" I said, "I think I do, but I'm not here to talk about me. I'd like to talk to you about Jim Lynes. He said, "Really."

His whole composure immediately changed. He no longer had a pleasant look on his face. I'm going to guess he was around fifty-five years old, 5', 8", 170 lbs. He had a full head of salt & pepper, medium length hair He was a nice looking guy.

I said, "Fr. Banks, I know that you and Jim don't get along. Everyone can't get along with everyone. It just doesn't happen. I think that you will agree with me when I say that Jim has that, you either love him or hate him personality." Fr. Banks interrupted me. He said, "Listen, I know that Jim is your friend. Maybe he was your best friend when you were here. I know that you think you know everything there is to know about Jim. But, you don't, Daze. There are things that you don't know. Life experience is the best way to learn things, in my opinion. It speaks volumes to me that you are here speaking up for Jim. I think that he is lucky to have you for a friend. We don't get along. Jim is highly outspoken, maybe too much so, in my opinion."

I said, "He has a strong faith." He said, "I know that." I said, "You're going to vote against his entrance into theology house." Before he could answer me, if he was going to answer my question, I said, "Aren't you suppose to put personalities aside when you vote for someone." He wasn't happy with that question. He opened up one of his drawers and pulled out a cigar. He said, "Do you still smoke stogies?" I said, "Yes, I do." He gave it to me and lit it for me. He said, "Relax, make yourself comfortable. I have to take care of something. I'll be back in a few minutes." The stogie was good. A lot better than the cheap ones that I bought. I should have visited him once in awhile when I was at St. Clement's Hall.

I finished the cigar just as the receptionist came in to Fr. Banks' office and said, "Fr. Banks told me to tell you thanks for stopping by. He got tied up with something." I said, "OK, thank you. Do you think Fr. Banks would mind if I grabbed a cigar out of his drawer for the road?" Before he could answer me, I said, "I'm only kidding …"

After reading what I just wrote, I can see that I hadn't demonstrated as much backbone as I thought I had. For a long time I had this scenario going on in my head about blasting the crap out of Fr. Banks, in a positive way. I guess I was up-playing in my mind, the things that I wanted to say to him about Jim, but ended up not saying.

Some other faculty members from St. John's were Msgr. Donnelin, Fr. Tom Daily, Fr. Bill Lucey, Msgr. Dwyer, Fr. Jack Farrell and Fr. McCormick, all from St. Clement's Hall. Other than the three priests I already mentioned, Fr. Banks, Fr. Lind and Fr. Ray Devitere, I can't remember any others from Bishop Peterson Hall.

Besides Fr. Ron Coyne, a couple other guys from theology house who I got to know a little bit were Fr. Mike Lawler and Fr. Rodney Kopp. All three were third year theologians, sub-diaconate year, when I was a freshman. In their fourth year of theology house they were assigned to a parish as deacons, and resided there. They kept their apartments at Bishop Peterson Hall as well.

I remember one other theologian. I don't remember his name. He was a terror on the basketball court. He suffered from SMD (Small Man's Disease). What he lacked in size, he tried to make up for with aggressiveness and talent on the basketball court. He had dirty blonde hair, a full beard, black framed, thick eye glasses, 5', 5", about 130 lbs. One of the few guys at school who weighed less than me. He was probably a decent guy. I only knew him from our annual basketball game, the college vs. theology house. I just remembered two more seniors. Dan Bettencourt, who played in our college against theology house basketball games and Peter (I forget his last name) who refereed the games. Two more sophomores that I just remembered were Bob Lally (non-athletic) and Ed Donnelly who played basketball with us.

Other than the BNBL (Boston Neighborhood Basketball League) who played some of their games in our gym, the college vs. theology house game attracted the largest crowd of the year. A lot of the theology house guys who weren't playing in the game, would show up in their black and whites-black suit, white clergy collar (their dress code in theology house some of the time, not all the time). Our freshman year, we just assumed they were coming to the game from somewhere where they had been wearing their black and whites. By sophomore year, we knew that was not the case. They would change on purpose into their black and whites before the game. It was a strategical tactic. God was on their side.

Fr. 'Belly' O'Hearn (big guy), another priest I just remembered along with Fr. Bourque (my Spanish professor) both from the college, would always show up to root us on. Fr. O'Hearn (one of my chess combatants, fiercely competitive-hated to lose in chess) took a page out of my book our second year there. After either seeing or hearing about me walking to the handball court one day with 'Ron Sucks In Handball' written on my T-shirt, he showed up at the b-ball game our sophomore year, with 'Theology House Sucks In B-Ball' written on his T-Shirt.

The college's track record against theology house in past years had been poor. I'm not going to say that they didn't have any good ballplayers. Some of the college's b-ball players went on to become theology house b-ball players. But … with the college's addition of Jim Lynes, things were different. One ballplayer does not make a team. There is no I in team. But … one very good ball player can be the impetus to launch a team into victory lane. And … when that very good ball player (with a little help from his teammates) likes to razz up the other team, in a good nature'd way, it sets up a whole different ball game.

I can remember our starting five, freshman year. Lynes, Dribsey (Fr. Driscoll), Bettencourt, Donnelly and me. There was no question in our minds that we were going to win. And we did … I didn't say it was easy. It was closer than we had anticipated. It was more physical than we thought it would be.

Besides Shorty being a terror on the court, their other guys weren't pansies either. Being freshmen, Jim and I were warned about how physical these guys liked to play. And so did we, especially Ed Donnelly. He was about 5', 10", 200 lbs, solid, blonde hair, medium looking, personable guy from West Roxbury. Short Stuff was causing all sorts of havoc on the court. He made more than his share of steals. His outside shot was OK. He was better at stealing the ball and then driving down to his hoop and laying it in.

Peter let a lot of fouls go. That's just the way it was when a bunch of guys got together for a b-ball game. It wasn't like we were playing a real college basketball game. Just having some fun. And also, he was the only ref (there are suppose to be two referees in a basketball game, sometimes three). One time, when Shorty stole the ball from Dribsey, it looked like he had gone right through Dribsey's legs. We were all over Pete for not calling a foul. Not long after that, Shorty stole the ball from Ed, and started heading the other way for his lay up. Not if Ed could do something about it. Ed went running after him. Just as Shorty was getting ready to lay the ball in, Ed tackled him. It was beautiful. A huge cheer went up from our side. Their side let out a groan that sounded like someone had just been killed. We loved it.

As Ed got his 200 pound body off of 130 lb. Shorty, he said, "You have to earn those two points from now on." Short Stuff looked at Ed in disbelief and then at Pete. Pete was already calling the foul. As Ed was walking away he yelled out, "The ref finally called a foul."

Just then, Steve (I don't know his last name), from theology house came running onto the court in his black and whites. Steve was a deacon. Deacons still maintained their student rooms at Bishop Peterson Hall while they were stationed at a parish. He started going at it with Ed. The yelling and screaming went on between Ed and Steve for what seemed like a good minute. Ed has probably had his share of physical fights while growing up. But I doubt if he's ever been punched by a priest. I think that's what he was going for. I think he was saying everything he could to try to get Steve to punch him.

We finally broke it up. He almost succeeded, though. As we were shoving Ed away, he yelled out, "The guys got a big bark for someone with no onions." Steve tried to come back at Ed. They had to physically drag him back to their side. Jim looked at me and said, "Now *this* is basketball …"

We huddled up while Shorty was taking his technical foul shot. Pete hit Ed with a technical foul, besides the regular contact foul during an attempted shot. Two free throws plus the technical foul free throw. Dribsey said, "All right guys, let's settle down." Jim said, "Fr. Driscoll, you're not about to lead us in a little prayer, are you?" Dribsey said, "I think not … great tackle, Ed. Let's go finish them off."

I am not prejudiced against short people. I like to kid and joke around once in awhile about all of our shortcomings, ooops … sorry! I can take it as well as dish it out. I think … My brother, Gene (oldest of the kids), was the recipient of some of my short people jokes all his life. He took it pretty medium, and sometimes he took it less than medium. Sometimes, I had to be careful with what I said to him. Dynamite comes in small packages.

He is 5', 1", 110 lbs. and solid. Not an ounce of fat on him, in his day. He has gained some weight over the years, but not much. He turns 56 in '06. Gene was the Bay State (Massachusetts) wrestling champ in his weight class all his three years at Braintree High School. He was talented and he had a good coach. Coach Joe Richardi, The human cannon ball, a great guy. Gene was also decent in gymnastics, but didn't try out for the gymnastics team. I watched him do a routine on the rings one time … holy mackerel. I have a lot of respect for gymnasts.

I challenged him to a contest once when we were younger, and got my butt kicked. I never challenged him in anything again, or hardly ever. I said to him, "Gene, pick something, anything, and I'll show you how it's done." He said, "Chin-ups." We had a chin-up bar in the cellar. I said, "Watch and learn." I knocked off about seven or eight chin-ups, pretty good, I thought. As he went to grab the chin-up bar, I said, "Do you need a hand getting up there?" He looked at me, smiled and did fifteen rapid fire chin-ups. He looked at me again and said,

"Should I keep going." How come short people can do more chin-ups than tall people? I turned and went upstairs to see if I could locate any vitamin pills.

Gene graduated from Northeastern University with an undergraduate degree in physical education. He was thinking about becoming a gym teacher. He has a good personality, outgoing and friendly, good looking, a pleasure to be around. He has that personality that makes anyone he's with feel good about themselves. Like my mother, Gene, most of the time gives people the benefit of the doubt. He does not stay on guard (except with me) with most people. Is that good or bad, I don't know.

Northeastern University is a co-operative educational school. Three semesters per year. Students go to classes for so many semesters at a time (I don't know exactly how it works) and then go to jobs for so long. All of Gene's jobs while at Northeastern University were student teaching jobs. He liked them. They liked him. Gene decided to go for a graduate degree after graduating from Northeastern University.

He went to the University of Michigan. He told me that it's one thing to watch the Wolverines (football team) playing on TV. He said it's an entirely different ball game when you're there at the stadium with tens of thousands of other people. I think that their football stadium holds about 100,000 people. A lot of them being crazy, yelling, screaming, students.

I asked Gene if he ever pictured me in his mind playing football there, when he was at a game. He said, "I could see you mowing the lawn and painting the stripes."

Gene's roommate was a guy from Texas. Toward the end of freshman year, he asked Gene what he was doing for the summer. Gene said that he would line something up to stay busy and make a few bucks. His roommate said, "Why don't you come to Texas with me. You can work for my father." Gene said, "What does your father do?" His roommate said, "He raises quarter horses (racing horses) on his horse farm." Gene said, "I don't know anything about horses, I've never been on one." The roommate said, "You don't have to know anything about horses to work there. You can shovel shit, can't you?" Gene said, "Ya, but I'm not sure. There are some folks in Boston who I miss. It would be a different experience, though. What are the ladies like in Texas?" His roommate said, "You won't find friendlier ladies anywhere else in the world. Some of them work for my father." Gene said, "I'm in."

They showed Gene how to exercise the horses, feed and water them, groom them and clean up their crap. And, Gene being Gene, he rode them a little bit whenever he could. His roommates father watched Gene riding one of his horses one day. He liked what he saw. He hooked Gene up with a veteran jockey and things took off from there.

Gene did not go back to Michigan University with his roommate. He stayed on the horse farm. Three or four years later, Gene was one of the leading jockey's at Pennsylvania National Race Track (Jockey Geno O'Donnell-1980 or 1981). Three or four years prior to that, he had never been on a horse.

Theology House was ready for us the next year. Dan Bettencourt was the only senior on our team my freshman year. After he graduated from the college, he did not go on to theology house. Bob Washabaugh took Dan's place as a starter. We had our same bench from the previous season. Big Bo Brazeau, Ed Kelly, Brian Donavon, and TimCollins. Most of Theology house was back including Steve, now a priest, who ran onto the court last season to yell at Ed for tackling Shorty. He suited up for theology house. He didn't live at St. John's Seminary anymore. He lived at the parish where he was stationed. We had no problem with that. If anything, we would have a problem trying to get guys to play. He was a little better than a medium ballplayer.

They beat us fair and square. We kept it close, it was a good game. I played less than medium. My outside shot was not going in. I think I missed 5 or six outside shots before Dribsey pulled me. On a time out he asked me if I was ready to go back in.

I said, "Not a good idea Fr. Driscoll, I don't have it tonight." I sat out the whole second half. Good thing too, because our bench was keeping us in the game. When Jim (Lynes), Ed (Donnelly), and me were on the bench at the same time, Big Bo, Brian (Donovan) and Ed (Kelly) were playing some decent ball. Tim Collins didn't do too badly either when he was in the game. Bob Washabaugh played decent the whole time that he was in there, which was most of the game.

Later on that evening, when Jim and me were in Jim's room, Jim started to say, "You know something …" I interrupted him and said, "if you give me any shit about the way that I played tonight, I'm going to rip your wastebasket off the wall and throw it out the window." He said, "Take it easy, relax. All I was going to say was that everyone has a bad game once in a while. It's no biggee … "And then I could have sworn that I heard him mumble under his breath, "You would have to pick tonight to suck …"

I received an e-mail last week from Plank (Steve Burke) that was pretty funny. I'd like to share it with you. Plank calls me Bodie. That's because all his younger brothers use to call me Bodie. I'm not sure why? I probably told them that I use to play Cheyenne Bodie in the TV show years ago. Ya, I think that's what it was.

Dave,

I'm continuing to enjoy the book. I look forward to each new section. I did have a problem with some of the recent text, though, and I'm afraid that in my confusion, I may have gotten you into some trouble. The text in question …

"I said, simply put, the percentage of good looking guys who become priests to the percentage of good looking guys who get married is disproportionate to the percentage of medium looking guys who become priests to the percentage of medium looking guys who get married."

I read and reread this sentence and then reread it again. It's meaning is, well, beyond my comprehension. Because it seemed pivotal to the story, and because Jim mentioned math, I brought the text to MIT and had one of the leading mathematicians in the world look the sentence over. He took a great deal of time examining the words, and finally looked up at me and said, "Why, a five-year old child could understand this." He then turned to his administrative assistant and said, "Go find me a five-year old child. I can't make head nor tail of this."

I then brought the sentence to Dr. Irwin Corey. He is the famous "double-talk" comedian who use to appear frequently on the Merv Griffin show, the Mike Douglas show, and The Tonight Show. I'm afraid this is where the trouble begins. Dr. Corey says that the sentence in question was first used by comedian Norm Crosby, the king of the malaprop, in his act, and that Dr. Corey stole it from him. Dr. Corey says that he has been using the sentence in question as part of his "double-talk" routine for more than twenty-five years. He's crying plagiarism!

Get a hold of a good attorney, Bodie. You know how these Hollywood types are. Steve Burke

Pretty good, Steve, pretty good.

There was one particular thing that I use to do while I was at St. John's that I enjoyed very much. On just about every other Saturday evening for two years, Tim Moran (senior) and I would walk from St. John's to Harvard Square. We would leave St. Clement's Hall, walk down Foster Street, cut through Brighton Center down to a main road. I can't remember the name of that road. We would walk along that main road past Sammy White's Bowladrome on the right and the channel 38 transmitting tower and studios on the left. I can't remember the rest of the route. I remember that it was about a forty-five minute hike, one way. In the fall and spring the weather was great. Our winter walks were fine, as long as we dressed accordingly. We walked to Harvard Square one Saturday evening during a snowstorm. There were hardly any vehicles on the roads that night.

When we got there, we would always go to Brighams. Tim liked milk shakes. I would usually get a Coca-Cola. Then, we would go and sit in the Harvard Square common. We would watch all the folks doing their thing. Chess is a popular event in the common. Unusual people are not unusual in Harvard Square. It is an interesting place to watch and observe human behavior, interactions, different types of wardrobes, unique hair colors and styles. We usually sat there for about an hour. We'd talk about anything and everything. Tim (Fr. Tim Moran) is truly a gentleman. One of the best. He was one of the first students at St. John's who I told that I was leaving the school at the end of my sophomore year. That was probably in April, '73, toward the end of my sophomore year.

He looked surprised when I told him. He said, "I'm sorry to hear that. Can I ask you why?" I said, "Of course you can. I want to tell you." Just then, a guy who was down and out on his luck approached us and said, "Can you guys help me out? I'd like to buy a cup of coffee at Brighams." He was around fifty, dirty, unshaven, probably homeless. I said, "I'm sorry, I don't have any extra money." Tim took out a five and gave it to him. The guy couldn't thank Tim enough. Tim had just made the guys day. I said to Tim, "If you did that to impress me, it worked." He laughed a little bit and then said, "I know you have something to say about that, so go ahead and say it." I said, "As a matter of fact, I do."

I said, "Number one, you're encouraging and enabling the guy to panhandle. You know he's going to the liquor store and not to Brighams. You know anytime he sees you in the future, you are now a target for him. If you don't have any extra money to give to him, he will not be happy with you. And one more thing ..." He interrupted me, and said, "No more things, I understand what you're saying. Try to understand this. The few times that I am able to help someone out with money, I do so. That man may or may not be able to help me out some day. It really doesn't matter. I have no control over what he spends the money that I gave him on. I had the extra few bucks in my pocket. I chose to give it to him. Sometimes, when you help out one person, you receive help back from an unexpected source."

It sounded good to me. So, anyway, I said to Tim, "I've had a couple of good years at St. John's. I've met some wonderful people and you're at the top of the list." I paused and looked at him. When he didn't say anything I said, "What ... you're not going to give me five bucks for that one?" Without changing the concerned expression on his face, he said, "Tell me why you are leaving?"

I had wished that I could have told him, the truth. But, I knew that I wasn't going to. I had just spent two of the best years of my short life at St. John's Seminary. I could not have been in a better environment. I could not have been around better people (most of them). I absolutely loved the area. The campus was gorgeous, just like I had been told. Boston College across the tracks was beautiful. I use to love walking around the B.C. campus, stopping in the cafeteria for a cup of coffee or going to a B.C. football game. I use to love going to Alumni Stadium just to watch the team work out or go there when the team wasn't working out and try to get into a tag football game. I don't know what BC's policy is today, but back in '71-'73, you could walk into Alumni Stadium at almost any time and if none of the school teams were practicing, there were always students playing on the field.

The whole Chestnut Hill area is gorgeous. There are a lot of wealthy people who live in that area. I remember one time when I was a kid. We were walking through the Chestnut Hill area on our way to a B.C. Football game. I said to my father, "Dad, who lives in these houses, movie stars?" He got a chuckle out of that one and said, "Could be Dave, I'm not sure. What I am sure of is that whoever lives in these houses will probably never live long enough to spend all their money."

The Chestnut Hill reservoir was a popular spot for joggers and walkers. Fr. Marc Noonan, my faculty advisor at St. John's, jogged every morning. He would get up at at 5 am and usually jog around the reservoir. Sometimes, if he had the time, he would jog there in the early evening, too.

I told Tim that I needed to start dating again. I missed the ladies. Being the gentleman that Tim was, he said, "I'll bet they miss you, too." I said, "I should give you five bucks for that one." He laughed, and said, "You are going to be missed … by a lot of people." What a nice thing for him to say. I was touched by that statement, and speechless. Which doesn't happen too often. I knew that my eyes were filling up with tears. Tim looked away because he knew that I was starting to feel embarrassed. He said, "You know where we live. I hope you visit us once in awhile. Maybe some Saturday evening, that is, if you don't have a date. We can go for a walk to Harvard Square."

We took our walk to Harvard Square one or two more times before that school year ended. I really enjoyed those walks, and I really miss them.

As good as things had been for me at St. John's, I was looking forward to inviting chaos back into my life. I wanted to start drinking again. I couldn't wait to start drinking again. I was an alcoholic. I knew it, and I didn't know it. I didn't know anything about alcoholism. I didn't know what AA stood for. I use to see AAA stickers on car bumpers. I knew they stood for American Automobile Association. When I saw AA stickers on cars, I thought that had something to do with automobiles, as well. I didn't learn what AA stood for until 1981.

I was moonlighting as a cab driver for Yellow Cab in Quincy, Massachusetts. Cab drivers spend the majority of their shift waiting for passengers or fares, not driving. One of our cab stands (areas designated by the city for taxi's only) was the Quincy MBTA station. While waiting for fares we would get in each others cabs to talk and pass the time. One of the guys, Larry L., almost always had a can of Pepsi with him. Me and a few of the other guys would usually have a Dunkin Donuts coffee cup in one of our hands, that had been refilled with beer several times during our shift. We worked twelve hour shifts. I would make a few pit stops per shift to the liquor store, usually buying two or three pounders (16 ounce beers) at a time. My shift was from 4 PM to 4 am.

One evening, Larry got into my cab, with his can of Pepsi. I was enjoying my beer.

After a little bit of small talk, Larry said, "Are you doing anything tomorrow at noontime." I said, "I've got a little contracting job going on, but, I'm the boss. I don't have to show up if I don't want to. Why, what's up?" He said, "Would you like to go to an AA meeting with me at the Faxon House (Detoxification Unit in Quincy)?" I was familiar with the Faxon House.

I knew it was a place to put drunks when their drinking got out of control. I thought they went there to learn how to drink like men and women. Not to detox and then learn how not to drink, one day at a time. But I still hadn't put the two together. Faxon House-AA (I never said that I was fast, did I?). I said to Larry, "Why would I want to go to an American Airlines meeting?" He knew I liked to joke around a lot, but, he could see that I was being serious. He said, "No, Dave. Now, don't take this the wrong way. An Alcoholics Anonymous meeting." I said, "Ooohhh.... that's what AA stands for. Thanks for explaining that to me, Larry, and no thanks."

Jim Lynes was disappointed when I told him that I was leaving St. John's. He said, "You have to do what you think is best. But, remember what you said to me one time?" I said, "What did I say to you?" He said, "You said that the reason you felt you messed up at Massasoit Community College was because you chose to drink instead of study." I said, "Ya, that's true. But, I think that I'll be OK this time (I was lying to Jim and myself again, whether I knew it or not). I've got two solid years of college under my belt." I probably didn't even realize that I was kidding myself. Maybe deep down inside I knew that as soon as I started drinking again, the rest of my college education was going to go down the tubes.

Something inside of me kept wishing and hoping that Jim, or someone, anyone would say, "You are making a huge mistake. DON'T leave St. John's. Get your undergraduate degree and then do what you have to do." Life would have been so much kinder to me if I had gotten that four year ticket. But no one told me not to leave. I would not have listened, anyway. But, sometimes when I think back I wonder if there could have been anything that anyone could have said to me to open up my eyes. Some kind of magical words. More than likely, not.

Most people do not abuse alcohol. Most people drink like men and women. I think it would be difficult for them to understand someone like me. How can you fully understand something or someone if you haven't been there yourself? The majority of the students at St. John's did not know about my drinking background. They saw me as a decent guy, average intelligent, willing to work extra hard to get B's. They had no idea that for the most part, I could have cared less about the courses that I took at Braintree High School.

I'm having a little trouble trying to organize my thoughts. I celebrated forty-five consecutive months of recovery a few weeks ago, August 8th, '05. I've done some damage to my brain. Thirty-seven years of drinking, the last thirteen of those years I was freebasing cocaine as well. Most long timers (women and men with twenty plus years of recovery) in AA say that it takes about five years of recovery to get your marbles back. And then another five years to learn how to use them again. If you think it's difficult trying to understand what I'm writing, try talking to me in person. You'll need a drink.

Well, maybe writing an autobiography at this stage of my recovery was a less than medium idea.... . and maybe not. Like my friend Millie from California said to me, "What if your book can help one active addict. Turn his or her life around. Then it's worth it." As hard as it is, sometimes, for me to write this, it's worth it. You will never fully understand the pain and misery of active addiction unless you have been there. You do not want to go there. God bless the souls of all the active addicts who could not deal with it anymore. May your souls rest in peace.

Time To Get A Job

My mother told me that when I was two years old I tried to disassemble a wrist watch my father had given to her. She told me that she had taken it off and put it on the coffee table. When she came back into the living room, I had her watch wrapped around my ankle. I enjoy taking things apart. I always have. And, putting them back together. Sometimes, that doesn't always work out. I end up with spare parts. I also like to push buttons and throw switches. I've been learning how to use my PC for about a year now. I'm trying to get into the habit of thinking before hitting a key. Especially, when I'm fooling around in advanced settings. I've ended up saying ooops, way too many times. I'm on my sixth computer. Last August I paid forty-five dollars for my first one. It was a 1993 Micros something or other. I wanted to use it to type my book and be able to save it to a floppy disk. The floppy disk part never worked.

A week later I paid 300 bucks for a rebuilt computer. Steve Ka, who didn't know me, let me walk out of his store, Worcester Wireless, with the used computer without giving him any cash. I don't think that happens too often these days. I paid him 150 a week later and another 150 a month later. The PC I bought from Steve was the fastest computer I have ever owned. He did the rebuilding. He is pretty sharp with computers. He has come to my place a couple of times to troubleshoot for me. I got on the internet with that computer and was able to type my book and save it to a floppy disk. Eventually, with help from friends, I learned how to send out attachments over the internet.

That PC lasted for about two months before I blew it up. I pushed too many wrong buttons, did too much exploring and experimenting. I did things that I should not have done with the little computer experience I had under my belt. I don't mind pushing a button to see what's going to happen or exploring areas I have no business exploring. It's a good way to learn. It would probably be better if I read the manual first.

My friend Patrick Smith gave me two computers after I blew up the PC I bought from Steve Ka. They were both the same, Gateway 2000's with Windows 98 operating systems. One was complete-server, monitor, keyboard, mouse, speakers and printer. And one was the server only. They were getting new computers where he worked and getting rid of the old ones. I tried being more careful this time, but I ran into a new problem, viruses. It seemed that every time I logged onto an adult web site, I caught a virus. And I caught viruses using other areas of my PC as well. My Gateway 2000 had a Norton Antivirus package in it. That helped a lot. But still, I was able to blow it up in a few months.

I hooked up the second Gateway server, turned it on and nothing. I opened it up and there was no hard drive in it, so I couldn't switch hard drives. The first Gateway hard drive was destroyed. I didn't have a PC for a few days. When I mentioned this to Rick (Kennedy) on the phone, he said, "I think I can help you out." He told me he would call me back in a few minutes. He called me back in five minutes and said, "Are you going to be home tonight?" I said, "Yes." He said, "Ryan (his son) and I will be there around 7 with Ryan's old computer. Ryan has a new computer." Ryan was a senior at Xaverian Brothers High School in West-wood, Massachusetts. He was accepted to several colleges.

He chose to go to Providence College. Rick moved him into his new dorm there last week. I said, "Beautiful, I appreciate it a lot." They brought over Ryan's computer. It was a Dell Dimension, Windows XP Professional Edition operating system, everything included. It's a beauty, I'm using it now. I've been using it since December, almost nine months ago.

My sixth computer was an Apple Mac OS X. Rick delivered it to me, via Carolyn Royce who got it from her friend, Deborah Bernard. Deborah bought a new computer. Neither Ryan, Carolyn nor Deborah charged me anything for their computers. I hooked up Deborah's computer one time, but ended up breaking it down. Trying to learn Mac OS X was like trying to learn a foreign language for me. I will give it to someone who can use it. I'm starting to feel comfortable about not blowing up Ryan's computer. I shouldn't have said that.

So, I'm comfortable about pushing buttons. It's still time to get a job. Maybe after I get my college degree. I transferred from St. John's to Boston State College where they accepted all my credits. I was a full time junior. Two more years of college and then easy street. I wish it had been that easy. Drinking and studying did not work out for me. I could do one or the other, I couldn't do both. I chose to drink. I did the same thing at Boston State that I did at Massasoit. I screwed up, for the most part. Alcoholism is progressive. There are stages of alcoholism. I was still in the early stages of my disease. I could attend my college classes and appear to be a normal college student. I don't think any of my classmates, the few I knew, at Boston State thought that I had a problem with alcohol. I didn't hang around there. I went to my classes and then I went home. I didn't get to know too many students. It's a lot different commuting to school versus living there.

I chose to major in psychology and minor in mathematics. I felt psychology was one of the easier majors. Read and memorize, I can do that. The math would be more challenging, but I liked math and felt that I could handle it if I put the necessary time into it. Someone should have told me about Set, Theory and Logic before I decided to minor in math.

I remember being confused and having a difficult time trying to understand Set, Theory and Logic. I also remember giving up on it before putting in the necessary time that I needed to put into it. The going got rough and I got going … right out of the class. Why study something that was difficult for me when I could drink, instead.

After two years at Boston State College, I had a bunch of college credits. Massasoit Community College, St. John's Seminary College and Boston State College. I never matriculated because I couldn't. I had not fulfilled my necessary major and minor area course requirements to be eligible for a degree.

OK, it's time to get a job. I was twenty-four years old, single and living in my parents' cellar. I just spent the last six years going to college with nothing to show for it. Hmmm …

I wonder if my drinking had anything to do with that? I know it did. I also know that I didn't fully understand it at that time. As a matter of fact, I believe that I thought I had it made. While attending Boston State, one of my side projects was remodeling my cellar bachelor's pad. I did a decent job. I used my father's Grossman's credit card to pay for the materials. I wired it, installed a half bathroom and partitioned off some rooms. A bedroom, bathroom, living room, laundry/boiler room and tool room. I knotty pined all the walls and installed a finished ceiling and tiled the floor. Not a bad pad. Unlike drinking and studying, which do not go together, drinking and contracting do go together. Quite nicely sometimes. I think a lot of folks will back me up on that one.

My cousin, Bill DiNatale, stopped by one day as he often did. I was half sitting, half lying on my couch watching a ball game and enjoying a beer. As he was coming down the cellar stairs he said, "There's no beer in the refrigerator (meaning my parents' fridge where I use to keep my beer). What's up with that?" I looked at him and then nodded in the direction of my new half refrigerator that I had purchased for my apartment. It was for beer only. If I wanted food, I would got to Esther and Bill's fridge. Bill opened the fridge, grabbed a beer and said, "You got it made, you know that don't you?" I said, "I like to think so."

Bill was having a rough time of it after coming out of the marines. He went in toward the end of the Vietnam Conflict. He did not have to go to Nam. But his mother, Eileen (God rest her soul), had passed away from cancer around that time. They were close. I was close to my Aunt Eileen. The three of us were close. I spent many nights sleeping over my Uncle Tom and Aunt Eileen's house when I was in my teens. My Uncle Tom and some of his buddies were hunters. During the hunting season, I spent a lot of Friday nights at their house. We would have to wake up at 4 am. I hated that part. We would arrive at our hunting destination, and set up camp. Tom and his friends would go off in one direction. Bill and I would go off on our own. I was fifteen and Bill was fourteen the first time that I went with them. Bill had been going on hunting trips for two or three years with his father. He knew how to handle a shotgun. The only hunting trips I went on with them were for rabbit, to be eaten. My Aunt Eileen made a great rabbit stew. I never went on a deer or bear hunting trip with them.

Before I was allowed to go on my first hunting trip, Uncle Tom, Bill and I, with our shotguns, went out to this huge field behind Uncle Tom's house in Randolph, Massachusetts. That's where Uncle Tom taught me how to handle a shotgun. He also taught me how to clean a shotgun ... how to clean three shotguns as a matter of fact.

I never shot a rabbit and neither did Bill. We would shoot at trees, rocks, cans, bottles, any discarded junk, the sky. One time, there was an old car at the bottom of an embankment. I dropped in a shell (I had a single barrel shotgun) and closed my shotgun. My Uncle Tom was strict about hunting rules. We had to carry our shotguns in an open, or 'broken' position. No ammo until we were ready to shoot. The first time that Uncle Tom told me to break my shotgun, I grabbed the barrel with both my hands and lifted my shotgun up over my head. Uncle Tom said, "That's very funny David. If you had a shell in your shotgun right now, and it went off, that hole that you have in your head right now would be much larger."

I took aim at the car when Bill said, "Hold it! How do you know someone is not in there." The car looked like it had been hit by a bomb. Completely rusted, no glass or tires, a couple of exterior parts missing. I said, "You're kidding me, right?" He said, "You never know. Go down there and check it out." I said, "Why, so you can put some bird shot into it while I'm standing next to it?" But he was serious. A chip off his father.

Uncle Tom was a Metropolitan District Commission Police Officer. He's a great, hard working guy. He always worked two jobs. He had to, to provide the nice things he wanted to give his wife and six children. But ... if you got pulled over by a police officer, you would not want it to be my Uncle Tom.

Many of Tom's family are in law enforcement in Boston and the surrounding area. One of his brothers, Anthony or 'Big Tony', was the superintendent of the

Boston Police, before he retired. I've met some of them. They're all nice people. Friendly, warm, emotional, love to hug, typical Italians. My Aunt Eileen and my mother, Esther, are sisters who were from Newfoundland. Eileen married an Italian. Esther married an Irishman.

The one time that I spotted a rabbit, I dropped in a shell, closed up my shotgun, and took aim. Just before I fired, I raised my shotgun. I love animals. We always had pets in my parents' house. Some pets are better than some people ... who am I kidding? Most pets are better than most people. I understood that we were hunting for food, not just for the 'sport' of killing defenseless, innocent animals. But, still, I'd rather let someone else do the killing.

My Uncle Tom had a large freezer in his cellar for his deer meat. Someone would butcher the deer for him. He would then store the meat in his freezer. I never saw any bear meat in there? I guess bears make better carpets or wall hangers than food? The reason I never went on a bigger game hunting trip with them was because I never saved up the money for a high powered hunting rifle. If I wanted to hunt, I had to pay my own way. Uncle Tom took me to get my firearms I.D. at the Braintree Police station. He took me to the sporting goods store for my shotgun, and I think, Braintree Town Hall for my hunting license. But I paid for everything. I bought a lesser expensive Ithaca, single barrel, 12 gauge shotgun, some boxes of shotgun shells, along with my orange vest, camouflage outfit (an orange vest with a camouflage outfit?) and some other gear. Uncle Tom told me not to bother buying any shotgun cleaning equipment. He said I could use his since I would be cleaning three shotguns (his, Bill's and mine) after every small game hunting trip.

My shotgun was kept at uncle Tom's house, in his locked cabinet. My parents would not allow weapons in their house. They did not like the idea of me buying a shotgun and going hunting. Uncle Tom talked to them and reassured them that it would be all right.

A high powered hunting rifle costs a lot of money. If I really wanted to, I could have saved up for it. Esther and Bill would help me out a lot of times with money. I did a lot of the maintenance on their house. Some folks in the neighborhood would hire me for maintenance work. I started off by mowing lawns and cleaning cellars and garages. I progressed as I got older and more knowledgeable to doing a lot of things that needed to be done. I took the time and put the effort into learning how to do things. I enjoy working with my hands.

The reason that I didn't save up for a high powered hunting rifle was my drinking. That rifle (inexpensive model) ran around 250 dollars. Saving up 250 dollars was a long term goal. Drinking interfered with all my long term goals.

There is no question in my mind that if I hadn't enjoyed drinking as much as I had, I would have purchased that rifle.

Writing a book is a long term goal. I have never attempted something like this before. If I stay in recovery, one day at a time, But For The Grace Of God, I will finish writing this book. If I fall off the wagon, another goal down the tubes.

It didn't matter anyway, about the rifle. I could never shoot Bambi. And I'm pretty sure that if a bear came toward me, I could out run her/him. I was pretty fast in those days. Just ask Gig (Gerry Cook) … wait a second … he was pretty fast, too.

My Uncle Tom is remarried and is living in Florida and Maine. He took an early retirement from the MDC. He was involved in an accident that has left him in pain, probably for the rest of his life. He pulled his cruiser over on Chickatawbut Hill, on the Braintree/Quincy line, to check out a parked vehicle. A lot of teenagers would drive there to park with their boy/girl friends. A lot of other teenagers would drive there to drink and drug. Tom got out of his cruiser and then leaned back into his cruiser to grab his flashlight. As he did this, a vehicle came speeding up over Chickatawbut Hill slamming into Tom's cruiser. The driver of that vehicle was drunk, a teenager. Tom was seriously injured, but survived. He has had many operations on his back. His back will never be the same.

I have done more than my share of underaged drinking and driving. Why I never injured or killed anyone while doing so is a miracle. It could have been me that slammed into my Uncle Tom's cruiser. It wasn't, but it could have …

Bill sat down with his beer and said, "What's up for today?" Before I could answer him he said, "When are you going to get a job. You have six years of college under your belt, right? You should be qualified for something." I said, "I have two full years and four part time years of college under my belt, no degree. I'm not qualified for crap." He said, "You mean that you are qualified for crap. You're not qualified for anything decent." I said, "Thanks for correcting me, professor." He said, "Six years of full and part time college and no degree. Hmmm … Why is that?" I said, "I don't know. Would you not mind getting me another beer?"

As I mentioned earlier, Bill was struggling himself. He had recently lost his mother. His father sold the house in Randolph and moved to Maine. His older brother, Tom (oldest of the kids), and his sister, Nora (oldest daughter), moved to California. His younger brother, Robert, moved into an apartment with his girlfriend in Avon, Massachusetts. His other two sisters, Joan and Susan moved to Maine. Joan, with her husband and Susan with a friend. Bill moved into an inexpensive apartment in a house that was falling apart on Pond Street in Randolph. I visited him there one time. It was in the winter. I kept my coat on. It was cold inside. I felt bad for him. He grew up in a warm, comfortable, cozy home. Now, he was living in a run down, crap hole apartment with no heat. He had been married for a couple of years, prior to his living in this dump. He has two beautiful, great kids from that marriage. Kerri and William Joseph, or BJ.

I remember the first time that I met Susan, Bill's first wife, Kerri and BJ's mother. I was in my cellar bachelor's pad watching a ball game on TV. It was probably around 2 or 3 o'clock in the afternoon, on the weekend. I had a few beers under my belt by then. I was tired. I had worked on a project earlier. Bill stopped by my parent's house with Susan. He introduced Susan to my parents and some of my brothers and sisters. He came downstairs to my apartment. He said, "I brought my new girlfriend with me. Let's take a ride to Stanley's Ice Cream Shoppe for an ice cream cone and you can get to know her. I said, "Sure." I grabbed my large, empty Dunkin Donuts cup. He looked at it and said, "You want me to stop at a package store first so that you can get some beer, right?" I said, "You got to have a beer once in awhile."

Susan was a pretty lady. I thought that the hour or so that Susan, Bill and me were together went OK. But … according to Bill, the ending wasn't so hot. He said that he pulled up in front of my parent's house to drop me off. I got out of his car and then I leaned back in and said, "It was nice to meet you, Susan." As I was saying that, I extended my right hand. Susan extended her right hand to shake my hand. Instead of shaking her hand, I squeezed one of her boobs. I don't remember it happening. I'm not sure to this day if Bill was kidding me or not. I never asked Susan if it really happened. As Susan and Bill were driving away from my parents house, Susan was staring at Bill with her mouth open. Without looking at her, Bill said, "So, what do you think of my cousin, David?"

During or around that period of time, Bill was not getting along with his father. His father could have helped him get a good job. Instead, his friend Phil, who went to cooking school, got Bill a job in the restaurant where he worked. Bill was a utility man. He did whatever they asked him to do.

He said to me, "Do you want me to ask Phil if he can get you a job at the restaurant?" I said, "No, thanks anyway. I'll just keep doing little jobs for the neighbors for the time being." Bill hung in at that restaurant for several years. He did a lot of cooking for them. He was always a good cook, just like his mother and his father. Eventually, he started talking to his father again. With his fathers help, and a lot of foot work on his own, he got a good job as an MDC police officer. The MDC and a few other police outfits including the Beacon Hill State House Police and Massachusetts State College Police Departments and maybe one or two others merged with the Massachusetts State Police. Bill has been a Massachusetts State Police Officer for over twenty years now. He got divorced from Susan. He remarried a wonderful lady, Chris, and they bought a house in Avon, Massachusetts. His younger brother, Robert, is also a Massachusetts State Police officer.

During that time period, my father was a teacher at South Boston High School. Besides teaching math, he also was in charge of the work-study program. He got to know the human resources people at the local area businesses. He asked me if I would be interested in getting a job with the Gillette Company in South Boston. I said, sure. Gillette had a great reputation, and like every other great place to work, without a degree or a skill, it was difficult to get a job there. Tons of competition for those jobs. You almost had to know someone to get your foot in the door. Here was an opportunity for me to possibly get my foot in the door of the Gillette Company.

I was interviewed by a guy named Ned Gillette. Ned was a starting defensive back for the Boston College football team a few years back. It was March of '74. I was twenty-four at the time, he was around twenty-eight. My interview was for an entry level, get my foot in the door, assembly line position. I knew I wouldn't be able to sit at an assembly line doing repetitive tasks all day long for very long. But once I got in the company, I could start bidding on other jobs.

The interview only lasted ten minutes. I'm pretty sure Ned had already told my father that he would hire me. All I had to do was show up on time for the interview and act pleasant and grateful. That was easy enough to do. He was a pleasant guy and a sports guy. For seven out of the ten minutes we talked about B.C. football. The other three minutes he spent saying some very nice things about the IF. In fact, I remember him saying to me, "If you're one-tenth the man that your father is, you will end up having a great career with us. One of our employee benefits is tuition reimbursement. I know you're not that far away from a degree." I said, "Thank you, that's very nice of you to say those things about my father. I plan on finishing up my degree requirements." That was thirty years ago. Cheeesch … I never did get that degree.

It's 5:50 AM, Wednesday, September 7, 2005. Nine days after hurricane Katrina struck doing most of her damage in Louisiana, Mississippi and Alabama. I was just watching more video on the news from the hurricane. Hurricane Katrina is the worst natural disaster in our country's history. They think that they are going to find a lot of fatalities after all the water is pumped out of the area. The video is getting harder and harder to watch.

I don't know if any of you have ever worked on an assembly line, but, it sucks. I started off on an assembly line in the Good News disposable razor department.

It was a new product at the time. I would have to snap the razor blade head onto the razor handle; for eight hours a day … five days a week. God love anyone out there who is doing assembly work. I was fortunate enough to bid on and receive another job after three months on the assembly line. I would not have lasted much longer. One of the ladies there had been working on assembly lines at Gillette for thirty years. I don't think she liked working on an assembly line. Who would? But, she accepted it.

That was in March of '76. I had been going to school full/part time, since graduating from Braintree High School in 1969, until May of '75. I was doing a lot more handy man work for the neighbors between May, '75 and March, '76, than I had been doing in prior years. When my father asked me if I wanted to work for Gillette, it was appealing. I liked the idea of getting vacation time, paid holidays, medical insurance, workman's compensation insurance, tuition reimbursement, a guaranteed pay check on time, company bonuses and incentives and pay raises. Contractors have to include many of those things I just mentioned in their estimates. I'm not sure that all customers understand that. I didn't include any of those extras in my prices because I never went through formal training for carpentry, electricity, plumbing and other things. I didn't have a contractors, electricians or plumbers license. I have never been afraid of electricity; I have always respected it and never did or never would attempt a wiring job unless I was sure about what I was doing—simple wiring jobs.

I read instructional manuals, how to books, worked with a couple of guys who were in the business and knew what they were doing. I did take an electricity course at the Blue Hills Vocational Technical High School one time. In their evening division, adult continuing educational program. I never took the final exam or got my certificate for taking that course. That was a short term goal. One certificate course that lasted a few months. There were other short term goals that I never completed because of my drinking. Why go to class or study when I could drink. I did most of my jobs first with someone who had done them before. Someone who knew what he/she was doing.

One time I was constructing a set of back door stairs for an elderly lady in the neighborhood. She asked me if I would take a look at her toaster for her. She said it wasn't working. I plugged it into a different receptacle and it worked. I put my testers on the first receptacle, it was gone. She said, "I'll call my electrician and have him replace it." I said, "You don't have to do that. I'll be going to Richmond's Hardware store later. I'll pick up a receptacle and put it in for you." She said, "I didn't know that you were an electrician, also." I said, "I'm not. I don't have a license. But it's a simple, easy job to do. I've done it many times in the past. If you don't feel comfortable about me doing it, call your electrician. He will probably charge you 25 dollars (at that time) for showing up and diagnosing the problem. Add another 2 bucks for the receptacle and whatever he charges for the work, maybe another 10 bucks. I can get the receptacle at Richmond's for 49 cents and I'll charge you another cup of coffee for my labor. It's up to you." She said, "You can do it."

That was around 8:00 am. It was about noontime when I replaced the receptacle. At about 2:00 PM, the electrician showed up. He heard me working and came around back.

When he told me that he was the electrician, I said, "I didn't know that Mrs. _ had called you. She asked me to take a look at one of her receptacles." He said, "Did you take care of it for her?" I said, "Ya, I'm really sorry." He said, "Don't worry about it, she's done this before. She's a nice lady, but, you must know that her memory is going? You saved her some money. I've got more work than I can handle." I said, "I'll tell her that you came by." He said, "Don't bother, she'll forget anyway."

I didn't have to charge the neighbors a lot of money. My parents weren't charging me for rent or for food or for anything else that I wanted in their house. I was taking care of almost all the maintenance that needed to be done on their house. If I didn't know how to fix something, I would watch and help the person who was fixing it, if he or she didn't mind. I remember one time the boiler went down. I went down stairs to look at it. I went back upstairs and told my father that I had no idea what was wrong with it. He called Barile plumbing, who he had a contract with.

When the service man arrived, I asked him if there was anything that I could do to help him. He said, "I drink my coffee with cream and sugar." When I came back downstairs with his coffee, the boiler was running. He said, "You're father has the maintenance contract with us. Since I didn't have to replace any parts, there is no charge for this job." I said, "That's good news. Why don't you come into my living room, sit down and drink your coffee and tell me how you fixed it?" He pointed to the red reset button on the control box on top of the jet. I said, "That's all it was?" He said, "That's all. It shouldn't happen too often. The jet cutting out once in awhile is normal. More than once in awhile and I can troubleshoot for other things. You'll know how to fix it next time. You can save me a trip. If it happens again and it won't reset for you, it may have to be primed first. Usually, it only has to be primed if you run out of oil. I know that your father never runs out of oil, so, when you hit the reset button you should be all set." I said, "You don't have time to explain to me how to prime it, do you?" And he did.

While working on the assembly line at Gillette, I bid on a Security Officer's opening for the Gillette Company's Andover plant. They were in-house security officers, not an outside agency. A good company job, a sought after job. A lot of people applied for that job. I had the least amount of seniority. But I was the only applicant with security guard experience.

During my second semester, junior year at Boston State College I was hired as a part-time security officer by the Pinkerton Company. They placed me at Simmons College, an all women's college (dorms located on Brookline Avenue in Boston, Massachusetts), to guard the dorms. "From A Seminary To An All Women's College." Our security control panel and main station were the front desk as you entered the main dorm, Simmons Hall. There were eight other dorms that made up that complex. Our security rounds took us through all of them, each and every floor. That's another book.

Besides my security guard experience, I had something else going for me. I did not drink during the three months that I worked on that assembly line. I know that had I been hung over and sick, there would have been no way that I could have worked on an assembly line for eight hours. Not just that. I wanted to put my best foot forward. I wanted to make a good impression, and I did.

I was interviewed in South Boston by Evo Bernardini, Manager of Safety & Security-Gillette Andover. My boss on the assembly line came up to me one day and said, "They want you in personnel. The guy from Andover is here to interview you for the security guard job." I was wearing a white T-shirt with a red heart on the front and yellow lettering that read, "Cigar Smokers Make The Best Lovers." I looked at my boss, then I looked down at my T-shirt, then back up at him. He said, "Don't look at me. You can't have my shirt." And he added, "Don't worry about it. This is the way it's done around here. The guy from Andover knows that you are working on an assembly line right now." Then he chuckled a little bit and walked away.

Personnel directed me to one of the interview rooms. I walked in and Evo Bernardini was sitting down at the table, with an ash tray in front of him (1976), smoking a cigar. We shook hands, he looked at my T-shirt, smiled a little bit and said, "My interviews don't last long. You haven't been here long. Only three months. No lates, no early quits, no misses, always filled your quota, your boss likes you and the best part; you're the only one who has applied for this job who has any experience. If I offer you the job will you take it?" I said, "Yes." He said, "Nice meeting you. I'll be in touch."

He hired me for the job. I enjoyed working at the Andover plant. It was fairly new at the time. One story high, spread out over a lot of land. There were two large warehouses for receiving and shipping. Their shipping warehouse was Gillette's main distribution center in the northeast. Three tractor-trailers made three trips a day always running together, five days a week filled with razor blades only, from Southie to Andover, with an armed escort in an unmarked vehicle. From Andover, Gillette sent out four teams of road (overnighter's) tractor-trailer drivers whose trailers were filled with razor blades from Southie, toiletries, shampoo, cricket lighters, and all the other products that were manufactured in Andover.

Those teams would deliver their loads to other Gillette company distribution centers across the country. I think that there were about twenty-five bays in the shipping warehouse, all with trailers backed into them almost all the time. A lot of the drivers who came to Andover to pick up Gillette loads were independent owner-operators. That was not an easy way to make a living.

We had a security post at the shipping warehouse entrance door. We had to sign everyone in, copying their name from their drivers license. A lot of the independent drivers had multiple licenses. Once in a while, one of those drivers would pull out a few licenses and say, "Which one do you want?"

Whenever one of them did that to me I would always say, "I'd ask you for your best looking picture … but, in your case … your not going to have one." I'd usually get a smile. That doesn't happen anymore. The Department of Transportation along with all the states Department of Motor Vehicles has corrected that problem. If a truck driver's license, a CDL(Commercial Drivers License), is suspended in Massachusetts, it is suspended in all the other states as well, because it is one license for commercial drivers that covers all the states. It use to be that a driver could lose his license in one state and just start using another license from a different state. He could continue driving. Even in the state where his license was suspended since he was now using a different license.

Once in awhile an independent driver could not back his trailer into the dock. They spend over ninety-nine per cent of their driving time going forward. They drive from the east coast to the west coast and everywhere in between. Backing up those trailers can be tricky. They have to turn their steering wheel in the opposite direction that they want to back up. It's a matter of experience for most drivers. Like most anything else, the more you do it, the easier it gets.

It was kind of funny when some independent drivers had just spent the last three days driving from California to Massachusetts, and then they couldn't back their trailers into the docks (not so funny for them). That's when our yard guy (moved trailers around in the shipping and receiving yards), Joe Spinetti, would take care of it for them. Sometimes, Joe spent more time at our security post talking to us than he did moving trailers around. But, that's just the way that job went. Sometimes there weren't any trailers to move around and sometimes Joe didn't have enough time to move around all the trailers that needed to be moved around. I got along pretty good with Joe.

A couple of Navajo (independent trucking outfit) drivers couldn't back their trailer in one time. They were young, maybe a couple of years younger than me. They were wearing cowboy hats and cowboy boots and cowboy shirts and cowboy belt buckles. They were probably wearing cowboy underwear, too. They had a cowboy accent. I decided to screw with them. After each one of them tried for half-an-hour to back their trailer in, they came back to the security post. Joe and I had been watching them for the whole hour. One of them said, "Do you boys know where the yard guy is at? We're having a wee bit of trouble trying to back our rig into the dock."

I said, "The yard guy is at home. He's out sick today." They turned around and looked out over the shipping docks to see which driver they would ask for help. I said, "I'm sorry, guys, company policy prohibits any driver from backing another driver's rig in. Only Gillette's yard man is allowed to do that." They stared at me, stared at each other, stared down at their cowboy boots and then looked back up at me. I said, "I tell you what I'll do, men. I'm not suppose to do this, so, don't say anything to anyone. I'll back it on for you." One of them said, "You know how to drive the big ones?" I said, "What do you have for a transmission?" He said, "A road ranger." I said, "I can handle it. You two wait here."

I went out the door and stood beside a tractor for a minute until Joe came out. He said, "All right, give me a minute to back it in and then you can go inside and tell them that you did it." I said, "You're all right, Joe. You're not a lefty are you?" Joe backed it in. I waited another minute and then I went inside and said, "You're all set guys." The two of them said, "We surely do appreciate it, partner." I said, "I'm happy to be able to help you boys out."

I worked in Andover for about three years. The commute from Braintree to Andover was about seventy-five minutes. It was almost all highway driving. My parent's house is a three minute drive to the highway, Route 128, to the Southeast Expressway through Boston to I-93 to Andover. There was hardly ever any traffic because I worked on the second shift. I enjoyed the drive. I have always enjoyed driving. I miss not owning a vehicle.

The other day I told Tom (Rowan) that I haven't owned a vehicle in nine years. I was wrong. I haven't owned a vehicle in about twelve years. I owned a

1974 MGB at the time that I worked in Andover. I had bought it the year before, sometime in the spring of '75. It was gorgeous. The best vehicle that I ever owned. It was Citron (yellow) with a black convertible top, nice wheel rims, black racing stripes on the two lower side quarter panels, extra comfortable black bucket seats and black interior, and a five speed transmission. It was one nice looking car. I bought it used from an MGB dealership in Waltham, Massachusetts. It had 6,000 miles on it. The '75 models were out, but this car was so sharp looking that it was one of the cars in the showroom at the dealership.

I didn't have a steady pay check coming in at the time that I bought it. Steve (Burke) use to say, "You're the only guy I know who bought a fancy sports car without having a job." I did have some money coming in from my handyman jobs. And, I had the Boston Teachers Federal Credit Union, for Boston school teachers and their family members. They didn't care that I didn't have a regular job. All they cared about was that my father co-signed my auto loan.

The car cost a lot of money, but, having 6,000 miles on it and being a year old, they were knocking a substantial amount off the original price. But, still, the main reason that I took the drive to their dealership in Waltham was to get some facts and figures. I hadn't planned on buying a car that day. I saw an MGB in a magazine advertisement. I wanted to see it in person.

I was looking at a maroon, '75 model in the showroom. I was writing down some figures and some other information. An attractive saleslady, about thirty-three years old, said, "That is one sharp looking car." She had an accent. I said, "Ya, but I really can't afford it." She said, "That one over there, pointing to the citron (yellow) '74 MGB, is a year older. It has 6,000 miles on it. We've knocked a lot of money off of the original price." I said, "Is there any reason that it was sold back to the dealership after being driven for only 6,000 miles?" She said, "That's because one of the owners of this dealership drove it. He always takes the sharpest looking car that comes in for himself. He drives it for a year and then he puts it back in the showroom. He owns more than one car, that's why the mileage is low for a year. When the new models come in, he does the same thing. Get in, check it out."

I sat in it and started to fall in love. I said to her, "By the way, where are you from?" She said, "France. My accent is French." And she added, "You're sitting in a French car." I know, I know, but I was gullible when it came to pretty ladies … and pretty cars.

I said,"I am?" She said, "If French girls see you in this car, you're going to have your hands full." I said, "I'll take it."

I remember one time when I was around seventeen years old, I was taken in by a salesman at Richmond's Hardware store store in Braintree, Massachusetts. It was the beginning of the winter season. The weather person was predicting the first snow storm of the year. My father said, "Go to Richmond's and pick up a snow shovel. You can use a new one." I went to Richmond's and looked at a medium priced snow shovel. It was OK, but, there was another one that was a lot better. A lot more expensive, too. It was a gravel shovel. I was checking it out, looking it over when the salesman approached me and said, "Son, you don't want that shovel." I said, "Why not?" He said, "You have to be a man to use it." I said, "I'll take it."

When I got home with it, the IF looked at it and said, "Did you get a truck to go with that plow blade?"

Out of the three years that I worked as a security guard in Andover, I commuted there from Braintree for about a year. In the summer of '77, the start of my second year in Andover, I met Jane. We fell in love. I moved in with her in Union Square in Somerville, Massachusetts. We were married on February 25, 1978. My commute to Andover from Somerville was a little bit shorter.

We decided to move into an apartment complex in South Lawrence, on the Andover-Lawrence line. I think that was in the fall of '78, shortly after our daughter, Shelley Anne, was born. Shelley was born on August 12, 1978, same birthday as my sister, Sheila. A lot of the folks who worked at Gillette in Andover lived in the Lawrence-Methuen-Andover area. Some lived in New Hampshire. One guy that I knew, Bob McKusker, the manager of one of the accounting departments and a hell of a nice guy, lived in an apartment complex in Andover. He told me that it was very expensive there. Gillette paid everyone well. But, the town of Andover was better suited for the Gillette white collar employee's.

I think that Gillette-Andover may have been one of the first outfits to have casual Fridays. On that day, you couldn't tell the office folks from the manufacturing folks. We all ate in the same cafeteria, one heck of a beautiful cafeteria.

I remember on our first casual Friday I showed up for work wearing bright white sneakers, baby blue Bermuda shorts, and a colorful Hawaiian shirt. Our Safety and Security office and control center was at the main entrance to the plant, Office North. As I walked in at my usual time of 2:45 in the afternoon (my shift started at 3), the guard at the control console, Tom, just stared at me. He didn't say anything. I walked into the Safety and Security control center. The shift supervisor's office was to the right, the manager's office to the left. I walked into the shift supervisor's office. My boss, Al Lawn, and the the first shift boss, John Langtry, were talking. They looked at me. I said, "Casual Friday." They both had a good sense of humor and enjoyed a good laugh. John went out to one of the bulletin boards and brought the casual Friday's bulletin back in with him. He looked it over and then handed it to Al who looked it over. Al then got up and went to get Evo, our manager.

When Evo saw me his cigar almost fell out of his mouth. I'm not sure why. He was wearing a pair of canary yellow Bermuda shorts and a fire engine red polo shirt. He said, "What do you think you're doing?" I said, I'm sitting here with two of my bosses discussing possible security problems ..." He said, "No, no, no ... Why are you out of uniform?" I said, "It's casual Friday, Evo. And, I like your outfit." He said, "It's not casual Friday for you." Al said, "Excuse me, Evo, but John and I were looking over the casual Friday bulletin. Neither of us could find anything in here about security officers being excluded from casual Fridays." Evo grabbed the bulletin out of Al's hand. He read it, turned around, then turned back around again and said, "I know that your uniform is in your car or your locker, isn't it?" I said, "It is, Evo, but, do I have to wear it today?" He walked away.

Our Safety and Security department had ten guards. Three per shift plus a guy who came in from 11 am till 7 PM. We had three shift supervisors and our boss, Evo. It was a decent department. It was a good job. Gillette-Andover was a good place to work. Being close to New Hampshire made it even better. I found my favorite grinder shop on Route 28 in Salem, N.H. The Atomic Sub Shop. Corbetts Pond in Windham, N.H., was a nice place to go fishing. One of the security guards, Rene Letournea, thirty-three years old, who worked on the third shift under Bob Griffin, lived on Corbetts Pond. He bought a bungalow there after his marriage went south. Before I got married, I moved in with him for a few months. Out of all the different addresses that I was about to have in the future, it was my only N.H. address. 7 Silver Road, Windham, N.H. Rene could be a sharp guy, and was sometimes. There were many things that he could do with his hands. He had a strong resemblance to Al Pacino. Many times he would get double looks from people. His father also worked at Gillette-Andover. A very nice guy, who, I believe did not drink. Rene had the same problem that I had. He loved to drink.

One of Rene's friends from Boston, Dan, bought a piece of land in New Hampshire, not far from Rene's place. There was a house on the property, but it was in rough shape. Dan could either knock the house down and build a new one or renovate the existing structure. He chose to renovate. He hired Rene for the job. Rene hired me to help him. Renovating is always harder than new construction, but you can save some money. It was a two story structure with a basement, a stone foundation that was in good condition and a wooden frame that, for the most part was solid. We gutted everything else.

Rene would get home from Gillette around 7:30 AM. I had to start work at Gillette at 3:00 PM. I would be awake and ready to go to work on Dan's house when Rene got home from Gillette. I would put in about four hours of work on the house, five days a week. On my two days off from Gillette, I would work on the house eight to ten hours each day. Rene worked eight hours at Gillette and another eight hours on the house, five days a week. He would put in eight to ten hours on the house each of his two days off from Gillette.

Our days off were not the same. The work schedule for the Safety and Security department at Gillette was different from all the other departments. One week, my days off would be a Tuesday and a Wednesday. The next week, a Monday and the coming Sunday. The next week, a Friday and a Saturday. That's just the way it was because the plant had to have security coverage 24-7-365. There was no Monday thru Friday (excluding the bosses) for our department. If all the guards worked Monday thru Friday like all the other departments, that would mean that we would have to come in on Saturdays at time in-a-half, and Sundays at double time. That would get expensive.

Safety and security departments, nurses, police, firefighters, EMT's, and other emergency personnel and certain other occupations know how that goes. We weren't excluded from overtime. There were vacations to cover and we had to fill in for guys and ladies (we had two female security officers) who were out sick. Gillette's annual stock holders meeting was held in Andover. All guards worked on that day. We were paid time in-a-half for most of our training sessions. If one of our scheduled work days fell on a holiday, we were paid double time in-a-half. And there were other things that would come up that required extra safety and security coverage.

I do not get up early in the morning if I drink the night before. I do not have the energy to get up. Alcohol does something to my system that makes it nearly impossible for me to get out of bed the next day. For the two months that I worked with Rene on Dan's house, I did not drink. I went on the wagon, again. I still didn't know what AA stood for and I didn't know anything about the disease of alcoholism. All I knew was that if I wanted to get up early in the morning to go work on Dan's house, I could not drink. Rene didn't go on the wagon. He did cut down on his drinking a lot. He couldn't understand why I went on the wagon. We had enjoyed drinking together. We had had some decent times. But, I know that he appreciated the ability and the quality of my work. And, he appreciated me being awake and ready to go to work when he got home from Gillette;

every day, day after day. We did a nice job on that house. Rene called in a roofing contractor and a few others once in awhile to help us out. But, we did most of the work ourselves.

Three years was long enough for me to be a security guard. I was getting restless. I wanted to do something that was more productive, more challenging for me. I bid on a job in one of the machine shops at Gillette-South Boston. Andover was a nice place to work. As far as opportunities to bid on jobs there went, there were not nearly as many as there were in Southie. The security guard job in Andover gave me an opportunity to become a Gillette permanent employee. I was a temporary employee when I first started working at Gillette on the assembly line. And, I enjoyed being an in-house security guard with a top notch outfit. There were challenges to that job that most people are probably not aware of. It was a good job.

I had no experience what-so-ever in a machine shop. But that wasn't going to stop me. I'm of average intelligence with a good set of hands. I can learn, if they are willing to teach me. And, I had perfect attendance going for me. I had never missed a day of work. Gillette was big on attendance. Gillette was huge on attendance. They had perfect attendance banquets every year. There is one and only one reason why I hadn't missed a day of work during those three years in Andover. Evening Shift. During my four part-time years of college I missed way too many morning classes. I couldn't get up in the morning after drinking the night before. I can remember one professor looking at me one morning, somewhere near the end of the semester, and saying, "Are you sure you're in the right class? I don't believe I've seen you here before." He checked his class list and I was on it. He said, "It's nice of you to join us, Mr. O'Donnell."

I drank as much as ever in Andover, with the exception of the two months that I worked with Rene. It was easy to get up at noontime, take a nice shower and hit the Atomic sub shop for a large grinder, bag of chips, and a Coca-Cola. I was rearing and ready to go to work. Three hours later I would have a great supper in Gillette's cafeteria. The cafeteria would shut down at 7, after the 2nd shift was fed. One of the benefits of being a security guard is having keys to everything, I mean everything. I would hit the cafeteria again around 10 o'clock for a snack.

I had heard one time that machinists are decent in math. And I think most of them are. With my attendance and decent math ability going for me, maybe I could talk my way into one of the several machine shops at Gillette-Southie.

The job I bid on was an NC (numerical control) turret lathe operator. I did not know that an NC turret lathe operator had at least four years of apprenticeship under his/her belt along with whatever other time after that, that he or she had been in the machine shop. Nobody told me. I focused on the word 'operator'. But, everyone who bid on a job, had to be interviewed for it, regardless of his/her qualifications. This time I traveled to South Boston.

The guy who interviewed me was Ray Lobbisser, the Manager of Piece Parts Machining, one of Gillette-South Boston's several machine shops. He was a decent guy. Working for a good outfit seems to bring out the best in people. After we realized that I had made a mistake bidding on that job, we talked about sports for a few minutes. I noticed that he had a blueprint on his desk. I said, "Is that a machine shop blue print. He said, "It is. As a matter of fact, it's a little test I'm giving to the guys and gals who are bidding on this job." I said, "Oh ya, I'm pretty good in math, what's the test." He said, "Your math ability won't help you on this test. Here, let me show you." He pointed to something on the blueprint and said, "How would you set this job up, and what tool would you use to machine it?" I said, "That's an easy one." He looked at me and said, "It is?" I said, "Ya, I'd find out who the best machinist in the shop was, and have him or her do it." He laughed.

I thanked Ray for his time and got up to leave. He said, "Sit down, hold on for a minute." He said, "You know, you've got terrific attendance, a nice write up from your boss and you're a young guy. I think most people would have settled into that nice security guard job that you have up there in Andover and retired from it. You don't want to settle for that. Nothing against those folks who do. You say that you are average intelligent; I think that you might be under estimating your intelligence." I wasn't and I don't necessarily wish that I were. There is nothing wrong with being average intelligent. Why do so many people want others to think that they are smarter than they are? What's wrong with being average intelligent-NOTHING IS WRONG WITH IT!.

"I think that you would do well in a machine shop. Tell you what I'm going to do. I've got a guy here who's been running my tool crib on the second shift for the last sixteen years. He's retiring next month. That job would get your foot in this machine shop. We have five other machine shops, and we all use this one tool crib. He pointed to the tool crib across from his office. There are other jobs that come up in the machine shops that don't require you to be an A/R (all round or all around) Machinist to bid on. There's one in my shop. A Blanchard grinder machinist. I've got two Blanchard grinders here. You don't need a four year machine shop apprenticeship under your belt to run a Blanchard grinder. If the right gal or guy bids on that job, we will train her or him for it."

It sounded good to me. I thanked him for his information. He said, "Watch for the tool crib attendant opening on the board." I said, "I will!" I thanked him again and said, "I'll see you again, soon."

I bid on and got that tool crib attendant job. I enjoyed it, a lot. I like putting things where they belong. It's nice to know that something is going to be where it is supposed to be. The first couple of weeks were a little rough trying to find out where everything was located. And, there were the guys who would ask me for tooling that didn't exist. I didn't mind. I got as much a kick out of it as they did. Being one who enjoyed pulling off a prank or two myself, I enjoyed the challenge.

One time, Marc Provost, a good guy, came up to my counter. He put his elbows on the counter and started rubbing his face with both his hands. He said, "Oh man, Dave, I screwed up!" I said, "What's wrong, Marc?" He said, "I screwed up, I screwed up! The only way that I can fix the job that I just screwed up is with an X-42 Ramification Reamer." I said, "Marc, if we've got an X-42 Ramification Reamer, I'll find it." Reamers are like precision drills. After a hole is drilled with a regular high speed drill bit, let's say a 3/8" diameter hole, or a .375 inch diameter hole, or 375 one-thousandths of an inch diameter hole. You can fine tune that diameter using a reamer. A .371 reamer will turn that .375 diameter into a .371 diameter, plus or minus a few tenths. In the machine shop, a tenth is not one tenth of an inch. It is one ten-thousandth of an inch.

I went to the reamer drawers. I spent at least five minutes looking through all the reamer drawers to try to find an X-42 Ramification Reamer. Nothing but the usual sized reamers, 3/32, 9/64, 1/4, etc., and the special sized reamers, .037, .649. .991, etc. I looked over at the counter. Marc had been joined by a couple other guys including the second shift boss, Steve Snyder. They were chuckling, enjoying themselves ... at what I was doing ... looking for something that didn't exist. I grabbed the biggest reamer in the drawer and walked towards them. They all scattered. X-42 RAMIFICATION REAMER ... holy moly!!!

I handed out tools for about six months on the second shift. One of the Blanchard grinder machinists had bid on and received another job in one of the other machine shops. His job went up on the board. It was for the second shift. Beautiful, my kind of shift. I came to work one day, stuck my head into Ray's office and said, "Is it too early to bid out of the tool crib?" He said, "Not at all. I'm expecting you to bid on the Blanchard job." He added, "There will be other applicants, but you still have perfect attendance going for you after four and one-half years. That's a huge plus. Another plus is that you already work in this department and you know the boss." I said, "Thanks, Ray" and started to leave when he said,

"There's one more thing, Dave." I said, "I'm good looking, too?" He said, "No, that's not it. Nobody can hand out a tool like you can." I laughed.

I was trained for four weeks on the day shift. I didn't go back on the wagon, but I didn't drink the night before a work day. I couldn't. I knew if I had, I might not show up for work the next day. Not only that, but I was learning a new trade. I had to be sharp. I'm not sharp when I drink. It seems to me that all aspects, ALL ASPECTS of my life are affected negatively when I put that first drink into my system. It was always the first drink that got me drunk. That is probably difficult for non-addicts to understand. The first drink I put in my system sets up a compulsion for me to take the second, third, fourth, etc., drinks. I'm an alcoholic. I cannot stop after one drink. I cannot stop after I take that first drink. That's the drink I have to stay away from. I don't even have to worry about the second, third, and fourth drinks if I stay away from that first drink.

As an alcoholic, I am an extreme example of self-will run riot. Driven by hundreds of forms of fear, self-pity, self-seeking and self-delusion, I step on your toes and you retaliate. You step on my toes. Sometimes I feel like you are stepping on my toes without provocation. Selfishness and self-centeredness are two of the roots of my problems. If I don't work on these two things, everyday, I will probably drink again.

I recently received an e-mail from a friend. She made the statement, 'Life should not be measured by the number of breaths we take. It should be measured by the number of times life takes our breath away'. I said to her, "That's pretty good." She said, "I read or heard it somewhere, I like it, too." When I drink and drug, life does not take my breath away. Life is a struggle, it is a hell, probably like no physical hell that may exist. When I am in recovery, I have moments of life taking my breath away. Not physical things like the red sox winning the world series. That was a beautiful thing, but I'm talking about mental moments where I might be sitting in my chair and all of a sudden a feeling comes over me that I can best describe by saying that feeling makes me say to myself, there is a God, and heaven is a beautiful place. Does anyone know what I'm talking about?

I worked as a Blanchard grinder machinist for two years. I liked that job. Everyday I was learning something new. The different jobs that I ran on the Blanchard grinder required different set-ups, presented new challenges. Besides having to grind high-grade tool steel on the Blanchard grinder (common material used in constructing machinery; a lot of our blueprints were for razor blade manufacturing machines that called for tool steel or high grade steel), sometimes I would have to grind bronze (non-magnetic), stainless steel (an extremely hard and very expensive material that the boss did not want anyone to mess up), and cast iron once in a while.

A Blanchard grinder has two main parts. The grinding wheel and the magnetic table. The control panel on one of my grinders (the big one) was to the right with a big, red, emergency stop button in plain view. I had to use that button a few times. The grinding wheel spins at around 2400 revolutions per minute. It is made up of eight grinding sections that had to be replaced as they wore down. If they weren't installed properly, the grinder would crash when the wheel made contact with the parts being ground. Stuff would go flying everywhere and everyone in the shop, about thirty guys and a few ladies, would stop what they were doing and look over at the Blanchard grinder ... at me. I would be on the floor with my arms covering my head. It happens so fast that there is no time to yell out 'fire in the hole.'

When that happens there really is little danger of me or anyone else in the shop being hit by flying debris. The grinding area is completely enclosed by steel walls with a sliding access door. The spinning, grinding wheel comes down on the parts to be ground from above. There is an area between the grinding wheel and the steel walls on the top where parts can come flying out during a crash. But, they go up and usually back down in the grinder. It's the loud noise during the crash that gets everybody's attention ... and scares the crap out of me.

The other Blanchard grinder in our shop was a small one that stood about six feet high by six feet long, maybe four feet from front to back. It had a circular grinding table that was about two feet in diameter. It was good for grinding smaller pieces. A lot of times we would get jobs that might be, maybe a hundred little blocks of steel, 1" x 1" x ½". We would Blanchard grind them to blueprint specs. We tried to do most of the small work on the smaller Blanchard. We would do on the larger pieces of work on the big Blanchard grinder. It stood about eight feet high, by twelve feet long by about six feet from front to back. It had a four foot diameter circular grinding table.

The grinding tables had a magnetic field that was manually controlled by an on/off switch. The magnetic field helped to hold down the steel pieces (not the bronze) while they were being ground. They also had to be blocked in or set-up. Poor set-up was the other main reason for grinder crashes. Blueprints told us what specifications to grind to, not how to set-up. That was up to the Blanchard grinder machinist.

Working on the second shift made it easy for me to show up for work every day. I probably would have shown up for work everyday no matter what shift I worked on, for two reasons. I enjoyed working in the machine shop a lot and I was married at that time. I will talk more about my four years of marriage in the next chapter. After I got married, I almost completely stopped drinking.

Somewhere around the beginning of October, 1981, I became aware that my marriage was falling apart. My ex-wife told me that she had been seeing a guy for a couple of weeks and that she wanted a separation from me. I'll talk more about it in the next chapter.

Almost five and one-half years of nearly perfect attendance with the Gillette Company. I had been late a few times. I never missed a day of work, until the beginning of October, 1981, due to marital problems. One day I didn't show up for work and I didn't call in. When my boss called my apartment, my ex-wife told him she didn't know where I was and she didn't care where I was and she hung up. I think that was a Monday. I started off that afternoon heading for work, and made it to work. At least I made it to the Gillette parking lot. After parking my car, I walked to the Triple O's club on Broadway Street in South Boston, which was nearby the Gillette plant. I spent the rest of the afternoon and evening there, drinking.

I showed up for work two or three times that week and did the same thing the following week. Five and one-half years worth of perfect attendance down the tubes. Gillette was a good outfit to work for. They were a good example of a non-union shop that worked. If you treated Gillette good, showed up for work and did what you were suppose to do, you were well taken care of.

One example of their several outstanding employee benefits was their paid sick leave policy. At the time I was working for them, they did not have a certain number of paid sick days per year. If you were sick, no matter how many days it took for you to get better, no matter how many times per year you were sick, you got a full days pay, a full weeks pay, a full months pay; if you were really sick and unable to work. That's why they were so strict about attendance.

The unusual part of that benefit was that you could break your leg skiing and you would receive a full forty hour weeks pay until you returned to work. It did not matter if you were injured on or off the job. If it was a serious injury or illness you would receive your full weeks pay until a time was determined for you to receive workman's compensation and if necessary, disability and retirement benefits. If you were healthy, Gillette wanted you to show up for work. If you couldn't, really couldn't show up for work, Gillette would take care of you. It was an interesting concept, policy. Healthy employees, by showing up for work every-day, are making it possible for the company to give a sick employee a full days pay, no matter how many days that employee is sick or injured on or off the job. I doubt it if they (Gillette was purchased by Proctor & Gamble) still have that policy today. There are too many people more than willing to take advantage of a policy like that in who knows how many deceitful ways.

Friday of that second week, as I walked past Ray's office, he yelled, get in here. I didn't even look at him. I wasn't planning on staying long. I walked down to my work station. I don't think that I said anything to anyone. I grabbed my tool box and headed back to the exit door. Ray was standing outside his office. He said, "Dave, can I at least talk to you for five minutes." I put my tool box down and let Ray talk for a little while. I wasn't listening, I wasn't able to listen attentively. I remember he was saying that he was going to put me in for a leave of absence, but it didn't matter. I knew I was leaving Gillette for good. I appreciated his concern, maybe not so much at that time. I was unable to. I appreciated his concern more so at a later time.

I'm not going to talk about what I think might be some of the psychological reasons behind my decision to walk away from a great job. Besides the obvious trauma (bodily or mental injury-I was devastated mentally) of my ex-wife leaving me, I will say this.

I have always, still am, and always will be my greatest critic. No one can beat me up like I can. I threw away five and one-half years with a good outfit because I had messed up for two weeks. Hard to understand, isn't it? You're lucky you're not living inside my head. I have been learning these days to put down the baseball bat, sometimes. I'm coming up on forty-seven consecutive months of recovery in nine days. I don't beat myself up as much as I use to, but I still do.

That was in October of 1981. Time to get another job.

After my separation from Jane, I rented a room in a private house in Holbrook, Massachusetts. Barbara, the owner, was separated from her husband. I no longer worked for the Gillette company. I traded in the car that I was driving at the time and purchased a Chevy S10 pick-up truck. I did some contracting work in the daytime and I drove a cab five or six nights a week.

I drove for a guy named George Parker, who owned Yellow Cab in Quincy, Massachusetts. At the time he hired me, he said the only hours he had available were from 4 PM to 4 am. He told me that his day guys drove from 5 or 6 am to 3 or 4 PM. One of his drivers came in at 4 am. His night guys drove from 2 PM to 1 or 2 am. He had three drivers that worked the 4 PM to 4 am shift. One of those drivers had left and needed to be replaced. I had driven a cab for Town Taxi in Boston when I attended Massasoit Community College my sophomore year. I was nineteen at that time. I believe the Boston Hackney Bureau has changed the law since then. A taxi driver in Boston now has to be at least twenty-one years old, maybe twenty-five. I had a little taxi driving experience under my belt and the crazy hours didn't bother me at all. I thanked George for the job offer and accepted it.

Bob Ruffo and George Dabrolet were the other two all night drivers, both Quincy boys. Bob was a few years older than me, about thirty-five. He had his CDL (called a Class 1 at that time), but told me that the one month he drove the big trucks, he hated it. He said he enjoyed driving a cab. And it showed. He was a nice guy, almost always in a pleasant mood. He was one of the few drivers who frequently received customer requests (customer calls for a cab and requests a particular driver) over the radio. George was around forty, 6', 2" tall, lean and sort of mean, sometimes. He had gotten into some trouble with the law when he was younger. He did some prison time, paid his debt to society. As far as I knew, ex-convicts were not suppose to drive cabs, but I guess it happens. He was reserved most of the time. Almost always on the serious side. I got along pretty good with both of them.

Driving a cab can be dangerous. I was young, thirty-one years old, and I didn't worry much about anything dangerous happening to me. I think most cab drivers worry about the folks who skip out on their fares, more than we worry about getting hurt. When someone does skip out on a fare, it's not worth it to have the dispatcher send it over a police unit.

Most of the time if a customer is planning on not paying, they will have given the driver a phony destination anyway. A place that is not their house, or apartment building or business building. They have the driver take them near to where they are going. The customer gets out of the cab without paying and just walks away. Unless the driver jumps out of his/her cab and tackles the customer holding the person down until the police arrive, there is nothing the driver can do. If the police are called, the first thing they want to know is what address did the customer give. When a driver tells the police that the customer did not go into the given address, but walked down the street instead, well, there's nothing the police can do. What can they do, put out an All Points Bulletin on a fare skipper. It's not fair, but, whoever said that life was fair?

Even if the customer walked into their house after not paying their cab fare, they don't have to answer their door when the police knock. What are the police going to do; kick down the door; obtain a warrant to enter the dwelling and question the person. What's to keep the person from saying that they never took a cab ...

Most folks are honest, decent people who would never do anything like that. But it does happen once in awhile and when it does, it puts a dent in the drivers day and in her/his earnings. It comes out of the cab drivers pocket, not the cab company owner's pocket. To be fair to the cab company owners, they have to deal with drivers who cheat them. Drivers who don't turn on their meters every time that they have a fare, or drivers who turn their meters off short of their customers destination once in a while so that he/she will get a bigger tip and the cab company will get short changed.

To have a weapon (hand gun) pointed at my head once should have been enough to last me for the rest of my life. But it wasn't. I think it was in the late summer or maybe the early fall. I had been driving for Yellow Cab for about a year. It had been a nice day, probably around seventy degrees. I was ten hours into my twelve hour shift. I was sitting in my cab at the Quincy MBTA station taxi stand. It was around 2 am. All the evening drivers had headed back to the garage. There was another all night driver sitting in his cab in front of me, Bob Ruffo.

I was enjoying my beer (large Dunkin Donuts coffee cup filled with beer) and a cigar when I felt something touch the left side of my head, not hard. It was the end of the barrel of an AK-47 rifle. The rifle was being held by a seventeen year old kid from Hingham Massachusetts. He had stolen it from his fathers gun case. He also had a hand gun tucked in his belt that the police later said was a BB hand gun.

Bob Ruffo had spotted the nut case in his side view mirror walking toward my drivers window, coming up from the rear of my cab, with the rifle in his hand. Bob did not drink while he drove as did not most drivers. There were only a few of us who did. There was nothing Bob could do to warn me. It had happened so fast. But he did try to help me. As the rifle was being pressed against the side of my head, I heard Bob's voice on my radio, in a calm, trying not to startle me voice, say, "Don't panic Dave, give him all your money. He won't shoot you as long as you don't try anything stupid." And then our dispatcher, Jim, jumped in and Bob filled him in quickly. We used codes when we were in trouble and for other things. My dispatcher said in a quiet, calm voice, "Dave, I've got a code 19 (or whatever the code was at the time, meaning driver in trouble and police are on their way) in, give him whatever he wants."

I won't say that I wasn't scared, I was. But if I hadn't had a few beers under my belt I would have been more scared. As soon as the barrel of the rifle touched the left side of my head, I instinctively turned to my left. And then, probably, almost immediately, my eyes left the barrel of the rifle and went right to the kid's eyes. I have always been able to read most peoples eyes. I am good at it. At least I believe that to be true. I think most people could have read this kids eyes. He was harmless. He wasn't going to hurt anyone, so I thought, and I was right. He said,

"I'm not going to hurt you. I need a ride to South Boston." And before I could answer him, before I even said one word, he lowered the rifle and leaned it up against my cab. He pulled what looked like a real hand gun (the police said it was a BB hand gun,) out of his belt and said, "If you take me to Southie, I'll give you this gun."

I had gone from feeling scared to feeling a little better, now. I finally spoke to him saying, "Listen, I really don't need a gun right now. But, the driver in front of me has been looking for a hand gun." The kid said, "Thank you." He grabbed his rifle and started walking toward Bob's cab. Bob went from zero to sixty in about two seconds. As Bob was doing that, I was going from zero to ninety in reverse, in about three seconds. I'm glad that no one was behind me, cause I never looked in my rear view mirror. I never took my eyes off of the kid. The kid just walked up the MBTA steps and into the station like he was a normal guy going to catch a train; who just happened to be carrying an AK-47 assault rifle and a handgun. It looked like a real handgun to me. Why steal a real rifle from his father and not a real handgun?

Then I saw the first Quincy police cruiser come flying into the parking lot driveway. He came in silent. Their dispatcher must have told them no siren since the kid had the rifle pointed at my head. Then, within seconds of the first cruiser coming in, I think about eight or ten more cruisers came from everywhere. It must have been the police departments whole third shift arriving. Quincy is a good size city with a population of 88,025 according to the 2000 census. They were coming in the driveway, they were coming from the other side of the parking lot where there is no driveway and they were coming up and over the curb on Hancock Street, across the sidewalk and across the parking lot islands taking out a few parking meters on their way.

Bob and I told them that the kid went inside the station. They were already told by their dispatcher that he had a rifle. They opened their trunks and they took out their shotguns before they headed inside the train station. They came out about five minutes later with the kid in handcuffs. I was praying that the kid wouldn't aim his rifle at a police officer. When I looked into his eyes earlier, I could tell that he had mental problems. I was relieved when they brought him out in cuffs. I had been expecting to hear a shotgun blast go off.

The night sergeant asked Bob and me if we were OK. We told him we'd be fine after we changed our underwear. He said he was glad that no one got hurt and took our statements. Then he said to me, "What time does your shift end?" I said, "4 am." He said, "I know you're not going to drive any more this morning, but, just in case you were thinking about it ..." I interrupted him, I knew he could smell the beer on my breath. I said, "I know, Sarge, I'm putting my cab up for the night and I won't ever drink and drive again." He said, "If you do, we will catch you, sooner or later … you just used up your one and only free ticket due to extraordinary circumstances."

I didn't have to make any court appearances for that incident. From what I read in the paper, the kid's parents asked the judge to sentence their son to a hospital for the mentally ill, where he had been in the past, where he could receive the treatment he needed.

I wish I could say that was the last time anyone aimed a weapon at me, at my head. It wasn't. In chapter seven I will talk about the third time that a gun was pointed at my head. It involved crack cocaine. And, I'll tell you about the time that a large knife was pulled on me. Another crack cocaine incident.

One final thing about that incident at the Quincy MBTA station. A few days or so after it happened, I arrived at work and my boss handed me a piece of paper with a name and phone number on it. He said, "This is the father of the kid with the rifle. He wants you to call him." I said, "OK." I gave him a call. He asked me if I could stop by his house sometime. I said I could. He gave me the directions. I went to his house a few days later. It was an expensive house, a wealthy neighborhood. I don't think anyone in that neighborhood had any money problems. The first thing that he said to me was, "Are you all right?" I said, "Ya, I'm fine, and yourself?"

He took me into his study. I don't know what he did for a living, but whatever it was, he made a lot of money doing it. I'm pretty sure that he didn't drive a cab for a living. He felt genuinely sorry for me, for the ordeal his son had put me through. He also did not want me to sue him. I never had any intentions of suing him. He showed me a personal check for what I thought was a large amount of money. He then asked me how I spelled my last name. He filled it in on the check and then he handed me a sheet of paper stating that by accepting the sum of three thousand dollars I would not pursue any legal action against him. I signed the legal document and he signed his personal check. I wasn't sure if I should have told him that I never had any intentions of suing him, possibly costing me three grand, but I did anyway.

I said, "I had no intentions of suing you." He handed me the check and said, "I just want to cover all my bases; put the money to good use." As we shook hands, I asked him how his son was doing. He said, "It's going to be a long process." I asked him one more thing. I said to him, "Your son showed me a hand gun that evening. The Quincy police stated in the newspaper that it was a BB hand gun. It sure looked like a real hand gun to me. Does a Quincy Police

Officer now have one of your hand guns in his private collection?" He looked at me, smiled, and said, "I'd rather not answer that." That was good enough for me.

It's a good thing I wasn't a crack addict at that time. I could smoke up (free-base) three thousand dollars worth of crack in four or five days. Some folks could do it in less time, some folks could stretch it out longer than five days.

I left Hingham around 1:30 PM and headed for Morey Pearls on the Southern Artery in Quincy. Morey Pearls was one of my favorite restaurants, eat in or take out. They specialized in sea foods and nobody served better fried clams than Morey Pearls; maybe just as good, but not better. Quincy, Massachusetts has a few great sea food restaurants that serve the best fried clams anywhere. The Clam Box and Tony's are two other great places to get fried clams in Quincy. And while I'm thinking of it, there's a place in Randolph, Massachusetts called Lynwood's, that makes the best pizza that I've ever had in my life. A lot of folks from the North End (predominately Italian section) of Boston are probably shaking their heads in disagreement right now, but if you've never had a pizza from Lynwood's, you don't know what you are missing. Probably the best pizza in the world.

Morey Pearls had a lounge to the left after you walked thru the front door. I would usually eat my food in the lounge, at the bar, with a couple of cold beers. It use to remind me of the many times that I went to the Braintree Five Corners Chinese restaurant (a two minute drive or seven minute walk from my parent's house) where I ate my chicken wings at the bar while having a couple of cold ones. The Braintree Five Corners Chinese restaurant in Braintree, Massachusetts, served the best chicken wings that I have ever had in my life. Probably the best chicken wings in the world.

I had probably been going to Morey Pearls two or three times a week for the past year. A nice meal, a few beers and then off to Yellow cab to drive for twelve hours. If you are wondering how much carpentry work I was doing during that time, it wasn't much. My landlady, Barbara, hired me to do a few things around her house. A few of her neighbors would hire me once in a while to do small jobs. I did not like getting out of bed in the morning after drinking the night before. Most folks who drink can get up in the morning the next day, even alcoholics. I never could. That should have been a sign post indicating to me that I shouldn't drink. In the Alcoholics Anonymous program they use the term 'sign post'. Something that tips someone off to possibly having a drinking problem. I ran over a stop sign one time. I guess running over a sign post is a sign post that I may have had a drinking problem.

I remember I ordered a seafood dinner plate that day. There was an awful lot of food on that plate. It was more than a two or three beer dinner plate. I have always been a slow eater and a medium to fast drinker. After eating everything on that plate and drinking five or six beers, I didn't feel like driving a cab for twelve hours. I had a check for three thousand dollars in my pocket. I didn't have to go to work that day. America is a nice place to live.

I decided to go on vacation. At least until the money ran out which was in about a month, I believe. After the money ran out, I started doing contracting work again on a fairly regular basis. One good thing about contracting work was, if I couldn't line anything up for myself, I could usually work for another contractor. When I did that, I had to force myself out of bed in the morning. That was hard. I tried my hardest not to work for other guys. I was working on a job for a guy one time in Avon. We were building a two car garage.

One day, when my boss left the job site for a little while. I approached the homeowner on his way out the front door. I asked him what my boss was charging him. After he told me I handed him my business card and told him to call me for any future work. I told him I was less expensive. He said, "I don't think that I can do that." I said, "Why not?" He said, "My wife would be pissed. That's her brother who you are working for." Ooops!

In the spring of 1984, I applied for a job with the Boston Gear Works Company located in Quincy, Massachusetts. I had heard about that outfit when I was younger. My friend Bob Cannon (God rest his soul), grew up in a nice, comfortable home with five brothers and one sister. They were a middle class family who would have been an upper middle class family if there weren't so many kids. Bob's father was one of the higher ups at the Boston Gear Works Company, possibly the plant manager. Mr. Cannon did not start off working there with a college degree. He got his degree the hard way. He worked full time and went to college at night, while he was raising a large family. You have to give the guys and ladies who did it that way an awful lot of credit.

Mr. Cannon started working there as a machinist. Some of my buddies fathers had work shops in their cellars. They had the usual carpentry and maintenance stuff. Half of Mr. Cannon's cellar was a family room, then a laundry room area, and his workshop, not large but fascinating to me. It was the first time that I had ever seen taps and dies and precision measuring instruments. It was the first time that I had ever seen a drill press and a small lathe in someone's cellar. A lathe is an expensive piece of machinery used for machining operations on steel and other materials. The work, almost always cylindrical, is placed in the lathe horizontally between the chuck and the tail, and then spun at different high speed revolutions while the tooling, which is mounted on a tool holder apparatus, is slowly fed into the work.

I knew that the Boston Gear Works Company was a decent outfit to work for. Their main product was the manufacture of gear boxes. I was hired to run a Blanchard grinder on the second shift. I got the job thanks to my Gillette machine shop background.

I liked it there. Who knows, I may have still been there today if the company hadn't decided to move down south where the labor costs were cheaper. A lot of the guys and a few ladies who worked there were upset with that decision. Many of them had invested almost all of their working lives in that outfit.

Business is business. We all know how that goes. I was laid off on January 28, 1986. That was the day the space shuttle Challenger blew up seventy-three seconds into flight due to a booster failure resulting in the breakup of the shuttle. School teacher, Christa McAuliffe, and six other astronauts gave up their lives for our country.

My buddy Gus, who had been with Boston Gear Works for about twenty years of his life, and I headed for the Golden Bowl in Quincy, Massachusetts, after we punched out of work that night for the last time. We drank beer and watched video of the shuttle blowing up over and over and over … and the hardest part was watching Christa's parents watch the explosion, along with the families of all the other astronauts. But Christa's parents were highlighted since Christa was the first school teacher in space, trained in a short period of time, to be an astronaut. It was hard to look at the pain on their faces.

Gus had been complaining for several months about the shut down. After watching the shuttle explosion video a few times, he turned to me and said, "What am I complaining for? I'm still alive."

I decided to go to truck driving school and get my Class 1 driver's license. It is now called a CDL Class A. I signed up with the New England Tractor Trailer School located, at that time, in Marina Bay, a part of Quincy, Massachusetts. I got my license somewhere around June or July of 1986. I found out what Bob Ruffo was talking about when he told me that he hated driving trucks. For the most part, I didn't care for it, with one exception. I enjoyed driving for Stop & Shop. But, as far as the other outfits that I drove for went, I didn't like it much. I was a new driver at thirty-six years old. I got the worst runs having the least seniority. St. Johnsbury Trucking, headquartered out of Vermont, hired me.

They had a good size terminal in the Campanelli Industrial Park in Braintree, Massachusetts. They went out of business as did some other trucking outfits back around that time. MacLean Trucking was another one that went out of business from the Boston area. I can remember them doing an awful lot of shipping for Gillette in Andover when I was a security guard there.

One morning (I still hated getting up in the morning) I left the St. Johnsbury terminal in Braintree with my trailer load and manifesto (shipping orders) and headed for the Norwood Industrial Park where I had to deliver my first load. Sometimes you can work around what's on the rear of your trailer and sometimes you can't. The third rear of my trailer was loaded up with stuff for Polaroid. I had no choice but to deliver there first. Polaroid had four or five different shipping and receiving docks in four or five different building locations in the Norwood Industrial Park. My manifesto did not state any building numbers and sometimes didn't even show streets. As a new driver, it was frustrating driving around in a forty-five foot trailer trying to find the correct Polaroid building. A seasoned driver would have had an easier time of it driving and would probably have known which building to go to first.

That example I gave was not rare, it was fairly common. Raytheon is another large Massachusetts outfit that almost always has more than one building in an industrial park. Sometimes I didn't mind driving and a lot of times I did. I had no idea there were so many industrial parks in Massachusetts, and other New England states. At least in the industrial parks there was no traffic to worry about when backing into a shipping or receiving dock.

Backing up a trailer is difficult to do when you're a new driver. Like anything else, it takes time to get use to it. There were times when I would have to back into a dock located on a main street with all sorts of traffic to worry about. The veteran drivers would just do it. Not me. I would always go inside the business I was delivering to and ask for help with the traffic. They were always willing to help out especially after I told them that I was a new driver. Sometimes I would say that it was my first day driving. When I said that, not only would the boss send two or three of his guys outside to help me, but he would come out himself as well to make sure that I didn't put the rear of my trailer inside his building.

Sometimes I was a full time driver for an outfit. Sometimes I was a spare driver. As a spare driver, I would have to call up different outfits or the drivers pool in Westwood, Massachusetts, the day before and ask them if they had any work for me the next day. There were no benefits for spare drivers but the hourly rate of pay was a little bit higher and I would have the option of still being able to do carpentry work if I wanted to since I wasn't committed to a company. Who knows, I might still be driving a truck today if it wasn't for my friend, Rick Kennedy. There is nothing wrong with driving a truck. A lot of guys and some ladies have made a good living doing it. One of the reasons I didn't care for it was because of my age when I started doing it. I'm sure I would have felt different had I started driving a truck at a younger age.

In May of 1990, I started working for the Boston Gas Company (currently Keyspan) thanks to Rick. It was the best job I ever had, even better than Gillette, for a couple of reasons. I worked out of the Commercial Point location in Dorchester, Massachusetts, off the Southeast Expressway. We were next to the LNG plant which is a landmark in Boston. The LNG plant has a gas tank (there use to be two tanks) that was painted by Corita several years ago. If you look close enough at the painting, you will see Ho Chi Minh in there. That paint job has been maintained throughout the years, to this day.

There were three trailers and a parts shed at Commercial Point. We reported to our respective trailers for work in the morning, afternoon, or evening, depending on our shift. Our boss would give us our jobs and orders and then we would roll out in our gas vans and service Roxbury, Mission Hill, Dorchester and Mattapan. That was the territory for Commercial Point. We also had barns, or locations that we worked out of in Braintree, servicing a lot of the South Shore area; West Roxbury, our headquarters, servicing West Roxbury, Boston, Jamaica Plain, Roslindale, Hyde Park and some other areas. I think there may have been a little barn in Concord, and maybe other barns that I forgot about. After seeing the boss in the morning, we wouldn't see him again until we rolled in at the end of the day. It was nice not to have anyone looking over my shoulder. If I had to have anyone looking over my shoulder, my boss at the gas company, Coly Joyce, would have been the one. I can't say enough nice things about that man.

Another advantage to working for the gas company was being able to pull over whenever and wherever we wanted to for our coffee, sodas and meals. Boston Gas paid me more money than anyone had paid me in the past. We didn't need college degrees to be gas service people, but, we did have to know what we were doing. I don't know if many people are aware of the exam you have to pass before Boston Gas will hire you, as a service person. I wasn't. When Rick told me about it, I said, "Crap." You can be related to the president of the company. If you don't pass that exam, you will not be hired ... as a service person.

You wouldn't want someone working on your gas appliances or repairing gas leaks in your house or on your street if that person wasn't qualified. The company provided full training, but they wanted to make sure you were capable of handling the training before they hired you. Not everyone who works for the gas company has to take that exam. If you want to be a gas service person, you do. To get to take that exam, you have to know someone, in almost every case. Thanks, Rick.

I had plenty of time to prepare for it. From the time that I filled out my application for the gas company to the time that I took the exam, six months had gone by. I wasn't told what questions were going to be on it, but, I could cut down on my drinking and drugging.

I had become a crack head by that time. I started smoking crack in 1988. Rick knew nothing about my crack habit. I was told later by one of my gas co-workers that it was an exam from Northeastern University that was given to freshmen engineering classes. That turned out to be a good thing for me. Math and mechanical questions. I knew I had done well on it. I felt good after the exam. I passed.

The Boston Gas Company fired me on August 10, 1992. I will talk a little more about my twenty-six month career with the Boston Gas Company in chapter seven. It was the fifth to last over the table paying job I held. From September, 1997 until March of '98, I drove a truck for the Salvation Army in Brockton, Massachusetts. From May of '98 until December of '98, I worked for the Harrington and Richardson (now owned by Remington) gun factory in Gardner, Massachusetts. From January of '99 until July of '99, I drove a cab for Smiley's Taxi in Gardner, Massachusetts. During the month of March, 2004, I drove a taxi for Yellow Cab of Worcester, Massachusetts.

I would like to close out chapter four with a list of things I came up with to have a medium day. Non-addicts may not understand everything on the list. Recovering addicts will have a pretty good idea of what I'm talking about. Active addicts will not ... let me re-phrase that. When I was active, I was not capable of understanding much of anything. All I wanted to do was get my next hit ... that's all I wanted to do. Yesterday, October 8, 2005, I celebrated forty-seven consecutive months of recovery. I'm proud of myself. It was hard work. It was the hardest thing I have ever had to do in my life ... BUT WORTH IT. If you are active, NEVER GIVE UP ON YOURSELF ... YOU ARE WORTH IT. There are people who love you and are rooting for you. You can do it, One Day At A Time, But For The Grace Of God, and Your Hard Work.

Ten Tips On How To Have A Medium Day

1. Stay on guard.

2. Always keep a healthy distrust of most people.

3. Ass kissers are good for your ego; but usually you don't learn much from them.

4. Stimulating folks can be beneficial if you know how to pick their brain.

5. Knucklebrains are good for nothing.

6. If you become engaged in a confrontation with someone, stop, think and say, "Let's see if we can figure this out together. Two heads are better than one." If the other person doesn't take the hint, say, "Excuse me, I'd rather share my time with someone else." Remember; most of the time you're better off if you bite your tongue, swallow your pride and walk away.

7. Spend as little time as possible with active addicts. Whether you know it or not, they are having an influence on you. Sometimes positive, most of the time negative. You know what 'they' say-it's easier for an active to bring you down than it is for you to bring them up. Only one out of thirty-six addicts will get straight and stay straight. You are a miracle. You are one of 2.7 % of addicts who knows how to stay away from that first one, one day at a time, on a consecutive basis for a lot of days at a time.

8. Do not give someone a free ride (with the exception of recovery meetings and extraordinary situations). Make them pay their own way. It might be hard the first time to tell the person you want gas money, but it gets easier. Otherwise, you open the door for someone to use you. No one wants to be used. Those who use people are usually very good at it. They know exactly what to say.

9. Always keep a can of air freshener in your bathroom. You never know when someone is going to stop by and give you some shit.

10. If you don't think others are talking about you … you don't think.

Time To Get Married

The Gillette Company in Andover, Massachusetts, was for the most part, a large, one-level complex. There were a few exceptions to the single level. Gillette had two large warehouses, one for shipping and one for receiving. There were two large office areas, Office North and Office South. There was a large manufacturing area with six production lines and twenty-six, newly installed (around 1979), injection mold machines. There was a smaller manufacturing area where they made the Cricket disposable lighter and other products, depending on what they were running at the time.

They had a huge dining hall and a large kitchen area. There was a tank farm where chemicals were stored. There was a leach field where some chemical waste was disposed. Other chemical waste had to be disposed of by stricter means. There was a power plant that had three huge boilers. The maintenance department had a good size storage shed located near the receiving warehouse, besides their maintenance quarters located inside the shipping warehouse.

The medical center was located in the Office North part of the complex. There were two employee parking lots, Office North parking lot and Office South parking lot, as well as a large parking area for trailers at the shipping warehouse and a smaller parking area for trailers at the receiving warehouse. Our softball field, with a dugout, was top of the line. The outfield fence was bordered by nothing but trees. I saw a guy pull over one time, get out of his vehicle and snap pictures of it. The landscaping surrounding the complex was always manicured, picture pretty.

As security guards, we would walk part of our interior security rounds, and drive part of our interior rounds in a battery powered cart, similar to a golf cart without the sun canopy. We had a security vehicle, a jeep, to do our exterior rounds in and to escort Gillette company trailers from the shipping warehouse to the highway (Rt. I-93), equipped with a two-way radio so that we could call in check points and/or emergencies. When driving on Interstate 93 in Andover, Massachusetts, you can see the Gillette complex from the highway. You might think that it would only be a matter of about three minutes to get to the plant once leaving the highway. It is not. It takes about twelve minutes traveling along a windy, country back road, unlit, and then another long road, Burtt Road, that goes by the Gillette softball field on the right and the leach field down a little further on the left, and then the plant.

I worked on the second shift. The receiving warehouse worked the first shift only, as did the offices. There was one exception to the receiving warehouse. I think almost all the other departments worked three shifts. The one exception in the receiving warehouse was Ralph. He worked the second shift doing inventory in the warehouse and paperwork. And he was there to receive a trailer in the rare instances when trailers made deliveries after the first shift went home.

Part of our safety and security round duties when checking the receiving warehouse was checking up on Ralph. Since he worked there alone on the second shift, we wanted to make sure that he was OK. That's all we were suppose to do, make sure that he was OK, not socialize with him or anyone else. Our security manual stated that for security reasons, security officers were not allowed to socialize with employees, while on the job. That was a gray area. I don't remember any guards following that rule. I never did.

Ralph almost always had a pot of coffee going in his office. Once in awhile, if I had time, I would have a cup of coffee with him. He was a good guy. Around my age, a couple of years older, maybe thirty, six feet tall, 170 lbs., medium length brown hair, average looking guy, nice personality. He was single. He had never been married. He grew up in Somerville, Massachusetts. He still lived there. After work on Friday evenings he would often go to a singles bar in Somerville called, Kevin's Corner. He asked me if I wanted to go there with him sometime. I said, "Sure. It's on my way home anyway." I'm not positive about the time line, but, I think that it wasn't long after I had first started working for Gillette in Andover. It was before I moved in with Rene Letourneau in Windham, N.H., for a couple of months. I was still living in my parent's cellar and commuting to Andover from Braintree.

I would not wear my security uniform when going out after work. I had a change of clothes in my locker. We picked a Friday night to go to Kevin's Corner. The place was crowded, just like any other singles club on a Friday evening. We probably got there around 12:45 am. That gave us about an hour and fifteen minutes to check out the scenery. The way Ralph put it to me was, "By the time we get there, the ladies won't even be able to tell what we look like." He was half kidding, half serious. Most ladies know how to drink like ladies, how to go out for the evening and have a nice time, not a stupid time.

You know the saying, 'It was love at first sight'. Well, I don't know any other way of putting it when I saw Jane that early morning. I can't say that I knew I was going to marry her because I didn't even think that she would give me the time of the early morning or talk to me other than to tell me to stop staring at her. She was the cutest little thing (petite) I have ever seen in my life, with a figure to match.

Jane grew up in Somerville and graduated from Somerville High School. Somerville is a city, one of the several communities that make up the urban Boston area. West Somerville, North Cambidge, Cambridge, Charlestown, Chelsea, Allston, Brighton, Brookline, West Roxbury, Roxbury, Hyde Park, Roslindale, Mattapan, Jamaica Plain, Dorchester, East Boston, South Boston are all part of urban Boston and are all served by the Boston Police and Fire Departments, I believe.

They are further broken down into areas by U.S. postal zip codes known as the West End, Hanover Street, Back Bay, Kenmore Square, South End, Roxbury Crossing, Grove Hall, Fields Corner, Uphams Corner, Mission Hill, Codman Square, Kendall Square, Central Square, Union Square (where Jane grew up), Harvard Square and Winter Hill.

I think I listed most of them. I've got a map of Boston in front of me. When I worked for the Boston Gas Company, we were given our job locations by building number, street and zip code.

After having a few beers, I felt comfortable approaching Jane. What's the worst that could happen? She could tell me that she was not interested. It would not have been the first time that someone wasn't interested in me. Unavailable ladies and guys go to singles bars all the time. It's fun, it's a night out. Someone may not be interested and someone may not be available.

A funny thing happened to me on my way over to talk to Jane. I bumped into her roommate, Judy. I didn't know that they were roommates at that time. She was an attractive lady. I said, "Excuse me, I'm sorry." She said, "Don't worry about it; there's no room in here to move around." I said, "Do you want to try to make our way to the dance floor?" She said, "Sure." If I couldn't get to the one who I wanted to dance with, why not dance with the one I was with?

After a couple of dances with Judy, the place was getting ready to close up. I asked her if she was up for an early morning breakfast. She said, "I'll meet you out front, I want to let my roommate know what I'm doing." I met Judy out front. As we started to walk to my car, someone yelled out, "Hey you ..." We turned around to see Judy's roommate, Jane, approaching us. Jane said to me, "She is my roommate, don't you dare get any funny ideas about her." I said, "It's good that you two look out for each other. I'll have her home in an hour." As

Judy and I walked away, I said to Judy, "For a little lady she has a big mouth." Judy laughed.

Jane stood about 4', 11' tall, maybe 90 lbs. Shoulder length, soft brown hair with a wave to it. Brown eyes, soft voice when she wasn't yelling. Very cute lady. I asked Judy how long she and Jane had been roommates. She told me about a year. She said they shared a one bedroom apartment in a four story brick apartment building in Union Square in Somerville. They would alternate sleeping in the bedroom and on the living room couch. She told me that neither one of them made a lot of money. The two of them together could only afford a one bedroom apartment. Jane was a nurses aid. I forget what Judy did.

I was twenty-six years old at that time. Jane and Judy were both the same age, twenty-three years old. I decided not to play games with Judy. When I was having breakfast with her, I asked her questions about Jane. She told me that Jane wasn't seeing anyone. And she asked me if I liked Jane. She didn't have to ask me that, I'm sure that she could tell I did. I told Judy that next to her, Jane was my most favorite lady in the world. She laughed, a little bit, and said, "It's OK, you're not hurting my feelings. I'm glad you told me." She gave me their phone number and said, "I'll put a good word in for you."

I found out later that Judy had met someone special a month or so before the night I met Jane and Judy. Judy and her new boyfriend had had a little fight. That's why Judy went out with Jane that evening. Judy's new boyfriend was there at Kevin's Corner that evening and Judy was trying to make him jealous. He was standing outside with Jane when she told me to watch my P's and Q's (an old English saying meaning pints and quarts) with Judy. I was using Judy to get to Jane. Judy was using me to make her new boyfriend jealous. Judy's new boyfriend probably went home with Jane that morning!

Within a matter of a couple of weeks I had moved in with Jane and Judy had moved in with her new boyfriend. Some people say that everything happens for a reason; that God has a master plan. If that's true, our daughter, Shelley, was the reason God put Jane and I together. Shelley had the sweetest, nicest, most gentle personality of any child I have ever known. I miss Shelley. I haven't seen her in over twenty years.

It was July of '77 when I met Jane. We were married on February 25, 1978. Shelley was born on August 12, 1978. Someone told me or I heard on TV or maybe read somewhere that in most relationships the wild, crazy, fatuous feelings about each other usually disappear in eighteen to twenty-four months. In order for that relationship to continue to work, a deeper, more responsible, more mature type of love then kicks in, or is suppose to. Relationships are hard work, to make work. You may have heard that the only reason most couples stay together is because of the kids. I don't know if that's true or not. I know that at the time that I was married, up until that point in my life, trying to make my marriage work was the hardest thing I have ever had to do. There were plenty of good times. Having someone I loved in my life meant a lot to me. I didn't take that for granted.

We had been together for a little over four years. From July of '77 to October of '81. That's when our marriage went south. It didn't have anything to do with my drinking. I pretty much drank like a man during those four years, when I drank which wasn't too often. I was working a lot of hours and so was Jane. We were saving up to buy a house. She went back to work after Shelley was around a year old. Jane's mother and father helped us out a lot by taking care of Shelley when we were working. Jane also worked on the second shift most of the time. Her father was retired from the post office. He was more than willing and happy to do whatever he could for us. He picked up Shelley if we were running late or for some other reason that we couldn't get her to them. George (Jane's father) bought his own car seat for Shelley and I think Lillian (Jane's mother) had more toys for Shelley in her house than we did. They loved their granddaughter very much, as did my parents.

It was a little different, though, for Jane's folks. Shelley was their first grandchild. Jane's older brother was not married at that time. She had one other sibling, a younger brother. My parents had two other grand kids at that time. And we lived in Somerville, as did Jane's parents. It was more convenient for them to help us out than it was for my folks who lived in Braintree. And most of Jane's relatives were from the Somerville area. I think a lot of them were more than willing to help us out, if they could.

Jane had a thing about a stranger watching someone else's kids. She didn't believe in it. It had to be a family member, a relative, or maybe a very, very, close friend. From some of the things that have happened to kids over the years by nannies and baby sitters, she had a good point. Jane was called into work early one day. She had to leave around ten in the morning. I could watch Shelley until two o'clock, the time I would leave for work. George and Lillian had a medical appointment that day. Before Jane left for work, she had arranged for one of her aunts to pick Shelley up around noontime. I had not met the lady, yet. I felt strange handing my daughter over to someone I didn't know, without Jane being there. Jane's aunt had already been to our place a few times to see Shelley during Shelley's first year. I wasn't there because I was working one of my weekend nights. Before I handed Shelley to Jane's Aunt, I considered asking her to show me her ID.

I'm not going to talk about why it didn't work out between Jane and me. There are two sides to every story. I loved her at one time, and still wish the best for her. We have a beautiful daughter. It would not be right for me to tell my side without her being able to tell her side. We had many nice, memorable, good times during our four years together.

Shelley, Where Are You?

When I walked away from the Gillette Company after working for them for five and one-half years, it wasn't because I didn't feel like working anymore. There was a reason for it. And by a reason, I mean it was more than just me messing up my five and one-half years of perfect attendance. A reason why I didn't show up for work most of the last two weeks that I worked for the Gillette Company.

I said earlier that Jane met someone. I'm not going to say anymore than that because it would not be fair to my ex-wife for me to tell my side without her being able to tell her side.

After leaving Gillette, I started doing contracting work, again, and I also drove a cab. After Jane and I had separated, the judge ordered me to pay eighty-five dollars per week in child support for Shelley. I was paying Shelley's child support, for awhile. After the judge granted a divorce to us, Jane remarried. I stopped paying child support, not because she remarried, but for another reason. I hadn't paid anything for approximately eighty-eight weeks. My arrears had reached about seventy-five hundred dollars on my last appearance in court for non-payment of child support.

The judge said to me, "Do you have a job, yet?" I said, "No your honor, I don't." Seventy-eight weeks ago, I told the judge I was no longer employed by the Gillette Company, that I didn't have a job. I did not tell him I was doing carpentry work under the table and also driving a cab. This time was my fourth or fifth appearance in front of him since I told him that I no longer had a job. My ex-wife had first taken me to court for non-payment after about ten weeks of me not paying child support.

The judge had had enough of me. He said, "I am ordering you to serve six months in the Billerica House of Correction." That sucked. I wasn't feeling so brave and confident anymore. I had been in jail in the past. A couple of overnighters. One time I was arrested on a Friday evening for starting a brawl in a Brockton, Massachusetts, barroom. I didn't call any family members to ask if they would bail me out, because I knew they wouldn't. I spent Friday, Saturday, Sunday and Monday nights in the Brockton jail. It was a holiday weekend. Court wasn't in session until Tuesday. I appeared in front of the judge that Tuesday wearing half a jacket. The other half of my jacket was back at the Alamo, the bar-room where I'm pretty sure I started the brawl.

As the bailiff started to put the handcuffs on me in that Cambridge court room, my ex-wife's attorney said, "Excuse me, your honor, would it be possible to have a conference with Mr. O'Donnell?" The judge said, "Sure."

The four of us, my ex-wife, her husband, Jane's attorney and I (I had hired an attorney out of my cousin Fred Barry's office, but that attorney knew I was a lost cause). Jane's attorney said that if I signed away my parental rights to my daughter, Shelley, to Jane's new husband, I would be off the hook for the arrears that I owed and any future child support payments, and I wouldn't have to go to jail for six months.

When the attorney held out his pen, I grabbed it out of his hand and signed away my daughter …

Shelley, Jane, her new husband and his children (he had custody of a couple of kids from his first marriage) ended up moving from Arlington, Massachusetts, where they were living, to Derry, New Hampshire. That was no surprise to me. Shelley, Jane and I use to take day trips to Canobie Lake Park in New Hampshire. It was as much fun for Jane and me as it was for Shelley. Jane grew up in the city. She had pretty much stayed in the city up until we met. She fell in love with everything about Canobie Lake Park and the other parts of New Hampshire that we visited. She loved the car ride out of Somerville to New Hampshire.

Canobie Lake Park had a petting zoo and animal food machines. We would put a quarter in the food machine, and then put the food in Shelley's hands. The animals would eat out of Shelley's hands. Shelley would get a huge kick out of it. I told Shelley that the name of one of the llamas was Fred. That's who Shelley looked for when we went there. Sometimes, when we were home, Shelley would say, "Can we visit Fred this weekend?"

One of the rides at Canobie Lake Park was the rocket ship ride. After we would get on board, it would go from a horizontal position to an almost vertical position and shake a little bit. Shelley thought we were going to the moon. She said that we couldn't stay on the moon too long, because we had to get home and feed Fluffernutter, her kitten.

We took day trips to other places in New Hampshire. Six Gun City and Story Land were two places we went to. There was another place where you could take a scenic train ride through some of the mountains of New Hampshire (I forget the name) and a few other places. Canobie Lake Park was our favorite. I think Jane enjoyed the boat ride around the lake, the best.

Another zoo that we would go to once in a while was the Stoneham Zoo in Stoneham, Massachusetts. Jane's parents use to take her there when she was a kid. It was a pretty nice place. Shelley loved animals.

Jane did not make my parents go to court to ensure their grandparental rights to see Shelley. They could see Shelley whenever they wanted to, and they did.

Well, let's see … I'm twenty days away from four consecutive years of recovery. By the way, recovery is the popular word these days. When I first started going to AA meetings in 1981, sobriety or sober were the most often used words in the fellowship. At that time, if a speaker talked about illegal drugs (alcohol is a drug; ethyl-alcohol) from the podium, there was a good chance that someone would yell out, "This is AA, not NA (Narcotics Anonymous)", and sometimes folks would get up and leave the meeting, if a speaker mentioned drugs. Alcoholics Anonymous meetings are more popular than Narcotics Anonymous meetings for a couple of reasons. AA meetings have been around longer, since 1935. They are better organized and structured and they put up with fewer shenanigans than NA, in my opinion and the opinion of a lot of other folks.

I don't know exactly why it is, but, for some reason, some of the folks at NA meetings think it is OK to give a big hello and hug to someone who comes in late to an NA meeting. It is disruptive to the speaker and disruptive to the rest of the folks at the meeting. And it's not just one person. Showing up late to an NA meeting almost seems like the popular thing to do, for some people. Why not get all your big hugs and huge hello's out of the way before the meeting starts, instead of waiting to do it when you know that you're disrupting the meeting, and everyone is looking at you? Try being on time for the meeting. That would be something different for some of the folks who attend NA meetings. This thing about saying hi to everyone like they are your best friends. Well, how many best friends do you have? I wonder how much of that is sincere and how much of it is showboating. Look at me everyone; I'm here, dressed like I'm going to the governor's ball.

For the most part, AA meetings start on time, and end on time, and most of the folks are on time.

Gradually, slowly but surely, speakers were saying from the podium that they were an alcoholic and an addict. Anyone can be addicted to anything. But, it was understood that by saying that you were an addict, you used illegal drugs. And then, they started to sneak in little stories about their drug use. They were alcoholics and drug addicts. Most people who are alcoholics and drug addicts prefer Alcoholics Anonymous meetings. A lot of folks do not care for NA meetings, unless they're into showing up late, huge hugs and hello's and showboating. I know that there are some folks who go to NA meetings who know how to act like ladies and gentlemen. I have been to enough NA meetings over the past twenty-four years to be able to do the criticizing that I just did. I can hear some of the NA gang right now after reading this. As a matter of fact, I'll bet some of their mouths are on the go while their sleeping.

Clean and sober then became the popular phrase. The long timers in AA accepted it and some of them got a kick out of it. Once in awhile you would hear a long timer say from the podium, "I'm clean and sober today. I took a shower this morning and I haven't had a drink of alcohol so far today." Over the past few years most folks have been saying that they are in recovery.

I feel good about having almost four consecutive years of recovery. I don't feel so good about signing my daughter away. How many folks do you know who signed away their children? It was a huge mistake, but not my worst mistake. Making the decision to freebase (smoke) cocaine was the worst decision that I have ever made in my life.

Before I close this chapter and talk about my thirteen years of freebasing, I would like to say something to my daughter, Shelley.

Nana and Papa stayed in touch with you, Shelley, until you were a junior at Penn State University. The pictures you sent them in your cheerleader's uniform when you were a cheerleader for the Penn State basketball team are gorgeous. You are a beautiful, young lady. You look like your mother. Everyone misses you. We don't know where you are. I know you don't want to have anything to do with me. I don't blame you. Maybe, if you get a chance, you could give Nana and Papa a call. I love you. Daddy

Thirteen Years of Smoking Crack and Cocaine (Freebasing)

It was a pleasant Sunday evening in the spring of 1986. I was sitting on an unfolded metal chair in the basement of a church in the Germantown section of Quincy, Massachusetts. I was at the Snug Harbor AA meeting. It was a Catholic church. I think the name of it was St. Bonaventure's, I'm not sure. I saw on the news one night a while back that it had been shut down by the Archdiocese of Boston. Sitting next to me was my AA sponsor, Scotty Joe. He was around forty-five years old, 6', 180 lbs., full head of medium length, salt and pepper hair. Not a bad looking guy. He came to this country from Scotland when he was younger. He came to Dorchester, Massachusetts, where he worked as a roofer.

Roofing is hard, dangerous work, especially in Dorchester and the surrounding area where there are three deckers all over the place. Many of them do not have flat roofs, but pitched multi-surfaced roofs. A lot of roofers like to drink, like a lot of people in other occupations. Drinking while roofing is not a good combination. It makes a dangerous job that much more dangerous.

I was thirty-four years old at that time. Joe was one of the heavy hitters of the Snug Harbor AA group. He had good sobriety time going for him. He had been sober for about fifteen years. The Snug Harbor AA group liked to think of themselves as the Marine Corps of AA, in the South Shore area. The church basement meeting hall would have three-hundred people there on any Sunday night. I think that was the largest AA meeting in the area.

They did not allow speakers from the podium to talk about narcotics at their meetings. Others group didn't either, but it was guaranteed that if you mentioned drugs from the Snug Harbor podium, one of the heavy hitters of the Snug Harbor AA group would yell out from the audience or the sidelines or the back of the hall, "This is AA, not NA!" or "We want to hear about alcohol, not drugs!" or "Sit down, you got nothing to say!" The long timers/heavy hitters from Snug Harbor were strict. And, the other AA groups in the area got to know this. Some of the Snug Harbor folks had a wee bit of an attitude … thought that they were a wee bit better than druggies. Hmmm … That's interesting, isn't it?

Scotty Joe and I became medium buddies. Alcohol had destroyed much of Joe's life. I had suffered some missed opportunities and some minor set backs up until that point in my life. Nothing I couldn't bounce back from, so I thought. That's one of the reasons I kept bouncing in and out of AA. I went there to learn how to drink like a man, to get in a little tune-up, or to get out of a jackpot.

A jackpot in AA means an unpleasant situation like, wife problems, boss problems, co-worker problems, children problems, parent problems, relative problems, friend problems, judge and or police problems. They're all telling you that you might have a drinking problem. Cheeeschhh …

Joe's ex-wife had tossed him out of the house years ago when he was drinking. That's when he went on the rooming house circuit. Living in one rooming house after another. One time I asked him why he didn't just stay in the same rooming house. He said, "Because the landlords always wanted the same thing; rent money."

Joe had a few brothers back in Scotland who died from the disease of alcoholism, either directly or indirectly. One of his brothers died from cirrhosis of his liver as a result of abusing alcohol. I had heard some things about cirrhosis of the liver in the past. I never looked it up in any dictionary or did any research on it until recently.

The liver is the largest organ in the body. It is also the largest gland in the body.[1]

There are many causes of cirrhosis. Alcohol is a very common cause, particularly in the Western World. The development of cirrhosis in alcohol consumers depends upon the amount and regularity of intake. Those individuals who drink at least eight to sixteen ounces of hard liquor or the equivalent daily for fifteen or more years will develop cirrhosis thirty percent of the time.[2]

Before I did my research, I had heard that cirrhosis of the liver had something to do with scarring of the liver tissue. One of my friends suffered from cirrhosis of her liver. She never drank alcohol. She had NAFLD, nonalcoholic fatty liver disease or steatosis. She told me that she had irreversible, advanced scarring of her liver.

I believe that Joe had two sisters. They came from Scotland to visit Joe one year, I think in the middle eighties. Joe bought a nice condominium on the South Shore. He had some nice stuff in it. He has good taste. He was looking forward to seeing his sisters and showing them his place. Joe said, when he left Scot-

---

1.   Leslie J. Schoenfield, M.D., Ph.D.
2.   Taken from HealthNews, Liver Overview

land for America, they had a party for him … after his plane took off. Nobody wants a drunk around.

Joe liked the ladies, like most of us. He was single, not bad looking in a rugged sort of way. With a lot of years of sobriety under his belt, he was back in the roofing business. He was working in a supervisory position now, and doing pretty good.

He asked me if I wanted to go with him to Tino's Lounge, a singles club in Randolph, Massachusetts, after the meeting. Tino's had become a popular place for single folks in recovery, as well as social drinkers. I had been to Tino's before. I said, "I didn't know that you went to Tino's." He said, "I go there once in awhile. It's a change of pace from the usual; coffee shops, Friendly's or Brigham's. Tonight is 'Parents Without Partners' night." I said, "No, not tonight. I like going there on a Friday or Saturday evening."

We usually went to a Friday night AA meeting together in my home town of Braintree, Massachusetts. The meeting was in the basement of my old church's school building, St. Francis of Assisi. I was always a little nervous going to that meeting not knowing who I was going to run into from my town. It would be different today. It would not bother me one bit. But, back then; I still thought I could learn how to drink like a man. I wasn't convinced that I was a real alcoholic. I was well aware of my screw ups as a direct result of drinking. But, didn't that go with the territory? Sure, I'd be better off if I didn't drink. But giving up alcohol completely? Isn't that a bit drastic? I'm doing the right thing now. I'm going to Alcoholics Anonymous meetings to learn how to drink responsibly, get my life back on track and try to avoid future jackpots.

Joe said, "How's this coming Friday night sound?" I said, "Good. This will work out pretty good for both of us. I can draw strength from your sober time. You can meet some nice ladies by hanging around with me." Joe shook his head and said, "That's right, Dave, that's how it will work out." I enjoyed listening to his Scottish accent.

That Friday evening, per usual, there was a decent size crowd at the meeting, maybe one hundred and fifty people. I knew some of them. I grew up with some of them. I went to school with some of them. I graduated from high school with one guy that was there. I played little league baseball with him. His father coached a little league baseball team as did my father. It was nice to see him there. In fact, I couldn't think of a better place for him to be. He was my age, thirty-four, and he already had a vehicular homicide under his belt due to the abuse of alcohol. I suppose it could have been me or any one of us when we drink too much alcohol.

He killed an elderly man at the intersection of West and Washington Streets, in front of the old Braintree High School. There is a stop sign there when you are coming down West Street to Washington Street, that he did not stop for. He broad sided the elderly man's drivers side, who was traveling north on Washington Street. The elderly man did not survive. Whether or not alcohol was directly or indirectly involved in the accident, I don't remember. I know that my friend loved to drink. Like me, if he wasn't drinking, he was thinking about drinking.

Maybe he had had a few drinks under his belt on the day of the accident and maybe not. He may have been in a rush to get to the liquor store. And, like I often was, he may have been hung over and sick from 'accumulative drinking', which could have knocked his guard off and made him not as sharp as he should have been. I had never heard of 'accumulative drinking' until an instructor or counselor talked to us about it in one of my rehabs. My friend did not do any jail time for the accident. I think he's fortunate that the accident happened in the late seventies or early eighties, and not today. He has to live with that accident for the rest of his life. Every single day of the rest of his life.

Joe and I bailed out of the AA meeting at half time and headed for Tino's. I met a sweetheart there. Yecha Ha, from Brockton. She was originally from Korea. She came to America when she was seventeen. She was thirty-one. She said to call her Suki, that was her nickname. Joe said, "Did you say your nickname was Sucki?" Suki said, "No, I don't say Sucki you stupid man, I say Suki, Suki, you understand me mista?" Joe looked at me and said, in his Scottish accent, "I don't know what she's saying. I don't speak Korean." I had trouble understanding both of them …

There were two other Korean ladies at the table besides Suki, Joe and I. Kim and Soonja, who also came to America when they were younger. Kim and Soonja were married to American men. Kim was her Korean last name, but it was also her nickname. Soonja's nickname was Sue. Suki was single. She had shoulder length black hair with a wave to it. Her face was very pretty. She stood about 4 feet, eleven inches tall. She might have weighed ninety pounds. I danced with her a couple of times. I didn't say much to her on the dance floor.

At the table, we all just goofed around with each other. The ladies were drinking alcohol, but they seemed to like the fact that Joe and me were ordering soft drinks. Both Joe's and my answer to anyone's question about why we were not drinking alcohol, usually was, "I'm not in a drinking mood," or "I'm a little tired right now, drinking alcohol will make me more tired."

I think Sue might have said something like, "You guys don't like to have a drink when you go out?" Instead of giving her one of his usual answers, Joe grabbed his club soda, raised it and said, "What do you think this is, my dear?" Suki said, "You know what she mean, you stupid man." Joe was getting a kick out of Suki.

I ended up taking Suki out on a date the next weekend. Or, at least we had originally planned on going to a restaurant for dinner. She owned her own home on Tosca Drive located on the west side of Brockton, near the Easton line, not far from Stonehill College. She lived in a nice neighborhood. She told me that she went halves on her house with her boyfriend, at the time. They got a good deal on it back in 1976 when she was around twenty-one.

She met her boyfriend shortly after coming to America. They had been saving their money to buy a house almost the whole time that they had been going out together. About four years. Suki was a seamstress. She worked for the MacIntosh Company. They made ladies coats. After they went out of business, she worked for her friends who had their own sewing machines in their houses. A time came when Suki bought her own sewing machines. I have never met a harder working lady in my life. She was almost always working on something. Sewing, vegetable gardening, flower gardening, aerobics, quilting, laundry, cleaning and cooking. When the relationship with her boyfriend wasn't working out anymore, she bought him out so that she could keep the house.

When I got there, she showed me around her house. It was gorgeous. She had some oriental ornaments, wall hangers, vases and carpets in her house that looked and probably were expensive. She was proud of her house and everything in it. She asked me if I would not mind her making dinner instead of us going out. I could see that she was tired. I said, "Why don't you lie down and rest and we can do this some other time." She said, "Do you like steak?" I said, "I love steak." She said, "Well, I bought a nice one at the market today. I am tired but I have to eat. Go watch TV and I'll call you when dinner is ready." We had steak, boiled potatoes and carrots and a Korean salad called kimshe. Suki ate kimshe every day. I had kimshe every time that I was at her place which was a lot over the next twenty-six months. It was a fantastic meal.

I have three, twenty-six month stretches of certain events in my life. I went out with Suki for twenty-six months. I worked for the Boston Gas Company for twenty-six months. I spent twenty-six months in the Aurora Project in Worcester, Massachusetts, my second time there. I was in the Aurora for sixteen months my first time there for a total of forty-two months all together in alcohol and drug rehabilitation in one program alone.

I was unemployed when I met Suki, sort of. I was a full time student at New England Tractor Trailer school. I worked part time doing carpentry and maintenance jobs, mostly for folks in my neighborhood, or, I should say, my parent's neighborhood. After I separated from my ex-wife in 1981, I moved into a room in a private home owned by a nice lady, Barbara, in Holbrook, Massachusetts. I moved out of Barbara's house after about a year and back into my bachelor's apartment in the cellar of my parent's house. Any time I moved back home I didn't have to call my folks to tell them I was coming. If no one was home when I got there, it didn't matter. The back door was always unlocked.

I don't believe anyone had a key for the back door. Sometimes both doors were unlocked when no one was home. Same with a lot of the folks in that neighborhood at that time. That's just the way it was back then. I remember the one time that I can think of that there was a house robbery in the neighborhood. Fred and Kitty Waterman lived on the same street as my parents, Addison Street, opposite side a few houses down from my parent's house. Fred was a professional photographer. Kitty stayed home keeping busy with cooking, laundry, cleaning and taking care of a lot of the wild birds in the neighborhood. She had several wild bird feeders in her back yard. That's where a lot of the wild birds in the neighborhood would hang out, in Kitty's back yard. They were an older couple. I don't know if they ever had any children.

Fred had some expensive photographic equipment in his cellar. They would lock their doors if they weren't home. When Fred and Kitty went on a cruise one time, their house was broken into and Fred's photographic equipment was stolen. It happened around 1969, my senior year in high school. The rumor going around the neighborhood about the robbery was that it was done by the kid of a family who lived in the neighborhood. It was a believable rumor. The family was nice, but this particular kid wasn't. He was a couple of years younger than me. I don't know if he ever straightened out or not. I don't think the police were ever able to pin the robbery on him, if he did it. When they searched the B_'s house, they didn't find anything.

I ended up getting my Class 1 license (it is called a Commercial Driver's License, Class A, today) in July of '86. I started off driving full time for an outfit until they went out of business nine months later. Then, I signed up with the drivers pool in Westwood, Massachusetts, and did some spare driving. The hourly rate of pay was usually higher for spare drivers, depending on the outfit they sent us to, because there were no employee benefits involved. I liked the idea of not having to drive if I didn't feel like it. If I felt like driving, I would call the drivers pool the afternoon before or early the same morning to see if they had any work. Sometimes I felt like driving and sometimes I felt like doing carpentry work.

Driving a tractor-trailer was more stressful then I had thought it would be. It was harder then I had imagined. Had I started driving a truck when I was younger, I think that I would have felt differently about it. A lot of the time that I drove, I did not care for it. But, I had no way of knowing that I would feel that way when I made my decision to go to truck driver's school. I thought it would be a fairly decent way to make a living, which, I'm sure it is for many truck drivers. There was one outfit that I enjoyed driving for. Stop & Shop out of Readville (a section of Hyde Park), Massachusetts. They had a huge barn in Readville as well as another large facility in Connecticut, possibly New Haven, that I ran out of once in awhile.

Their equipment was top of the line, I thought, and they ran their operation the way an operation should be run. I made several runs for Stop and Shop hauling produce to their Massachusetts, Rhode Island and Connecticut stores. Stop and Shop was a sought after truck drivers job. To go from a spare driver for them to a full time Stop & Shop driver, you had to watch your P's and Q's, do the right thing all the time. During the three years that I spared for the driver's pool, I never turned down a Stop & Shop run. I knew the dispatcher at the driver's pool, Wayne Benner, from playing softball with him one year. I also knew his sister, Donna. They were from Braintree. I got along well with both of them.

Wayne treated me pretty good at the driver's pool. I cannot remember having any kind of a major problem with any of the outfits that Wayne sent me to. Especially Stop & Shop. Wayne asked me one time if I was going to try to make the list (full time, permanent driver) at Stoppy. I said that I was and I appreciated all the Stoppy work that he had given me. He told me that it was looking good for me. He had never received a complaint or an incident report from any of the dispatchers at Stoppy, on me. That's because I was putting my best foot forward at Stoppy, going the extra mile. There is no such thing as a forty hour work week for a tractor-trailer driver, local as well as over the road. Sixty or seventy hours a week would be normal. Everything over eight hours a day is time-and-a-half. The hourly rate of pay was decent. Ten and twelve hour days were normal. There was money there to be made for guys and gals with a high school education and a Class 1 license (CDL today).

I was about to make the Stop & Shop list in the spring of 1990. Trucking outfits do not give you physical exams as a pre-requisite to driving for them. That is done by the D.O.T. (Department of Transportation). All tractor-trailer drivers have to pass a Department of Transportation physical exam and carry their D.O.T. cards on them whenever they are driving. It is a comprehensive exam, as it should be. No one wants a tractor-trailer driver to have a medical problem while she/he is driving.

The reason I was able to pass that physical exam was because my nephritis with nephrotic syndrome symptoms had dropped to accepted levels. The protein and creatine levels in my urine were down thanks to years of medication and drinking a lot of cranberry juice and drinking an extra lot of cranberry juice before I took any physical exam.

Stop & Shop set up an appointment for me to go to personnel and fill out the paperwork to become one of their company truck drivers. It was only a matter of days after Stoppy called me that the Boston Gas Company called me to tell me to come in and take a physical exam. I had been waiting for about six months to hear from the gas company after having taken their gas service persons exam, and passing it. It was six months before that, that I had filled out the paper work for Boston Gas.

They were both good outfits. I decided to pursue the gas company job. I wrote a nice letter to Stop and Shop declining their offer. I could work for the gas company and drive a truck on my days off if I felt like it. All I had to do was call the drivers pool and ask Wayne if he had any work for me. I started working for the gas company on the Tuesday after the Memorial Day weekend in 1990. I drove a truck for Stoppy once in a while on my days off from the gas company. I did that for the first several months that I was working with the gas company.

Things were progressing nicely with Suki. We enjoyed each others company a lot. I could be a character sometimes and so could she. During the twenty-six months that we were together, from April of '86 till June of '88, I spent a lot of time at her place. Carpentry was my hobby as well as a means of making money. Suki had lived in her house for ten years, most of those years by herself. There was no man there to do the things that needed to be done to maintain a house.

Two years before I met her, she hired a roofer to strip two layers of shingles off her roof and lay down new shingles. When she told me what he charged her I shook my head. She said, "Did I pay too much money?" I said, "No, that's what roofers get for stripping two layers and then laying down new shingles on a roof your size. The reason that I'm shaking my head is because out of the $3700 that you paid him, about $2900 of that was profit for a weeks worth of work." Back then, roofers did not have to deal with the proper disposal of roofing shingles like they do today. Asbestos roofing shingles are hazardous materials. That's another expense that roofers have to pass on to customers today. "He probably paid around eight-hundred dollars for the materials." She said, "Shit ... well, what I suppose to do, David, climb up ladda with hamma and nails?" I said, "Don't forget the shingles."

I spent the night with Suki maybe once or twice a week during the first year of our relationship. I was hired by St. Johnsbury trucking in July of '86. That was a few months after I met Suki and shortly after receiving my Class I license. They were located in the Campanelli Industrial Park in Braintree, Massachusetts, five minutes away from my parents house where I was living. When St. J's went down the tubes, I signed up with the drivers pool in Westwood, Massachusetts. I drove a truck whenever I felt like it. I started to spend a lot of time at Suki's place. She would be working in her cellar at her sewing machines and I would be doing something on her house.

One time she said to me, "You know that this your house too, David?" I said, "No it's not. It's your house, Suki. Everything I'm doing for you, I want to do for you, no strings attached, no expectations." She said, "If that the case, I have to pay you for all the work you doing." I said, "This is my hobby. I get to be near you when I'm doing my hobby. And, you are the best cook in the whole world as well as the nicest, sweetest, hardest working, prettiest lady that I have ever known in my life."

During our first year together, Suki never saw me drink a beer. I could drink at home. Now that we were spending more time together, I decided to tell her that the reason I never drank around her was because I thought I might have a little problem with booze. She said, "Easy to solve, never drink again." I said, "Easy for you to say. I go to Alcoholics Anonymous meetings once in …" She put her hand up in the air and said, "You don't need meetings, you need good woman, me. I never let you drink again."

If it were only that easy. It was for George, Sue's (Soonja) husband. When Sue told George it was either her or the booze, shortly after they met, he picked her. He had a decade of sobriety under his belt when I met him, with one exception. They had two beautiful Amerasian children. Georgey Jr., eight years old, and a ten year old daughter (I forget her name). The one exception was every July fourth. On that day, George was allowed to have three beers.

When George and I were tossing a football around in his back yard one day, I said to him, "How the hell could you have had a problem with alcohol if you are able to drink three beers every July fourth and then stop. He said, "Trust me when I tell you that I did have a problem with alcohol and I do only have three beers a year now, and I have been doing that for the past ten years."

Then he walked up to me and said, "You're an honest, open guy. You have shared a lot about yourself not only to Suki, but, to Sue and me as well. You see how beautiful Sue and Suki are. You see how beautiful my children are. You know how hard Sue and Suki work and they will work like that for their entire working lives. It's a part of their culture. They can't help working hard and doing anything and everything that they can for their men. Do you understand what I'm saying to you? I would have to be out of my mind to throw that away. Ya, it requires some will power to stop drinking after you've started, when you have a drinking problem. But, it can be done. You don't need meetings, Dave, you need Suki."

I can't remember exactly when, but, one weekend morning after Suki and I woke up, she told me that she was pregnant. I had never smoked a cigarette inside Suki's house, up until then. I remember saying to her, "Are you sure?" She said, "Yes." I got out of bed to go to the bathroom lighting up a cigarette on my way. When I came back, she was sitting up in bed, looking at me. I said, "How do you feel about an abortion?" She started crying, and then went into the bathroom and stayed there for awhile. I told her through the bathroom door that I was sorry, I hadn't meant what I had said, I wasn't thinking clearly. She told me to go home.

I left and headed for George and Sue's house. Sue worked at home so she was almost always there. It was a weekend morning because George was also home. It was the first time I smoked a cigarette in their house, too. I lit up without think-ing. They didn't say anything. Sue got me a saucer for an ash tray. I didn't have to tell them what had happened. Suki had called Sue. I explained to them that I hadn't meant what I said. I told them I didn't know why I had said it. I said that I was looking forward to having our baby.

Sue got up and left the living room leaving George and me there alone. George did not look pleased. He said, "It's too late." I said, "What the hell are you talking about … it's too late." He said, "Suki wants you to take her to the abortion clinic in Brookline." I said, "That's not going to happen. We are going to have a baby." He said, "I know you didn't mean what you said to Suki. But, you shouldn't have said it. Suki will always believe that you do not want her to have your baby." I said, "What the f___ are you talking about. I want her to have our baby." He said, "You don't completely understand their culture yet, do you? Once you say …" I interrupted George and said, "I will never completely under-stand their culture. Please tell Sue to tell Suki that I will see her sometime tonight." I headed to Santy's in South Braintree for a few beers.

I ended up having a few too many beers at Santy's. The bartender shut me off and took my car keys. One of the guys gave me a ride home. Now I remember that it was a Saturday. I ended up falling asleep or passing out sometime Saturday evening and waking up around noontime Sunday. My mother had cooked an eye of the round for Sunday dinner, one of my favorite meals. Sometime after dinner the IF gave me a ride to Santy's. It was the first time that I smoked a cigarette in his car. I lit up without thinking. I'm good at that, doing things without thinking. He didn't say anything. He rolled his window down and told me to do the same. He said, "Things must be going pretty good with you and Suki. You have been spending a lot of time at her place." I said, "Ya, Dad, things are going pretty good between us."

All the apologizing I said to Suki did not do any good. I tried to explain to her that I had made a terrible mistake by saying what I said to her. I told her that I had no idea why I said it. I don't believe in abortions. I did not want her to get an abortion.

We went to an abortion clinic in Brookline, Massachusetts, where Suki had an abortion. We went back there two more times. Suki had another abortion. The third time we went there was a false alarm, she was not pregnant.

I signed my daughter away. I'm partly responsible for two babies not being born. I'm about to get involved with crack cocaine. For anyone who is judging me right now, screw you. What's in your closet?

No one is perfect, right? But, some mistakes are worse than others. There are some of us, that, for what ever reason, we make more than our share of bad decisions. Why is that? I don't know, you tell me.

Yesterday was November 24, 2005. Thanksgiving. I hope everyone had a nice Thanksgiving, except those of you who are judging me. I turned down the few invitations I received from family and friends to join them for dinner, as I have done for the past several years. I helped to serve dinners to the homeless folks at the PIP Homeless Shelter across the street from where I live, here on South Main Street in Worcester, Massachusetts. I don't do it for them. I do it for me. If I felt better having dinner with my family or friends, I would have dinner with my family or friends (nothing what-so-ever against my family and my friends). It makes me feel good helping to serve dinner to the less fortunate. Do I hear someone judging me, again?

Most of the intimate feelings that Suki and me had for each other were now gone. For the most part, our relationship was over. It was in June of 1988 when we decided to part ways. A few days after we broke up, I received a call from Suki. She had received some bad news from Korea. Her mother was very sick and was probably going to die. Suki had not been back to Korea since coming to America about sixteen years ago. She asked me if I would do her a favor. She asked me if I would not mind baby sitting her house for her while she was in Korea. I told her that I would be happy to do that for her. She told me that she would be in Korea for at least two months. I told her that it didn't matter how long she was in Korea. I would take care of her house for her.

I remember that it was a beautiful spring day when I drove Suki to Logan Airport. There wasn't a lot of conversation between us on the way. Suki had a lot on her mind. I could see the concerned look on her face for her mother. I felt bad for Suki. Her mother was about to pass on (God rest her soul) in a few weeks. At least Suki got to see her mother for one last time.

On my way home, to Suki's house, I stopped at my favorite grinder shop in Brockton, that was on Suki's side of town in West Brockton. I had a favorite grinder shop in East Brockton, as well. I can't remember either of their names. During the two years I spent with Suki, we did not get take out food that often. She preferred to cook. But, she knew I enjoyed grinders. So, once in a while I would walk from her house to a little strip mall where the grinder shop was. It was about a ten minute walk. Walking there gave me an opportunity to fire up a couple of smokes, round trip.

I ordered a steak bomb with extra steak and was just about to grab a jug of Coca-Cola when I hesitated. I paid for my steak bomb, got in my car and headed for the liquor store. I had drank three beers in Suki's back yard on July fourth, 1987. That was the first and only time that I had drank beer at her house, up until then. It was only the second time that she saw me drink beer, and she watched me carefully, again, to make sure that I didn't go over my three beer limit.

The first time was on July fourth, 1986, in George and Sue's backyard at their cookout. I remember that day saying to George after cracking open my first beer, "Three beers, George?" He said, "That's right, Dave, three beers." I said, "Ya … right …" He smiled and said in a quiet voice, "Will power."

After my third beer I said, "Well … that's two beers, I might as well have my last beer (which would have been one of George's beers since we only bought one six pack)." Suki said, "Who you think you talking to? You think I not watching you?" And then, she said something in Korean. Sue and George got a big chuckle out of whatever she said. I poured myself a glass of Coca-Cola.

I arrived at Suki's house with my grinder and six pack of pounders (sixteen ounce beers). It felt strange being there. I had been in Suki's house alone before, but she was always nearby and coming home soon. She would be at the market or doing some other type of shopping or at a friend's house. This time, Suki was on a plane that was heading out of the country. And, we had broken up. We weren't even a couple anymore. I ate my grinder and drank a couple of beers. All of a sudden I was exhausted. I fell asleep watching TV on her couch. Before I fell asleep, after I ate my grinder, I accidentally started to go outside for a smoke. I caught myself, grabbed a saucer from the kitchen cabinet for an ash tray and enjoyed a smoke or two … inside her house. Her phone rang so I got up and unplugged it.

I had been baby sitting Suki's house for about a month. With the exception of a couple of times, I stayed there overnight. She called me a few times. The second time was when her mother had passed away. The first time was when she safely arrived in Korea. The third time she called she told me she would be staying in Korea probably until the middle of August.

She asked me if I was going over to Sue and George's, or Kim's, or two other of her Korean friends who lived in Bridgewater, I forget their names. I use to call one of them Bulldog, not to her face. I told Suki that I had not been visiting any of our friends. I told her that I was working a lot. Driving a truck and doing a few things around her house to stay busy. I said there was one problem. She said, "What is it?" I said, "The large bowl of kimshe you made for me before you left, is all gone." She laughed a little bit.

I asked her how she was doing. She said she would be OK, that her mother had lived a long, hard working, good life. I told her that I missed her a lot and that I was looking forward to her coming home. It took a few seconds before she said, "David, things never be same again." I quickly said, "I know Suki, but we can always stay good friends." She said, "Yes."

On a Friday evening, probably towards the end of July, 1988, I stopped at the Alamo barroom on my way home from work. It was a neighborhood barroom located in downtown Brockton, Massachusetts. I had been driving a truck all day. The Alamo was the type of barroom that you would not have to take a shower before going in. You would be better off showering after you left. I was to receive a lifetime ban from the Alamo a few years later for starting a brawl there. It was because of my smartass mouth after having a few beers. I remember that one of the regulars had walked in and said to everyone, "Hey … what do you think of my brand new sneakers?" He had on a pair of bright white, expensive looking sneakers. He was a good size guy with an extra good size beer belly. I said, "I like them Joe. But, how the f___ can you see them?" That was the same thing that I said to Kevin C. when I was a kid. I got in trouble with Kevin for saying it and I got in trouble with Joe for saying it … twenty something years later.

This Friday evening was my first time at the Alamo. I was being inspected by several people, especially a guy named Santos. He seemed nervous and on edge because of my presence. I found out later that he was a drug dealer. He sold crack at the Alamo. The regulars were always suspicious of a new guy, wondering if the guy was a cop. Some working girls would bounce in and out of the Alamo all day and all night long. I had a good idea about the working girls at the Alamo, but I had no idea about the drugs.

I didn't like weed the few times that I tried it in high school. It made me paranoid. I smoked hashish once and it made me sick. I turned down LSD a couple of times. My drug of choice was beer. I loved it. It made me feel like everything I couldn't feel like when I wasn't drinking. I didn't need illegal drugs.

I was enjoying my beer at the bar when Deanna came in. She was a nice looking black lady with a killer body. She sat down beside me and said, "Buy me a drink?" I said, "Nice to meet you, too." She said, "I'm sorry. I'm Deanna, everyone calls me Super Dee." I said, "I can see why." She smiled and said, "What brings you here?" I said, "I'm here with my friend, Budweiser, waiting for someone as pretty as you to come by." She said, "Are you a cop?" I said, "Not the last time I checked."

She started to get off her bar stool before we had finished our drinks. I said, "Hey ... let a guy finish his beer, will ya ..." She sat back down and said in a low voice, "I'm jonesing for a hit." I said, in a low voice, not that it really mattered, "Does jonesing mean that you can't wait and a hit of what?" She said, "Right and crack." I said, "I'm a beer drinker. I don't know too much about other stuff. What's crack?" She said, "I'll tell later."

We headed to Deanna's room which was in a rooming house off of Spring Street which was off of Main Street, not far from the Alamo. The MainSpring homeless shelter in Brockton is located on the corner of Main and Spring streets. She lived in a crack house. The majority of people in her building smoked crack. I would later get to know many of the crack houses in that neighborhood of Brockton and other neighborhoods in that city. There were a lot of them. Some people use to call Brockton, Rockton (crack rocks).

On the way there she said, "Can you spend forty?" I said, "Sure." I parked near the front of her building. There were a couple of guys hanging around outside. As we walked by, Super Dee said to one of them, "Bring me up a forty." When we got inside her room on the second floor, she said, "T. J. will be here in a few minutes with my crack." I gave her forty bucks and said, "What the hell is crack?" She said, "Do you know what cocaine is?" I said, "Ya." She said, "It's cocaine cooked up. You smoke it. I'll show you how, I'll let you try a couple of hits." She broke out her crack pipe. It was a plastic nip bottle that use to have vodka in it. She had put a hole in the side of it using a lit cigarette. Some folks put two holes in their pipe, using the second hole as a carburetor. There was a piece of aluminum foil tightly wrapped on the top of the nip bottle with little pin holes in the foil.

Some people put a rubber band or a piece of tape on the foil, around the neck of the nip bottle. She told me to save my cigarette ashes, to flick them on a piece of paper with a crease in it that she had on her coffee table. She put the ashes that we saved on the top of her pipe. T. J. dropped off her crack. She opened up her package and emptied the contents on a small plate. It was a big rock and a couple of little rocks (crumbs). She cut a piece of rock off the big rock using a razor. She put it on her pipe and fired it up. She lit the piece of crack on the top of her pipe with a cigarette lighter, by holding the lighter upside down and at an angle. There is a technique to it.

She was in heaven. Everything in the world was now OK with her. I said, "You look serene." She didn't answer me. She had crack smoke left in her pipe, more crack from her first hit to smoke. She fired it up again. She looked like she was in a different world. But, those feelings that she was experiencing from firing up her pipe, were not lasting very long. The extreme rush that she was getting lasted less than ten seconds. She fired her pipe up twice, sometimes three times for each hit she put on. That forty dollar piece of crack gave her eight, maybe nine medium size hits, for a rush that lasted less than ten seconds.

I thought to myself that she paid an awful lot of my money for something that didn't last very long. She was finished smoking that forty dollar rock in forty-five minutes and that's because she started to slow down after her first couple of hits and stretched it out to try to make it last as long as she could. Everyone is different. Some would have smoked it faster, some would have taken longer.

I could have bought forty dollars worth of Budweiser's that would have lasted me for hours and hours and hours. I pretty much sat there on her couch during that time doing nothing but getting restless and bored. She put her third to last hit on the pipe and handed it to me. I picked up my lighter and she said "Put your lighter down, I'll light it for you."

Anyone who smokes crack for the first time has trouble lighting the hit. I put my mouth on the hole, she lit it, I sucked in the crack smoke. Nothing much happened, I didn't feel anything. There was still crack smoke in my pipe. I hit the pipe again and again nothing. She put up her last couple of hits and smoked them. She said, "How did you like it?" I said, "I didn't get high, I didn't feel anything." She said, "Some people don't feel anything the first time they smoke crack. It takes a few hits before you experience the crack high." Whatever she had been experiencing must have been a hell of a rush for those brief periods of time. I wanted to experience it. I wanted to feel those feelings she was feeling.

She said, "Do you want to get down to business?" I said, "No, I'm not in the mood anymore." I took out forty bucks, handed it to her and said, "Buy another forty."

Had I known how powerful the crack high was and how highly addictive it was, I would like to think that I would not have taken that first hit. I knew nothing about crack until that evening. I had cracked open plenty of beers and had been cracked on the side of my head a few times, but I had never heard the word crack used in a drug context, before. I did not have the information available to me that is available to everyone today. If you have never tried crack, don't. If you do try it, it will get you. It will affect every single aspect of your life, negatively. It will destroy the relationships you have in your life with everyone … everyone … If you start smoking crack, there will come a point in time when the only thing that matters to you is getting that next hit. It will completely destroy your life. No one survives crack.

I ended up experiencing the crack high that night with Super Dee. It was a powerful high, like nothing I had ever experienced before in my life. We ended up buying a third forty rock and we would have bought more if I had had more money. The next time I got paid and most of the times that I got paid for the next thirteen years, I spent some or most of that pay check on crack. If heaven is similar to being on crack, then that's where I want to be. I can't imagine hell being worse than the feelings that I suffered through when the crack was gone. Only an addict will be able to understand what I'm talking about.

If I were able to add up all the money that I spent on crack, it would be way too much. Besides taking away my money, crack took away my self-worth, self-esteem, morals, values, principals, beliefs, integrity, friendships, honesty and all the things that make someone a decent person. When someone smokes crack, he/she is no longer a decent person. I was far from perfect before I started smoking crack. But, there were plenty of times when I was a decent person. That did not happen for the next thirteen years while I was smoking crack. The only thing that mattered to me was getting my next hit.

I know that you non-addicts are shaking your heads. I don't blame you. I can't figure out why I did the things that I did. It is very sad. It is very, very sad. Have you heard the saying, 'God does not make junk'. I can't speak for other addicts, but, I know that when I smoked crack, I was a piece of junk. God didn't make me a piece of junk. I made me a piece of junk.

I don't think that there is anything wrong with wanting to feel good. We all want to feel good. Using drugs to feel good is the wrong way to go about it. The consequences are horrendous, devastating and many times fatal. Why do drug addicts become drug addicts? I wish that I knew the answer. Does anyone really know? Why do most folks live a good, decent life from birth till death? You work hard, make the right decisions, do the right thing, live a decent life. I don't know why, but, thank God that you do.

I have a great deal of respect for those of you who have demonstrated day after day, the stick-to-it-tiveness to put your elbows to the grindstone and accomplish the things that need to be accomplished to make this world a better place to live in. You deserve a lot of credit. You are the ones who have the backbone needed to keep our country, the United States of America, the greatest country in the world.

One important loss that all addicts suffer is our loss of gratitude. We have no gratitude whatsoever, none at all. Our appreciation for everything, everything, goes down the toilet. I mentioned earlier in my book that I was involved in a gun incident for a third time. I think that I came within a second or two of taking a bullet in my head. No, I don't think, I know. It was in the beginning years of my cocaine addiction, probably 1989. I had learned that crack was becoming increasingly popular, especially with street ladies. To support their crack habit they had to work the street. At that time, I was the only person I knew in Braintree who smoked crack. To get my cocaine, I was dealing with the street ladies in Brockton or Boston. I knew that this thing called crack was way too expensive, illegal and would bring me nothing but trouble. I knew that from the beginning.

After I had smoked crack for my second time, I believe, I said to myself that I can't do this anymore. I'm going to end up in a world of crap if I don't knock it off. And I had meant what I had said. There was one problem. ALCOHOL. Almost every single time I chased crack for thirteen years it was after putting alcohol in my system. I would say to myself, I'll have a few beers and call it a night. That rarely happened. Those few beers I would have set up a compulsion in me to chase heaven. When I smoked crack I was in heaven. I could not do one without doing the other.

It was payday. I cashed my check and went to a bar for a few beers. After drinking a few beers I got in my car and headed for Boston. I was driving down Blue Hill Avenue in Mattapan checking out the ladies. I pulled over to let a lady get in my car. Her name was Jennifer. She said, "Hi, are you a cop?" I said, "No, can you get me some crack?"

No matter how much money I had in my pocket, once I took that first hit of crack, I would spend all my money, every time. Jennifer said, "What do you want to get?" I said, "A forty." I had about two hundred bucks on me. And I added, "Can you get it from the car and do you have a place where we can smoke?" I learned the hard way, like I seem to learn everything the hard way that it was not a good idea to hand money to a stranger for crack and let her go into a crack house to buy it. Most of the time she didn't come back.

Jennifer said, "No problem", and directed me to a street.

We pulled up to a few guys hanging around on a street. I had the money in my hand. She rolled down her window and asked for a forty. I handed her the money, a guy handed her the crack, she gave him the money. We headed to Logan Street in Roxbury where she lived. Jennifer was a pretty young lady with a pleasant personality, probably about twenty-three years old. She hadn't been smoking crack for that long. She told me that she started a couple of months ago. She lived in the cellar apartment of her mother's house, a two story, single family home in Roxbury.

Jennifer was the oldest child in her family. She had some younger brothers and sisters who lived upstairs on the second floor of her mother's house. She had her own apartment entrance on the side of the house. There was no direct entrance to her apartment from the first floor of her mother's house. The set of stairs going from the first floor to the cellar led to the other part of the cellar where the furnace and hot water heater were located, designed that way for tenant privacy. She kept the inside door in her apartment that led to the cellar utilities room locked. One of her brothers, Junior, was nineteen years old. He also smoked crack and he carried a gun. Jennifer told me that Junior smoked crack, but she didn't mention anything about his gun.

It was probably around 8 or 9 at night. I asked her about her mother. She said we didn't have to worry because her mother worked the second shift at Boston University Hospital Medical Center (today it is the Boston Medical Center). And that her mother rarely bothered her in her apartment. Her mother must have been a hard working lady. Raising the kids, working full time and owned her own home.

When we got to her street she showed me where to park. It was next to her mother's house. There was an empty parking spot in front of her mother's house. She said no one takes her mother's parking spot. I said, "It's still early, it won't take us that long to smoke what we have." She said, "I know, but, not taking my mother's spot is a good habit to get into." Hmmm ... A good habit to get into? Her mother sounded like a strict lady. That turned out later to be a good thing for me, possibly a life saver.

We hadn't been in her place too long when Junior knocked on her outside door. She told him to go away, that she was busy. He kept knocking. She kept telling him to go away. I said, "Open your door, I want to talk to him." She said,

"No way." I said, "Do you want to get an eight ball (about 150 dollars worth of crack) after we finish this?" She said, "Ya." I said, "Then open your door." She opened her door and let Junior in. I said, "Junior, we only have a couple of hits between us. We're getting more after this. I'll cut you off a twenty dollar piece when we get back. Is that cool?" He said, "OK, I'll be waiting."

We finished our forty, and went back out and bought an eight ball. When we got back, I didn't see Junior hanging around outside. I said to Jennifer, "Where's Junior, in the house?" She said, "He's probably hanging around with his friends. It doesn't matter anyway cause we're not giving him anything." I said, "I told him that I was going to give him something and …" She interrupted me and said in a loud voice, "If you give him something he will keep coming back. He will bug us for the rest of the night." I wish she had mentioned to me that he carried a gun.

We spent a few hours smoking the eight ball. I can't remember exactly how long it took us. Maybe four or five hours. Junior knocked on Jennifer's outside door several times and her inside door a couple of times. We ignored his knocks. After we finished smoking, not right after, but sometime after, we fell asleep. I think that it was around 10 am when we woke up, but, I can't remember for sure. Jennifer asked me if I was supposed to be working. I told her that I drove a truck whenever I felt like it. I added, "I don't feel like driving a truck today. I feel like smoking more crack." She said, "You don't have any more money." I said, "I do in my bank. We have to take a ride to the South Shore Plaza in Braintree. We have to go to my bank and get more money. Do you know how to drive?" She said, "I have my driver's license." I gave her my car keys and we left her apartment.

I had forgotten all about Junior. He hadn't forgotten about me. Jennifer got in the drivers side. I got in the passengers side and rolled down my window. Just as she started my car, Junior, appeared from out of nowhere and put a 9 mm handgun to the right side of my head. He was yelling something about me not giving him any crack and getting ready to squeeze the trigger. A split second before he tried to install air conditioning in my head, Jennifer screamed, "If you shoot him I'm telling mummy." That threat from Jennifer was enough to make him think twice about shooting me. He raised his gun and whacked the side of my head with it. Jennifer threw my car into drive and took off. I didn't say anything for a few seconds. Jennifer said, "Don't worry, Dave, the gun wasn't loaded."

I said, "You stupid f_____ bitch. I nearly got killed because you wouldn't let me give him a little crack." She said, "It wouldn't have been a little crack, you don't know him. He would have been bothering us all night long. And the gun wasn't loaded." I said, "Like hell it wasn't. Why did you scream at him not to shoot me?" She said, "Well, I know when he bought the gun a while back he didn't have any bullets for it." I said, "Just drive, head for the Southeast Expressway." She said, "I've been to the South Shore Plaza, I know how to get there." I leaned my head back and massaged it. I was thinking more about getting more crack than I was about almost just getting killed … thinking more about getting more crack …

Jennifer said, "He hit you pretty hard. Are you OK." I said, "Ya, I'm OK. After we go to the bank we are going to my apartment. It's in the cellar of my parent's house, just like your place." She said, "We have to get the crack first." Jennifer was the first of many ladies that I brought to my apartment in the cellar of my parent's house in Braintree to smoke crack. We had to do some extra driving. We had to go from the South Shore Plaza in Braintree back to Boston to get the crack, then back to Braintree again. But it was better than going back to Jennifer's place where Junior was.

We bought another eight ball of crack. We smoked it in my apartment. Afterward, I drove Jennifer home. I saw Jennifer a couple of weeks later. I went to her apartment at her mother's house. I was looking forward to running into Junior. I had bought an eight ball of crack from Santos, the guy who dealt crack out of the Alamo barroom in Brockton.

I took it home, smoked a little bit and cut off a piece for Junior. Then I drove to Roxbury. I didn't see him around when I pulled up to Jennifer's mother's house. But that son of a gun saw me. Less than two minutes after I was in Jennifer's apartment, he knocked on her door. I gave him a decent piece of crack, probably about a quarter of the eight ball I bought. I told him, no, I asked him not to bother Jennifer and me for awhile. He said, OK, and he didn't. He didn't ask me how my head was feeling …

Probably about a week or so after that, I was driving along Blue Hill Avenue looking for a nice lady to smoke crack with. Jennifer was a nice lady, but, I've got nothing against being with a different lady. And, I didn't want to have to give Junior a piece of crack every time I saw Jennifer.

I picked up Tanya. What a cutie pie. She was around thirty years old, pretty, attractive figure, medium length black hair, brown eyes, light skinned black lady. When she got in my car, she said, "What are you doing, what's going on?" I said, "Not much, I'm Dave." She said, I'm Tanya and it's nice to meet you." I said, "Same here. I'm driving around looking for a nice lady to keep me company because my girlfriend left me a couple of days ago." Tanya said, "I'm sorry to hear that, what happened?" I said, "Nothing happened, she just had to leave for a couple of days to take care of some business. She called me this morning and I said to her, "Sweetie Pie, you wouldn't believe how miserable I've been since you've been gone. It's almost as if you were still here."

Tanya looked at me for a few seconds and then she burst out laughing. She said, "I was believing what you were saying You got me good." And then she added, "You can't be a cop. They never tell jokes." I laughed and said, "Sure they do, but no I'm not a cop and do you smoke crack?" She smiled and said, "I do, but I never would have figured you for someone who smokes crack." I said, "Why, do people who smoke crack have a certain look?" She said, "Ya, at least the people I've smoked crack with have a certain look. But, I can't explain it. Anyway, do you have any?" I said, "No, can you get us some without leaving my car?" She said, "No problem."

And it wasn't a problem. I saw Tanya a few times in a row over the next few weeks. One time when I saw her, there was a problem. She had given me her mother's phone number and I had given her my phone number. She called me one night, around 6. I had just got home from work. She asked me if I was doing anything. I said, "Besides talking to you, I'm eating a grinder." She said, "What kind?" I said, "Meatball with tomatoes, pickles, hot peppers and cheese on it." Tanya said, "Hmmm, that sounds so yummy." I said, "Would you like half of it?" She said, "No, you eat the whole thing. You worked hard today." I said, "I never work hard. Meet me at Pop Eye's Chicken (in front of Orchard Park) in about an hour." She said, "I'll be there. I'll be the black lady." I laughed and said, "You're funny. You will be the prettiest black or white lady there." The Orchard Park projects in Roxbury, Massachusetts, are predominately black.

When I worked for the Boston Gas Company, a year or so after I met Tanya, my partner and I and a few other gas crews went there one time to do a job. The Orchard Park Projects maintenance department normally does most of their own gas work. But, in an extraordinary situation, we would be called in. There had been a gas leak in the main gas line coming into the Park. It had to be shut down while our gas street crew repaired it. After it was repaired, we were called in to light everyone up. Light the range and oven pilots in all the units.

There are way too many apartments there for the Orchard Park Projects maintenance men to handle it in a timely fashion. I remember that out of all the apartments that my partner and me lit up, and we lit up a lot, I don't remember seeing any white families, latino families, oriental families or any other families there; only black families.

I met Tanya in front of Pop Eye's. I said, "Did you eat anything?" She said, "I ate earlier, I'm good." I said, "OK, I was going to offer to buy you a meal in Pop Eye's." She said, "Thanks anyway, I'll take a rain check. I'm in the mood for smoking." I said, "Me too. Where should we go to get it." Tanya said, "Do you mind driving down that street?" She pointed to a street. I forget the name of the street. It was a narrow side road that ran down the length of Orchard Park, not one of the main Orchard Park perimeter roads. "I'll run in and out in less than five minutes." At this point in our relationship, I trusted Tanya with my money. Even though we had not known each other for very long, and even though the major part of our relationship consisted of smoking crack together, I trusted her.

I think that I am better than medium when it comes to sizing up people. I didn't think that Tanya would take off with my money. I said, "No, I don't mind. Just, try to be as quick as you can." She knew that I was nervous about driving down that street, and about letting her leave my car with my money. She said, "David, I'm not going to take off with your money. I'm not going to screw up a good thing with you." I said, "I know." What she forgot to say and what I forgot to do, was lock my driver's door. I'm not use to locking my door when I'm sitting in my car. Tanya just forgot all about reminding me. Those things happen when people are excited about smoking crack.

We headed down the side street. She told me where to pull over. She exited my car and headed into the projects. I remember seeing a guy across the street on the sidewalk, in front of the projects, standing there, checking me out. It was at that point that I remembered that my door was unlocked. No big deal. I'm keeping my eye on him. I didn't lock my door. I wish I could tell you exactly what happened over the next fifteen seconds, but I can't. I don't remember looking away from the guy on the sidewalk. I do remember my driver's door being opened and the guy from the sidewalk standing there with a large knife in his hand. It had to have been ten inches long. I knew right away that it was the guy from the sidewalk because he was ugly and his right ear stuck out and it was slightly bent over at the top.

I've been away from my writing for a couple of days. Today is December 19, 2005, six days before Christmas. It is a busy time of the year, even for those of us who are poor. It seems like every day there is something to do to keep me from my writing. I have had time to remember, to be pretty accurate about how I lost track of the man on the sidewalk.

I had been watching him out of the corner of my eye the whole time. I remember that he started to walk down the sidewalk, away from me and my car. That is when I took my eye off of him. He must have doubled back as soon as he noticed that I wasn't watching him anymore, crossed the street and slid up along-side my car. Whether or not he knew that my door was unlocked, I don't know. I do know that the amount of time that it took for him to do that was fifteen seconds or less.

When my door flew open, I immediately looked to my left. The guy said, in a demanding, forceful voice, "Give me your wallet, I'm not f_____ around with you." He wasn't yelling, but, he was talking in a louder than normal voice. He didn't raise or point his knife at me. He just made sure I saw it. I immediately went for my right rear pocket where my wallet was, with my right hand. I tried not to move my left hand and arm, too much. I wanted him to be sure that I was going to do exactly as he told me. I handed him my wallet. I didn't say anything to him, and he hadn't said much to me. He didn't grab the wallet from my hand. He calmly accepted it and started to walk away as if I had just given him a cigarette.

At that point, I realized that I had probably cheated death again. I yelled to him, "Hey buddy, there is only ten bucks in there, no money hidden anywhere else. Keep the ten bucks, can I have my wallet back, please?" He ignored me and calmly walked into the Orchard Park Projects.

I sat in my car for about a minute or two, thinking. Then I got out of my car. I leaned up against the driver's side door of my car, folded my arms, lit a cigarette and I stared into the projects. Why did that man rob me? What did I do to him? Is this the world that I am now a part of since choosing to smoke crack? I would not have been there if I were not trying to buy crack. What if I were there for some other reason. I still would have been robbed. I believe this happened probably in the summer of 1989. I know that I wasn't working for the Boston Gas Company, yet.

I started working for them on the Tuesday after Memorial Day weekend in 1990. I had now been smoking crack for about a year. In that year, I nearly got my head blown off and I could have been stabbed with a large knife. Those two things are what are known in the programs of Alcoholics Anonymous and Narcotics Anonymous as sign posts. It sounds simplistic, doesn't it? SIGN POSTS. Maybe even common sensible. You should try thinking with my brain. Or any addict's brain. There is a reason that Alcoholics Anonymous and Narcotics Anonymous keep their programs simple. As simple as possible.

I was talking on the phone to my youngest brother, Billy, the other day. Like me, he likes to joke around with people and goof off once in awhile. He lives with his wife, Linda and their two children, Anne Marie and Danny, in Whitman, Massachusetts. Billy and Linda started dating when he was twelve and she was eleven. Linda's family lived three houses away from our family. Her mother, Anne (God rest her soul), a very, very, nice lady, died from cancer when she was way too young. Linda's sister, Kathy (God rest her soul), died from diabetes complications. She was a sweetheart. Linda's other sister, Karen is married with a couple of kids and lives in Connecticut. Al, Linda's father, is an awfully good guy. I respected that guy when I was a kid, and my respect grew for him as I grew older. He was not a man to screw around with, and I never did.

I called to thank Billy and Linda and Anne Marie and Danny for their Christmas presents. I had received a large box in the mail from them earlier that day. A present from each one of them. They do it every year. They have never not done it. Since I live alone in my studio apartment, there is no reason for me to wait till Christmas morning to open the few presents that I receive. What a nice feeling it is receiving presents. What a sucky feeling it is not being able to afford to give presents. I also received a couple of presents from two of the eight ball. An awful nice thing for them to do, but ... it really sucks that I can't return the favor. And I know that they don't expect me too, that they gave me the presents because they want to, but, it still sucks ... wish I wasn't poor.

I thanked Billy for their presents and asked him if he and Linda had had a chance to look over the book pages that I had been mailing them. He said, "As a matter of fact, Dave, Linda and I were planning on sitting in front of the fireplace this evening to read your book." I was just about to say, "That sounds nice" when I could hear Linda laughing in the background. Freaking Billy, what a clown. He must get it from me.

I had been leaning up against my car for, probably a couple of minutes when I could see some kind of an emergency vehicle coming down the street. At first, I wasn't sure of exactly what kind of an emergency vehicle it was. I could see the emergency lights on the roof. It was a white 4 x 4 with red stripes down the sides. It wasn't a Boston Police cruiser. They are white sedans with blue stripes down the sides. I wasn't sure who it was, but I figured it must have had a two way radio. I stood in the middle of the street and stopped the vehicle.

It was a Boston Emergency Medical Technician's vehicle. The emergency medical technician got out of his vehicle and said, "What's wrong?" I said, "I've just been robbed. I wasn't hurt, but, can you get the Boston Police here."

He said, "Sure." In those days, they didn't wear their radio microphone's on their shoulders like a lot of them do today. He got back into his vehicle and radioed for the police from his vehicle's two way radio. He got back out of his vehicle, walked over to me and said, "They should be here soon. I'll wait with you until they get here." He could see that I had been pretty shaken up over the incident. He said, "Are you sure that you are OK? Do you want me to check you out? I'm an emergency medical technician." I said, "No, thank you anyway. I wasn't hurt."

The Boston Police and Tanya both showed up at about the same time. When I gave the police officers my description of the guy who robbed me, everyone there knew who he was. Tanya, the officers, the EMT. His street name was Cowboy. His real name was Tony Tony. That's right. Tony Tony. I don't know how his last name is spelled, but, it is Tony. And his parents named him Anthony. Anthony Tony, or, Tony Tony. One of the officers said, "I don't think Cowboy has an address." Tanya said, "He is living with his girlfriend in building _, unit _." Out of the five of us that were there, I was the only white person. I was robbed by a black person and now four black people were trying to help me. The EMT took off. I thanked him for his help. The two police officers, Tanya and I headed for Cowboy's girlfriend's apartment.

Cowboy's girlfriend finally answered the door after the police knocked several times. One of the officers said, "Tell Cowboy to come out here." She said, "He doesn't live here, he's not here." I said, "Just tell him all I want is my wallet back, I don't care about the ten bucks." She said, "He's not here." One of the officers said, "Tell him we will be looking for him." There was nothing else the police could do. On our way out, one of the officers said to me, "I guess you won't be coming back to Orchard Park anymore to buy your crack." I looked at him and the other officer and I looked at Tanya and I said, "No, you're right, I won't."

After finishing the police report, Tanya and I drove off. She said, "Is ten bucks what he really got from you?" I said, "Ya, I had seventy, gave you sixty, Cowboy got my last ten." She said, "How did it happen?" I told her that I hadn't locked my door and then I said, "Forget about that. Did you get the crack." She said, "I always do." I said, "You got balls walking around with the cops with crack in your pocket." She said, "No, not really. It wasn't that big a deal. If the cops were looking for me or if I had been giving them a hard time in the past, then it would have been a big deal." We drove away from Roxbury and headed for my apartment in Braintree.

A few days later I was at one of the Boston police stations, I forget which Area. The police stations are named for areas, Area A, B, C, D, etc. The detective who was working with me put several mug shots in front of me. I picked out Cowboy. The detective said, "Tony Tony." I said, "His name is Tony?" He said, "His first and last names are Tony." I said, "You're kidding?" He said, "Nope. Anthony Tony. That's his name." Then he said, "When we pick him up, are you willing to go to court and testify?" I said, "If you can get my wallet back for me, sure I'll testify." He said, "You think that you're going to get your wallet back? You're kidding me, aren't you?"

I've told a few people about this incident over the years. When I told them that I got my wallet back, I'm not sure if they believed me. I got my wallet back. Everything in it had been rearranged. I don't think that anything was missing. But, at least I got it back. It was a few nights after I was robbed when I received a phone call from Tanya. She said, "Do you feeling like taking a ride to Roxbury?" I said, "No, not tonight, Tanya. I'm too tired." She said, "Are you too tired to come to Roxbury to get your wallet?" I said, "For real or are you kidding me?" She said, "For real."

I met Tanya a little later that evening. She handed me my wallet. I said, "How the hell did you get my wallet back from Cowboy?" She said, "I didn't." But I have friends." I said, "Thank God for friends." I took Tanya to one of my all time favorite grinder shops, possibly my favorite, Ugi's in Boston. They had a couple of grinder shops in Boston. The one I use to go to most often was located at the corner of Massachusetts Avenue and Washington Street, right next to Skippy White's Records. They can say what they want to in Philadelphia, but nobody made a better steak and cheese grinder than Ugi. Those of you who have been to Ugi's know what I'm talking about. It was the last meal that Tanya and I had together. It was the last time that we saw each other. We hadn't known each other for very long. But, we enjoyed each others company very much. Who knows, maybe if we had met under different circumstances, who knows …

I'm not sure exactly how long it was after I had been robbed by Cowboy. Maybe a week in half. I received a phone call from Detective _____. He said, "David, where were you on such and such a night." I told him and asked him why? He said, "Well, I know you had nothing to do with this, but it's part of my job. I had to call you to ask." I said, "You know I had nothing to do with what?" He said, "Cowboy was stabbed nine times." I said, "What?" He said, "They were all non-life threatening stab wounds. He is going to live. Someone was giving him a message." I immediately thought of Tanya's friends. Then Detective _____ added, "I knew that you had nothing to do with it. We have a couple of good suspects. I not only called you because it's part of my job, but also because I thought that you would like to know what happened to the guy who robbed you." I said, "Thank you Detective. I really appreciate you calling me." He said, "Your welcome, and …" I interrupted him and said, "I know, I know, stay away from Orchard Park."

Whether or not Tanya had anything to do with Cowboy being stabbed nine times; who knows. Maybe she did and maybe she didn't. Cowboy probably had a lot of enemies. If he changed his ways, good for him. If he didn't, he's either dead or in prison. Anthony Tony, if you are in one of the Massachusetts Correctional Institutions and you happen to be reading this, you owe me ten bucks … plus interest.

I don't know how anyone else who smoked crack felt in their beginning crack smoking years, but, I can tell you how I felt. After every single time that I did it, I told myself that I would never do it again. And I meant what I said, at the time. There was no feeling that I had ever experienced in my life that was comparable to a crack high, for me. As I have said before, if there is a heaven, I can't imagine it being better than smoking crack. We all like to feel good. We are all dealt a certain hand of cards in life. We play the hand of cards that we were dealt. Some can play better than others, with the same hand. Some have a better hand. You know what I continually think about? What if I hadn't had a kidney disease? Just, what if? I was dealt a kidney disease and it screwed up my dreams. Up until that point in my life, I had no complaints. I could not have asked for better parents. I got along OK with my brothers and sisters, some better than others. I can't say that we were close. We were medium. Sometimes it seemed as though we were close, and sometimes it didn't. I can say that each and every one of us knew how lucky we were to have the parents that we had.

If I hadn't come down with a kidney disease, where would I be right now? Would I have been offered a four year football scholarship, after having been an outstanding high school football player? No question about it. The talent I have in football is something that I was born with, God given. There are things that you can practice and work hard at, and get better at. And then there are things that you are born with. I did not have to work hard at catching a football, almost any pass that was thrown anywhere near me. I did not have to work hard at running pass routes. I could lose anyone who was trying to cover me. Those were talents given to me by God. I did not have to work on them.

I use to kid Tyracks (Tom Rowan) once in awhile. During our high school and college years, the eight ball had our own tag football league. The TAFL, or Thayer Academy Football League. We played our games at Thayer Academy in Braintree, Massachusetts. Plank (Steve Burke), Gig (Gerry Cook), J.C. Nickel (John Cumming), Kennard (Rick Kennedy), Duck (Don O'Leary), The Arm (Rich Pompeo), Tyracks (Tom Rowan) and me. Plank's brother, Al Burke (Big Al) and Jawba (Jack Devine) also played in our informal league. It seemed as though we had a game every Sunday in the fall and winter, for years.

They weren't five on five games because not every one would show up on every Sunday. They were usually two on two or three on three games. Tyracks,

Plank, Gig and I probably showed up the most. And, nothing against any of the other guys, they were all decent athletes. But, the best two on two battles that we had, I think, were Plank and Gig against Tyracks and I. Sometimes, we played those games like we thought that we were playing in a Super Bowl. Tyracks and I played in the Boston Park Football League a few years later. Many times Tyracks and I were on the same team in the TAFL, Tyracks quarterbacking and me receiving. Once in awhile, after having made a pretty darn good catch, when I returned to the huddle, Tyracks would say, "How the hell did you catch that pass, Chelch?" I would look at him with a huge smile on my face and say, "Pennsylvania football blood, T", (we also called Tyracks Big T or T). I would say that in reference to my father being from Pennsylvania.

There are a few states in this country, that, for some reason or other, seem to turn out more than their share of football talent. Pennsylvania, Ohio, Texas, California and Florida. I know that football players from states that I didn't mention will want to give me an argument. And I know someone else who may want to give me an argument as well. I don't know too many people who are more informed than Plank (Steve Burke) when it comes to all sports. He is a walking book of sports information. How did I do naming those football states, Steve? Any feedback?

Big T and I played for different teams in the Boston Senior Park Football League. T told me a funny story one time. He had taken the snap from center and was rolling out when one of the opposing teams linebackers caught him from behind and ripped his football jersey right off of his back. He was wearing number eleven. The only spare jersey available on the sideline was number twenty-six; not a quarterbacks normal number. A few plays later, T lined up over the center. A couple of the opposing linebackers were busting T's onions, saying things like, "Number twenty-six is going to regret the day he was born", and, "you cave in twenty-six's left side and I'll cave in his right side."

T was trying to remember which one of his running backs wore number twenty-six. He couldn't remember who it was. He called for the snap and started to fade back when those two linebackers came flying in and cremated him (there were some awfully big boys in that league). As the linebackers were helping T up, T looked at them and said, "Oh, that's right. I'm number twenty-six." They slapped him on his shoulder pads and said, "We'll be back."

I told Tanya, two Boston Police Officers, and one Boston Police Detective that I would not go back to Orchard Park. Well, me being me ... I didn't lie, but I went back to near Orchard Park. I'm not sure when this was, but it was before I was hired by the Boston Gas Company and probably a few months after I was robbed by Cowboy. I drove to Pop Eye's Chicken across the street from Orchard Park to get a meal and scout out some friendly looking ladies. I took my license out of my wallet, put it in my pocket along with enough cash for a chicken meal and a forty rock of crack, and left my wallet on top of my bureau; just in case I ran into Cowboy or someone like him.

After I finished my meal, I left Pop Eye's and I was walking to my car in Pop Eye's parking lot. I saw a nice looking lady walking by on, hmmm, it might have been Harrison Avenue or Dudley Street or Washington Street. I forget. It was the main street that goes by Orchard Park that Pop Eye's Chicken was on. She didn't look like the type of lady who smoked crack. But, I didn't look like the type of guy who smoked crack. I stared at her. When she looked at me, I nodded and said, "How are you tonight?" She said, "OK, and you?" I said, "Better, now that I'm with you." She smiled and said, "Do I know you?" I said, "I'm Dave, do you like beer?" She said, "Yes, once in awhile."

I opened the passenger door of my car, grabbed my Dunkin Donuts coffee cup that was sitting on the floor, and she got in. I got in the driver's side and reached behind me on the floor of the back seat to grab her a beer. She said, "I'm Mary." I said, "It's nice to meet you. I don't have a DD cup for you, do you want mine?" She said, "No, I'll drink it out of the can. Is it cold?" I said, "I bought it in Braintree about forty-five minutes ago. It should be all right." She took a sip and said that it was fine.

We talked for awhile, and drank beer. Some how or other, our conversation turned to football. She loved watching football. I told her about my dream, and my kidney disease. She said, "That's too bad. I bet you would have made it in the NFL." That reminds me. Recently, maybe within the past two weeks, I saw Michael Irvin on the news. He was a wide receiver for the Dallas Cowboys. They showed police cruiser video tape of Michael being arrested for drunk driving. The police found a crack pipe in his fancy car. The newscaster referred to Michael as a great wide receiver. They like to use the word, great, an awful lot, don't they? They and everybody else. He was or is a great wide receiver; he's a great quarterback; he's a great linebacker; he's a great actor; she's a great actress; he's a great talk show host; she's a great talk show host; she or he is a great gal or guy ... Michael Irvin was a better than medium wide receiver. He made some terrific catches.

Our conversation turned to crack. Mary said, "You don't look like you smoke crack." I said, "I know. You neither. Can you get us some, from my car?" She said, "They are selling some dynamite stuff in the projects." I said, "I'm not going in there, nothing personal." She said, "I don't blame you, and, you don't have to." And she stared at me. I said, "Listen Mary, you are probably a trustworthy person. But, when it comes to crack, no one can trust no one." She reached into one of her pockets and pulled out her house keys. She handed them to me and said, "You can trust me. I will be back."

Now, she could have stolen those keys from someone else. Those are things that crack addicts think of. There was an initial on her key ring, an M. But, that didn't mean anything. She would have seen that when she stole the keys, hence telling me her name was Mary. But you know what? She wasn't lying to me. Those were her house keys. She was going to come back ... so I thought. And she would have, except for one thing. Something bad Happened to Mary.

I gave her forty bucks and held her house keys. She said, "See you in five minutes." Ten minutes went by. I was nervous. I was beginning to think that I had been ripped off. Then I heard it. An ambulance siren off in the distance. It was getting closer and closer. It was right on top of me. The ambulance turned into the projects, right into the emergency vehicle access path that Mary had walked through. I knew that it was for Mary. Someone had hurt her for her money. Maybe killed her. There was nothing that I could do. I waited another ten minutes. I left before the ambulance drove out. Hopefully, Mary wasn't killed or hurt too bad. Maybe the paramedics were able to work on her right there, and she refused to go to the hospital. Maybe ...

I must have held onto Mary's house keys for months before I threw them away. I had put them in the glove compartment of my car. I think I drove by the Orchard Park Housing projects at least a half a dozen times looking for Mary, before I finally threw her house keys away. I know that there were other things that I could have done to try to get her keys to her. But I didn't do them. I could have called up Detective _____ from that Area police station and told him what had happened. He would have known about the incident. He could have told me Mary's full name, if she was in the hospital and what hospital she was in. I probably could have brought Mary's keys to him and I'm sure that he would have seen to it that she got them. If she were alive. Detective _____ would have told me that, too.

I don't think that she was killed because there was nothing on the 6 or 11 o'clock news the next day about anyone being killed in Boston. I hope that she just gave up the money and wasn't hurt too bad, if she was robbed and attacked.

I know that for me, when I was actively drinking and using drugs, there were a lot of things that I should have done, that I didn't do. It goes with the drinking alcoholically and drugging (I haven't met any social crack or heroin users) territory. It's just the way it is. Am I blaming myself for what probably happened to

Mary? It's partly my fault, it's partly Mary's fault and it's mostly the fault of the person or persons who robbed and possibly hurt Mary, if that's what happened. I'm sorry for what may have happened to Mary and I'm sorry that I did not try harder to get her house keys back to her.

Speaking of robberies. Today is Tuesday, the 27th of December, 2005. Yesterday, the 26th of December, a former professional baseball player walked into a jewelry store and robbed it.

Jeff Reardon, a four-time all-star, who played for the New York Mets, Montreal Expos, Boston Red Sox, Atlanta Braves, Cincinnati Reds and the New York Yankees walked into Hamilton Jewelers at the Gardens Mall in Palm Beach Gardens, Florida, and handed an employee a note saying that he had a gun and that the store was being robbed. He fled Hamilton Jewelers with an undisclosed amount of cash. He was found at a nearby restaurant by the police who recovered the stolen money and charged him with armed robbery. Lt. David O'Neill said that Reardon didn't have a gun and that he didn't resist when he was being handcuffed. O'Neill also said, "He said it was the medication that made him do it, and that he was sorry."

Reardon's twenty year old son died of a drug overdose in February, 2004. I can't imagine what he went through when that happened, and what he is still going through and what he will continue to go through for the rest of his life because of his son's death. I feel bad for him. We all do. But, to say that he robbed a jewelry store because of his depression medication? I wonder if there is more to it than that.

The Associated Press stated that Reardon "… was one of the top relief pitchers in the history of the game." "… one of the top relief pitchers in the history of the game." Here we go again. He wasn't better than average or a good pitcher. He was "… one of the top relief pitchers in the history of the game." Hmmm …

His career record was 73-77. He lost more games than he won. But, according to the associated press, he was one of the top relief pitchers in the history of the game. I don't understand, do you? His career ERA was 3.16. Not bad, better than average, but he was one of the top relief pitchers in the history of the game. He had 367 career saves which is the sixth best in baseball history. That is a way better than decent statistic. That is a pretty darn good statistic. But, he lost more games than he won? In the 1992 World Series, the Atlanta Braves played against the Toronto Blue Jays. Reardon pitched for the Braves. He gave up a two-run homer to Toronto's Ed Sprague in the ninth inning allowing the Blue Jays to tie Atlanta, one game apiece. Toronto eventually won the World Series in six games.

But, Reardon was one of the top relief pitchers in the history of the game. Why not just say that he was a good relief pitcher?

According to baseballreference.com, Reardon made more than 11.5 million during his career. Reardon's attorney, Mitchell Beers, said that Reardon was not having financial problems. He also said that the incident involving his son's drug overdose has been "very difficult for him and his family". Mitchell added that Reardon is married and has two other children. He said he underwent a heart angioplasty last week and has been taking medication for that condition. Beers also said, "He asked me to apologize to his fans and friends" and "this bizarre incident is completely uncharacteristic of Jeff Reardon".

I take medication for depression. I know others who also take medication for depression. My depression medication has never made me want to rob a jewelry store, any other kind of store or person. No one else who I know who is taking medication for their depression has ever told me that their depression medication made them want to rob anything or anyone. I wonder if Jeff Reardon was telling the truth. Are we going to hear about him entering a rehab in the future? And then again … I never lost a child. That I know of.

I can tell you what did make me want to rob anything or anyone. Running out of crack. There are no words to describe that feeling. You coconuts know what I'm talking about. Why I never robbed anything or anybody; there is probably more than one reason. I was afraid of being caught, and I would like to think that I hadn't lost all my morals, values, feelings for others. I would like to think that.

Some of my crack associates can't say the same. I received a Christmas card last week from Mark G. The card came from the Worcester County House of Correction in West Boylston, Massachusetts. Mark is doing eighteen months for something that he should not have done due to smoking crack. He has been bouncing in and out of recovery for way too many years. I'm glad that he isn't giving up on himself. I hope he gets straight while he is still alive.

When he is in recovery, I like the guy. We have worked out at the YMCA together. At one point, when I was clean and sober for seventeen months which would have been about thirty-three months ago, I worked out for sixty-five consecutive weeks. I did not miss too many scheduled work outs. Four a week, three full work outs and a half a work out on Saturday. I missed under five scheduled work outs during those sixty-five weeks. I get dedicated to something when I want to. If I'm not drinking and drugging. Mark was in and out of the gym like a boomerang. I would see him there for three weeks in a row, going all out. And, then, I wouldn't see him for three weeks.

Many times, it's a blessing when an addict ends up in jail. As long as that addict didn't hurt anyone to get there. I have done overnights and entire weekends in jail. Never, an extended period of time or "sentence" or "bid" as they call it, yet. If I stay in recovery, one day at a time, but for the grace of God, and my hard work, I probably will never have to worry about doing a "bid".

Today is Wednesday, December 28th, 2005. In eleven days I will have fifty months of recovery under my belt. I hope everyone had a nice Christmas, Kwanza and Hanukkah. I turned down the invitations that I received from my family members and friends to spend some time with them. My parents live in South Dennis, Massachusetts. That is about a two hour drive from Worcester, Massachusetts. They are always willing to come and get me. I won't allow them to do that. Same with my brother Gene and his wife Joan who also live on Cape Cod. They recently sold their house in Dennisport and purchased a house in West Yarmouth that is a little bit bigger than the house that they had in Dennisport. My brother Billy, his wife Linda and their kids, Anne Marie and Danny have also offered at times to come and pick me up. It is a wonderful feeling for me to know that they are willing to do that. A very nice, warm feeling.

My AA sponsor, Kevin O., who has been my sponsor since the first week that I arrived in Worcester, which was on August 25, 1999, has invited me to his place a few times. Kev is an AA long timer. He is younger than me by about five years. He has twenty-two years of recovery under his belt. There is no one better in AA or NA to have as a sponsor than Kevin, as far as I am concerned. I will get to Kev's place one of these days. For one thing, he has a bird named Marshmallow who talks. I love birds, especially talking birds. I have a few things that I want to tell Marshmallow about Kevin.

There is one advantage to being poor. I have less stress and do way less running around in my life now than ever before. I know, I know. Many of you are shaking your heads in the negative right now. But it's true. You might be saying to yourselves, ya, Dave, you do less running around and you have eliminated some stress in your life. But, that's because you still don't have a life.

You might be right. All I know is that I like the less stress part and I love the less running around part. This is a hectic world that we're living in. One person climbing over the back of another person to try and get ahead. Hmmm ... I wonder if that has anything to do with why there is so much drinking and drugging in our country?

... I remember as I was pulling the gun out of my coat pocket, everything seemed surreal (having the intense irrational reality of a dream). But, everything was real. I was sitting in the drivers seat of my car, he had just gotten into the passengers seat of my car. The gun that I was pointing at him was a Raven Arms, .25 caliber, semi-automatic, which means that you have to pull the barrel back and then let it slide forward the first time for the first shot and the next six out of the seven shot magazine discharge by pulling the trigger only. Was I really pointing a loaded handgun at another man? Wasn't I in a seminary one time …

I stated a short while ago in this book that I had never robbed anyone. I was wrong, or, at least partly wrong. I failed in trying to rob a guy one time. To the best of my recollection, it was the only time that I ever tried to rob someone.

I was driving a tractor-trailer for an outfit called MIT (Mystic Island Transport) out of Avon, Massachusetts. They were over-the-road haulers (long distance) for Marshall's clothes, as well as other companies. Marshall's clothes had a huge warehouse located in Woburn, Massachusetts. Our tractors, all Kenworth's (K-Whoppers) were parked at our barn in Avon. We would get our paper work from the dispatcher in Avon, fuel up, load up our tractor with our gear and usually bobtail (no trailer) to Woburn (I think that Marshall's had another warehouse in Chelmsford) to pick up a trailer load of Marshall's clothes.

Once in a while the trailer would be in Avon, ready for us. Our first stop was always Bridgewater, Virginia. It was a twelve hour run. There was another huge Marshall's warehouse in Bridgewater, Virginia, where we would drop our trailer. Sometimes, we would have orders to hook up to another trailer right away and sometimes not. If not, we would bobtail to a nearby truck stop for a shower, a great meal, video game machines, phone calls (no cell phones back then that I can remember; around 1988), and wait and wait and wait. When dispatch finally gave us our orders, we could be heading anywhere. California, Georgia, Illinois, Ohio or New Jersey were common runs for us. I never made a California run. The one time that we received orders to head for California with a load, we couldn't go because my partner had some kind of a conflict. I forget exactly what it was. I think that he had to be back in Massachusetts on a certain date for some kind of a commitment.

One time, when we left Bridgewater, Virginia, we headed for Georgia. We stopped at a town outside of Atlanta, I forget the name of the town. MIT had a maintenance contract with a tractor-trailer garage in that town, or near that town. We drove our whole rig into the garage so that the guys could do their maintenance on our tractor and trailer. This garage could have fit about ten rigs in it. It was a good size building.

As my partner and I were walking around the garage, my partner pointed to one of the mechanics and said, "That's Red. He sells handguns if you're interested." I don't want to say anything negative about the speed of these mechanics in Georgia, so let me put it this way. I walked up to Red and said, "Red." He said, "Did my hair give me away?", in his southern accent. I laughed and said, "My partner told me to see you about a handgun." He said, "I am the one to see about that. If you'll just give me one minute to finish up this here little chore that I'm working on ..." Two hours later, Red came and got me. I was sitting in the coffee room drinking my third or fourth cup of coffee. I'm pretty sure that they had spiked the coffee.

Red brought me to his tool chest. He opened the bottom drawer. There in the bottom drawer were brand new hand guns. Colts, Smith & Wesson's, and others. I had never owned a handgun before and couldn't tell one manufacturer's handgun from another. Red was giving me a play by play as he was pointing to the different guns. I was nodding in agreement until he started giving me prices. Then I nodded in disagreement. I thanked him for his time and was going to walk away but he said, "Something a little less expensive, my good Yankee friend?" I said, "I hate the Yankees, but ya, you got anything cheaper?"

He was trying to figure out what I meant by what I had said. I don't think that he was a sports fan. He opened the second to last drawer of his tool chest exposing a number of smaller handguns and said, "Everything in this here drawer is fifty or under." I said, "Do you have any mechanics tools in your tool chest?" He laughed and lifted up a nice little hand gun, brand new. It was in its box, the top underneath the bottom exposing the gun. He held the box out to me. I took the hand gun out of the box and asked Red if it was loaded. He said, "No, you're on your own for ammunition." I liked it. A Raven Arms chrome plated, pearl handle .25 caliber pistol. He started to reach for another gun to show me when I said, "I'll take this one." He said "That'll be forty-five bucks and no permit to carry required."

I had that gun for a couple of years before I bought ammunition for it. I'm not sure why I waited so long to buy ammo. Probably, because I didn't belong to a rod and gun club. And, I didn't have a permit to carry a handgun. I had a Firearms Identification card issued by the Braintree Police Department that was signed by Detective Frank Novio. I had to get that when I purchased my shotgun. Whether or not that ID would allow me to purchase ammunition for a handgun, I'm still not sure to this day.

When I was working for the Boston Gas Company, I had mentioned to my partner, Tom W., that I had purchased a handgun a couple of years back, illegally, but I never bought ammo for it. I told him that I had a firearms ID, but I didn't know if I could use it to buy ammo for a handgun.

He said, "There's one way to find out." We drove to a gun and ammo store in Dorchester. The instructions for disassembly and cleaning that came with my gun said to only use full metal jacketed ammo, whatever that meant. My partner came into the gun store with me. I had my firearms ID in my hand. The clerk was a young guy, maybe around twenty-five years old. I showed him my ID and said, "Can I buy ammo for my handgun with this?" He looked at it for longer than he should have before saying, "What kind of ammo do you want?" That's why I'm not sure if the clerk just wanted to make a sale or if my ID was legitimate for purchasing handgun ammunition. It was the one and only time that I bought ammo for my gun.

I had been smoking crack this one particular night with Jim P. and Paul A. They were the first two guys I met from Braintree who smoked crack. They both lived in the rooming house that was next to the rooming house where Beaker (Richie Vernon) lived. Beaker's rooming house was fifteen or nineteen Holbrook Ave. in South Braintree. His room number was either fifteen or nineteen. I have mixed those two numbers up in the past, and I'm not sure about what they were right now. More than once Beaker told me that I mixed up his street and room numbers on the Christmas cards that I had sent him throughout the years. I think that his building number was fifteen and his room number was nineteen.

Beak had lived in that rooming house for about fourteen years. He moved in after he and his wife, Holly, separated. He was drinking a lot at the time. I don't think Holly ever visited Beak at his rooming house or had much to do with him after they separated and eventually got divorced. But, his two beautiful daughters, Jody and Cherrie did. They both had a strong resemblance to Beak. They were good looking young ladies with golden blonde hair, just like their father had when he was younger. Beak's golden blonde hair had darkened somewhat over the years. His brother John's blonde hair has stayed blonde over the years and maybe even got more blonde. Maybe he colors it?

Besides drinking a lot, Beaker had developed some mental health problems. He had to be looked in on a medium amount of the time. He was suppose to get a shot from his doctor once a month to help him to cope. Sometimes, he wouldn't get his shot.

His best buddy, his life long buddy, Pat McKenney, would take Beak out every Friday night after Pat got out of work. They would go to a restaurant or grinder or pizza shop. Sometimes, Pat would pick up Chinese take out food and bring it to Beaker's place. Beaker's older brother, John, would show up whenever he could. Between Jody, Cherrie, Pat and John, the Beak was being looked in on.

He had two other brothers, James, who lived in Maine, and Paul (I forget where Paul lived). They would visit Beak whenever they could.

He had three sisters, Joan, who was married and lived in New York. Anne (I don't know where she lived), and Carrol, who was a police officer in one of the Bridgewaters, either Bridgewater, East Bridgewater or West Bridgewater. I'm sure that Beak's sisters helped him whenever they could.

His father had passed away a few years back. His mother sold the house they grew up in Braintree. I forget where Mrs. Vernon moved to. I would visit Beak on an irregular basis. It was a pleasure for all of us any time that we had a chance to be with the Beak. The only other guy I knew who was as fast, clever and witty as the Beak, was Tyracks (Tom Rowan).

I can remember one time, Beak saying something pretty clever and funny to me that required my response. After he said it, he stood up and headed for the door. I said, "Where are you going?" He said, "To the bathroom. By the time I get back, you will have thought of your come back line."

The first time that I visited Beak wearing my Boston Gas uniform, was on a Thursday, payday. He was happy for me. He knew that Kennard (Rick Kennedy) had gotten me the job. You just don't get into the gas company without having a connection. He said, "You owe Rick big time, don't you?" I tossed him a beer out of the twelve pack I brought with me and said, "What makes you think that I didn't get the job on my own?" He said, "I'm going to say it one more time, Dave. You owe Rick big time, don't you?" I said, "Ya, ya, ya; shut the freak up and drink your beer."

One of the guys who lived in the rooming house next to Beak's rooming house, Paul A., stopped in to visit Beak one time when I was there. Beak introduced us. We had some beers together, shared some laughs and then I told Beak that it was time for me to head to Brockton. Paul said, "What's up in Brockton?" Beak said, "That's where Dave goes sometimes to pick up his medicine." Paul said, "What kind of medication are you on?" I said, "Crack." Paul's face lit up. He looked like a little kid who just woke up on Christmas morning. He said, "You don't look like you smoke crack." I said, "I know, but I do. What about you?" He said, "I've been smoking it for about a year now." Beak said to Paul, "I didn't know you smoked crack." Beaker only drank and smoked weed. Paul said, "Jimmy does too." Jim lived in Paul's rooming house. Paul added, "Jimmy is smoking crack right now."

It still wasn't that popular a way to get high in 1990, but, it was getting there. Paul was the first guy I knew who wasn't from Brockton, Roxbury, Mattapan or Dorchester who smoked crack. I said, "Where does Jimmy live?" Paul said,

"Down the hall from me." I said, "How come you're not smoking with him now?" He said, "I don't have any money. Jimmy gave me one hit and then he told me to screw. That's when I came over here."

Over the next two years I must have given Paul over two thousand dollars worth of crack. I didn't like to smoke alone. And, I wasn't always with a lady when I smoked it. Sometimes, I just liked getting high with the guys.

Paul was a good guy. He was a big, dumb sometimes, Italian. I liked him. He was poor. He was receiving the minimum amount paid by social security. Paul wasn't the only guy who I gave crack to. If I were to draw up a list of all the guys I smoked crack with, on me, cheeesch.... way too much money. But, there is no question that Paul headed up that list. I liked the guy, I enjoyed his company, I felt bad for his financial situation. I spent tons and tons of money on crack for ladies. But that was different. I had a motive, even though most of the time that motive didn't work out for me. I can't speak for anyone else, but, I can tell you as far as I go, after three or four hits of crack, turn out the lights, the party is over, as Dandy Don would say. And I don't mean that I would fall asleep. I would continue smoking crack with my lady friend, but that's all we would do, most of the time. Not all of the time. A lot to be said for female companionship.

I said to Paul, "How much does Jim have?" Paul said, "I'm not sure. There was only a little bit on the plate (we always put the crack on a plate instead of right on the table in case we have to move it in a hurry) when I was there. But, who knows how much more he had hidden." I said, "Why don't you go back to Jim's place and tell him that Beaker's buddy, Dave, wants to talk to him. Make sure you tell him that I have money."

Paul started to say something and I interrupted him and said, "Yes Paul, I'll take care of you." It's funny sometimes how fast a big guy can move when he wants to.

I asked the Beak about Jim. Beaker said that he didn't know him all that well. He said that he seemed like an all right guy, from what little he knew about him. He said that Paul was a decent guy, but always broke, a big time mooch.

Paul introduced me to Jim, who I ended up smoking crack with several times over the next couple of years. And, Paul too, even though he was usually broke. After thinking about when that time period was, I now remember that I first met those guys in the spring of 1991. I started working for the Boston Gas Company after Memorial Day weekend in 1990. I remember that for the first six months that I was with the gas company, I did a pretty decent job with them. I was watching my P's and Q's. I still smoked crack once in awhile, but way less than I normally would have been considering the amount of the pay check that I was getting. And, I had kept my crack habit to myself.

No one I worked with knew about it, for about six months (I think). It must have been in the spring of 1991 when I met Paul and Jim. That's when I went from the second shift to the first shift. As a helper, I would be put on different shifts whenever they wanted to put me on a different shift. The Class A, B and C service people would work on whatever shift they wanted to, if that shift was available, according to their seniority. Our work day started at 8:00 am and ended at 4:30 PM. It was around that time period when I started to visit Beak every Thursday, payday, after work. After meeting Jim and Paul, I visited them every Thursday after work, as well. Paul and Jim were always waiting for me.

Jim's family was originally from Dorchester. He had several brothers and one sister. His mother bought a condominium in Braintree, I'm not sure when. I went there several times. I was usually a character, but so was Jim's mother. In fact, she was a double character. I hit it off pretty good with her. Jim had his own room in his mother's condominium. But, if he was being bad, if he was on the crack, he couldn't stay there. He had an extremely attractive sister, I forget her name, who kicked the crack habit a couple of years back. She had started her road to recovery in Worcester, Massachusetts, at Adcare Hospital. She ended up getting married to an attorney. Before she did, I thought that I had a shot at winning her heart. When I mentioned that to Jim, he said three words. "Not gonna happen." So I said, "Well, do you think that she would be up for a roll in the hay?"

Through Jim and Paul, I met another guy from Braintree who smoked crack. JB, who lived in Beaker's building. JB was originally from South Boston. He was a pretty decent guy. Pleasant personality, a fun, nice guy to be around. He was a painter, and had made some decent money at times when he was painting on a union job. He drank a lot and was thrown out of his house in South Boston by his wife. He too, had not been smoking crack for that long. Now that I'm thinking about it … I believe that when Paul, Jim and I went to JB's room to smoke crack, even though JB had said that he smoked, I'm pretty sure that we had to show him what to do.

Yup, I remember that I took a nip of vodka out of my pocket. That was one of our crack pipes. Paul and Jim did the same. They drank their nip of vodka first before rinsing out their bottles and turning them into crack pipes. I can't stand liquor, never could. I said to JB, "Do you drink Vodka?" He said, "Sure do." He drank the nip of vodka and threw the nip bottle into the waste basket. I said, "JB, what did you do that for?" He said, "What did I do what for?" I said, "Throw away the nip bottle?" He said, "Why, do you collect them?" I said, "That's our crack pipe." He said, "Oh, it is." He retrieved it and took it to the community bathroom to rinse it out.

The four of us spent many nights in JB's room smoking crack. Beak would come down once in awhile to have a few beers, but he would never stay long. It was one of those nights when we had been smoking crack in JB's room that, after we ran out of crack, and money, I did not want to stop. It is a mental obsession, not physical. I just did not want to stop.

I said to JB, Paul and Jim, "I own a handgun. I'm going home to get it. Anyone want to take a ride to Dorchester with me. I'm going to rob a crack dealer." Jim said, "Don't do it, Dave. You'll end up getting yourself killed." Paul said, "I don't want to stop either, but I don't want to have anything to do with that." JB said, "Me either, but if you succeed, I'll be up for awhile."

I drove home and got my gun. I checked the chamber to make sure that it was empty. I inserted the magazine, fully loaded, seven rounds in it. I left the safety on. I did not cock it. I did not want a round in the chamber. I think Jim was right. If this didn't go the way I wanted it to go, the other guy would probably shoot me first. I don't think that I could shoot someone after I had been the aggressor. My plan was to make the other guy think that my gun was cocked and ready to fire. Things didn't go exactly the way that I had planned them.

I'm not sure what time of the evening it was, 9, 10, 11? I don't remember. I was driving down Talbot Avenue in Dorchester when I saw my victim. He was standing on the corner of Talbot Avenue and a street that runs off of Talbot Avenue. He was a black man, probably a few years older than me. He was wearing a baseball cap and he had a three or four day old beard in the works. I slowed down, he nodded, I pulled over. He came up to my passengers side window. I rolled it down. He said, "What do you need?" I said, "Can you sell me six twenty's for a hundred (six twenty dollar pieces of crack for one hundred bucks)?" He said, "Go around, I'll be back here in five."

I drove to the end of Talbot Avenue where it intersects with a main street, I can't remember the name of it. I've been on it over a hundred times when I worked for the gas company. Where the Franklin Field Housing projects are. Blue Hill Avenue? I turned around and headed back at a slower than normal speed. I wasn't sure of what the hell I was about to do. All I knew was that I wanted more crack.

He was standing there on the sidewalk. I made a u-turn and drove up to him. He came up to my passenger's side window. I opened the passenger's door and said, "Get in." He was extra nervous, which was not a good sign. Most of the time when I've been ripped off trying to buy crack from someone that I didn't know, that person was extra nervous or giving off bad vibes. I knew that something was wrong.

I said, "Let me look at it first before I give you any money." He said, "I couldn't get crack, I got powder." That didn't matter that much because Jim had taught us how to cook (turn powder into rock). It meant extra time cooking it up, but if it was real coke, that's all that mattered to me. He had four in the palm of one his hands and one in his other hand that he was getting ready to hand to me to check out. That turned out to be the real coke. The other four were fake.

As he started to hand me the real bag, I pulled my gun out from my jacket pocket and said, "I'm undercover, hand them all over." He immediately dropped the four he had in one of his hands onto the floor of my car and almost simultaneously ripped open the real bag of coke and threw it out the window. I knew that the four bags on my car floor were fake. I knew the twenty that he ripped open and threw out the window had been real. He said, "What are you going to arrest me for. There's no coke in your car." I said "Get the _____ out of here, you caught a break tonight."

He got out, but I kept my eye and my gun on him. I know that he wasn't sure if I really was a cop or if I just tried to rip him off. He left my passenger's door open and he backed away from my car, keeping his eyes on my gun the whole time. I was worried that if he had had a gun and had decided that I wasn't a cop, he would start shooting at me as soon as he had an opportunity. I think that's why he left my passenger's door open. I was no longer concerned about smoking crack. I was concerned about getting shot. When he backed away from my car by about five feet, I threw my car into drive and took off making a u-turn because I was going to head back in the direction of Braintree. My passenger's door was still open and I never took my eyes off of him and I kept my gun pointed at him.

I never looked to my left. I was making a u-turn cutting across a lane of traffic that would have been heading right at me. Had another vehicle been coming when I banged my u-turn, it would have broad sided me on my drivers side and I probably would have been killed. I never looked …

My original plans were to write about all thirteen years of my freebasing cocaine. But, you know what, I don't think I'm going to do that. There are a couple of reasons. I think that I've told enough war stories to get my points across. Freebasing cocaine will eventually lead you to death, jail, or a mental institution. And, if I am fortunate enough to get this book published, I think it's best to keep the number of pages down to a minimum. I remember that the times that I was in rehab, I would not even begin to read a book if it had too many pages. I would not be capable of finishing it. I didn't want to start reading a book that I knew I wasn't going to be able to finish.

I think that it's time to wrap up chapter seven and begin writing chapter eight, the final chapter.

Recovery

I'm not sure why I went to the Alcoholics Anonymous meeting at the Faxon House, in Quincy, Massachusetts. When Larry L. had made that suggestion to me the night before while we were sitting in my cab, to go to an AA meeting with him, I thought he was nuts. Yet, at the same time, I also thought that he had given me a good suggestion. What did I have to lose? An hour or maybe an hour and-a-half out of my day for the meeting plus travel time. It wasn't going to kill me to go there. Drinking and driving might kill me, or worse. I could kill someone else when I was drinking and driving.

It was in 1981. The Faxon House, at that time was an old, maybe four or five story high brick building that was a part of the Quincy City Hospital. It was a detoxification facility/combination Alcoholics Anonymous meeting place. That building is no longer there and there has been a whole bunch of construction work done at the Quincy City Hospital. The hospital was sold. I don't know if the name was changed or not.

The Faxon House had its own parking lot, separate from the hospital parking lot. I parked there and I saw Larry standing around with a few other people near the front door entrance. I walked over to them and said hi to Larry. He introduced me to the others. If I'm not mistaken, I think it was a one hour meeting that started at 2 PM, five days a week. The coffee was free and they sold raffle tickets for AA books. The tickets were twenty-five cents per ticket, three for fifty cents and seven for a dollar. That's the same price as they are at an AA or NA meeting today, twenty-five years later. I wish everything else cost the same today as they did twenty-five years ago.

It was a discussion meeting. One person would lead the meeting or facilitate it. She or he would pick people to share their thoughts on a topic, or talk about whatever they wanted to talk about that was related to alcohol. The facilitator usually picked from those who raised their hands. It didn't always work out that way. As I became more familiar with meetings I began to realize why it didn't always work out that way. I found out why I and others could be sitting at a discussion meeting, listening attentively, more or less minding our own business, not raising our hands and yet still be called on by the facilitator to share with the group.

There are folks who go to meetings who raise their hands every single time they are at a discussion meeting, sometimes multiple times at the same meeting. They like to tell you that they have to open their mouths to save their butts. BULLSHIT. There are always one or two of them at every single discussion meeting, who have to open their big mouths to hear themselves talk.

God forbid, should they just sit attentively at a meeting and listen. Maybe even give others a chance to share. The more meetings someone goes to, the more he/she realizes that there are always going to be a couple of loud mouths there. You can't avoid them. I get so sick and tired of listening to their same bullshit all the time that I couldn't wait for the meeting to end so that I could go out and have a drink.

A good facilitator is aware of who the big mouths are and will call on someone who doesn't have her/his hand up to share in order to save us all from having to listen to a big mouth … again. Part of sharing is sharing time.

I think it might be best for me to share my feelings on the "fellowship" of Alcoholics Anonymous before I write any more about recovery. I have already shared with you a little bit about my feelings on Narcotics Anonymous.

AA is a good outfit. It is, however, not the eighth wonder of the world. No one or no thing is perfect. Not even Mother Theresa. There are people and outfits who think that they are perfect. We all know someone or something like that. Everyone, every outfit makes mistakes. That's the way it is. One mistake that I believe AA makes is to remain anonymous on the level of press, radio and films. The eleventh tradition of Alcoholics Anonymous states, "Our public relations policy is based on attraction rather than promotion; we need always maintain personal anonymity at the level of press, radio and films."

Whenever I hear something like that, my first thoughts are, WHY? Does AA have something to hide. I have talked to people in AA who have said, I don't care if anyone knows my last name. I have talked to people in AA who have said, I would rather have my family and friends see me at an AA meeting than sitting on a bar stool getting drunk. I have talked to people in AA who have told me that one of the the first things that they do when they get home from an AA meeting is tell their family or call their friends and tell them details about the meeting. That's just the way it is.

I think, at least I hope that the eleventh tradition of Alcoholics Anonymous does not carry as much weight these days as it may have in the past. Times are changing. AA is a good outfit. It is not the eighth wonder of the world.

I wonder if I am even suppose to be saying what I just said about AA in a book? The fourth tradition of Alcoholics Anonymous states, "With respect to its own affairs, each AA group should be responsible to no other authority than its own conscience. But when its plans concern the welfare of neighboring groups also, those groups ought to be consulted. And no groups, regional committee, or individual should ever take any action that might greatly affect AA as a whole without conferring with the trustees of the General Service Board." Who are you shitting? Who the freak wrote this crap. I'm suppose to ask the TRUSTEES of the general service board if I can write about AA in my book. That's funny. Sue me.

By the way, you TRUSTEES who are sitting on the General Service Board. Are you recovering addicts? Are your TRUSTEES positions full or part time? Do you get paid for being TRUSTEES? I'm not sure if I trust you.

AA is a good outfit. In 1951, AA was given the Lasker Award. Part of that citation reads, "The American Public Health Association presents a Lasker Group Award for 1951 to Alcoholics Anonymous in recognition of its unique and highly successful approach to that age-old public health and social problem, alcoholism … In emphasizing alcoholism as an illness, the social stigma associated with this condition is being blotted out … Historians may one day recognize Alcoholics Anonymous to have been a great venture in social pioneering which forged a new instrument for social action; a new therapy based on the kinship of common suffering; one having a vast potential for the myriad other ills of mankind."

Well, I guess, here we go again. "… a great venture …", not a good venture, but, "… a great venture …" Hmmm "… vast potential …" Not good potential, but, "… vast potential …" Hmmm Well, there are a lot of 12-Step programs around, aren't there?

AA is a good outfit. It is not the eighth wonder of the world. I wonder if there are many folks from the Lasker outfit who go to AA meetings?

I've been away from my writing for a few days. Today is January 8th, 2006. I have fifty months of recovery under my belt. I feel good. The New England Patriots won their playoff game against the Jacksonville Jaguars last evening. I have food and Coca-Cola in my refrigerator. Snacks in my cabinet, clean clothes on my body. My bills are paid up to date. My parakeets are singing. I feel a hell of a lot better than I did fifty months ago, November 8th, 2001.

I was living in a subsidized apartment, through the Worcester Housing Authority. My address was 275 Pleasant Street, Worcester, Massachusetts. There were a lot of elderly folks living in that nine story tall building. There were other folks who weren't senior senior citizens like myself, who also lived there. I received my subsidy because of my disability, as did the others who were under sixty-five. I moved into that building after graduating from the Aurora Project for my first time. I came to the Aurora Project from the Leominster Detox in Leominster, Massachusetts. I was at that detox for fourteen days from August 12th (my daughter's birthday), 1999 till August 25, 1999 (inclusive). On August 25, 1999, I came to the Aurora Project for my first time. I stayed there for roughly sixteen months. I remember moving out of the Aurora Project a few days before the new year; 2001. I think it was December 28, 2000, when I moved to 275 Pleasant Street.

I stayed clean and sober for about a month and-a-half at 275 Pleasant Street before relapsing on February 10, 2001. It was two days before I would have had eighteen months of recovery under my belt. From February 10, 2001, until November 8, 2001, were the worst nine months of my life. 'They' say that every time that you relapse, it gets worse. 'They' aren't kidding. Boy, does it ever get worse ...

My friend, Mary Beth, was living with me. She was my drinking and drugging buddy. I'm pretty sure that she moved in on February 11, 2001, the day after I relapsed. MB was a prostitute, capable of making some decent money. She was tall for a lady, about 5 ft, 8 inches, probably 140 lbs, nice figure, medium length brown, curly hair, attractive eyes, better than medium looking face. I think she was about forty years old. We made love, or had sex the first day she moved in and never again. Sex was low on my list of priorities at that stage of my drinking and was always low on my list of priorities when I was drugging. I enjoyed female companionship, not necessarily sex, but rather, someone to be with. Most of the time I wasn't capable of having sex after my third hit from the crack pipe. I wanted company, someone to talk to, someone to tell me that I was OK, that I was a good guy.

Mary Beth was a good girl who was an addict. She was not a bad person. She had a disease. She preferred heroin to crack and she drank vodka. She is the only active addict that I have ever met in my life who could read an entire medium length book in one day. I had never in my life seen an addict finish doing his/her drugs and then pick up a book, until I met MB. She was also a clean person. A lot of active addicts are not.

Personal hygiene is not important when we are active. In our nine months living together at Pleasant Street, I hardly ever cleaned my apartment. She did. I did a medium job keeping it clean for the first month in a half that I was there by myself, when I was clean and sober.

I almost never did any laundry my last nine months that I was there. MB did it. I rarely cooked and I hated taking showers. I didn't have the energy to take showers. She cooked and she made me take showers, sometimes. She could make money seven days a week. She didn't have to walk the sidewalks all the time. There were guys who would call for her on my phone, maybe three or four times a week to get together with her.

There had been times in the past when a lady would treat me to crack. It didn't happen too often, but it had happened. With MB, it was a whole different ball game. Now, I didn't have to worry after we had spent my whole disability check in two days, three days tops. I'm not saying that we were doing drugs every day, we weren't. I'm saying that not too many days would go by where we at least had alcohol. Vodka for her and beer for me. And she was good about making sure that we had at least one decent meal almost every day whether she cooked it or we got take out. And some snacks in the evening. And cigarettes, too. God forbid should MB ever allow us to run out of smokes.

Non-addicts probably cannot understand what I'm talking about. You addicts can.

So, I told you that those were the worst nine months of my life. And yet, from an active addicts point of view, I had it made … wrong. The progression of my alcoholism and cocaine addiction had occurred. I learned in one of my detoxes that when an addict relapses, he/she picks up their addiction right where they had left off when they went on the wagon. It does not matter how much time went by while they were in recovery. I did not believe that when the instructor in one of my detox classes stated it. I thought it was a crock of crap. I had put together eighteen months of recovery. That was the longest stretch of recovery that I had ever had in my addicted life, up until then. I was a good boy for eighteen months. I got in a decent tune up for myself. My mental and physical health were better than medium, I thought. I was ready to rock-n-roll.

I don't remember planning on relapsing. It just happened. Stuff happens, especially when you're an addict. I have stated in this book that all I wanted to do was feel good. Drinking beer made me feel good, for a little while. Smoking crack made me feel like, if there was a heaven, I was there. For a little while.

I never put much thought into what I was doing to my family and friends. In fact, I didn't think that I was hurting anybody but myself. As far as being an unproductive member of our society when I was drinking and doing other drugs; who cared. I didn't care. Let someone else do what needed to be done so that I could go to the market and buy my food. Someone will build the market. Someone will deliver all the items to the market. Someone will organize everything and stock the shelves and run the cash registers. Someone else will do it. I don't have to worry about it. I can drink and drug whenever I've got the money to do so. Someone else will do everything for me. I don't have to do anything.

You know, no one in this world can make it on their own. We all need help. We need to help each other. One of the saddest aspects of my being an active addict, I believe, was my unavailability to others. No active addict; sorry. I should rephrase that.

When I was active, I was never available to do anything for anybody, never, not once, it never happened. All I wanted to do was my next drug. My favorite drug was more. Just give me more, that's all I want. I don't want to stop, I can't stop ... give me more ...

On the evening of November 8, 2001, probably around 9 o'clock, I was standing on the heating unit next to my window in my apartment for the second time. The first time I climbed onto it, I fell off. I had drank during that day with MB, but, I wasn't drunk. She wasn't drunk either. She hardly ever got drunk. I have a bad left hip. I fell off the heating unit the first time that I climbed onto it because of my bad left hip.

When I was climbing back onto it the second time, MB said, "Try not to fall off this time. It's distracting to me while I'm reading." I said, "I'll do my best." I opened the inside window and was working on opening the storm window when MB said, "David, are you really planning on jumping out an eight story window?"

At least, that's what MB told me later. I don't remember. I don't mean that I don't remember climbing onto the heating unit a couple of times. I mean, I don't remember MB saying anything to me. What I do remember is MB tackling me from the side. She knocked me off the heating unit the second time that I climbed onto it. Decent tackle for a lady. It knocked the wind out of me. As I was lying on the floor, she yelled, "Don't move." She put the inside window down and then got on the phone and called Kevin O, my AA sponsor. Kevin told her that he was on his way over and told her to call 911. She did.

MB told me later that when she looked up from her book and saw the look that was in my eyes, she flew off the couch and tackled me. She said that she knew I had been deeply depressed, but she had never seen that look in my eyes before.

When the police and the paramedics arrived, I had no choice but to go with them to the University of Massachusetts Medical Center, Emergency Mental Health. I remember seeing Kevin there, in front of my building as they were walking me to the ambulance. He grabbed my shoulder and said, "It will be all right, Dave." I don't think that I said anything back to him. The paramedic who sat in the back of the ambulance with me was a kind man. I forget what we talked about, but I remember that he was a kind man. I have never seen him since, but, I know what he looks like. I will always remember his face. I hope I see him again sometime, under different circumstances. I want to tell him that I'm doing OK today. I want him to know. I know that he was genuinely concerned about me. I want to tell him that I wish every paramedic in the world was like him. I really do.

I remember I was sitting in an examination room, waiting. A man in a white coat came in. He was the emergency mental health psychiatrist working that evening. He asked me some questions. I answered them. He said, "I'm going to send you to Worcester State Hospital for a few days." I said, "OK." He left the room.

A little while later a nurse came into the examination room to get some more information from me. She was a nice lady. She told me that an ambulance would be taking me to the state hospital soon. She brought me into another room, a larger room where there was a table and chairs and a refrigerator and cabinets. She told me that there was juice in the fridge and snacks in the cabinets, to help myself.

I think that I had thought that I would probably be put in a straight jacket, or maybe injected with some kind of a knock out medicine. But, I was being passive and compliant. That's probably why I wasn't restrained or knocked out.

The doctor had committed me to Worcester State Hospital because he thought that I was a threat to myself. He had felt that I had made a serious attempt at committing suicide. Had MB not been there in my apartment, I might not be here today.

I had to stay at the Worcester State Hospital for three days. I could stay longer if I wanted to. It was up to me. My doctor told me that he thought if I got back into a rehab and then a long term program, and continued to take my medication, I had a good chance of being OK. OK. Not good, not bad, OK, medium. I'll settle for medium. I won't be shooting for the stars anymore. My dreams as a kid are long gone. My outlook on life as a kid is long gone. Anything that I hear on the news today will not surprise me. I am living in a tough world. Everyone is imperfect, everyone. Especially me.

Most of the time I readily admit my imperfections to most people. I have hardly ever had a problem doing that. Some people hate to do that. They hate to say that they were wrong or that they made a mistake. I think it's easier to say, my fault, I was wrong, and move on from there.

A guy told me one time that he *never* apologized to anyone for anything. I said, "You never apologized to anyone for anything?" He said, "That's right." I said, "You have never been sorry for something or made a mistake or were wrong." He said, "I didn't say that. I said I never apologized to anyone." He added, "Whenever you apologize to someone for something you are setting yourself up for a future apology." Hmmm …

I think I understood what he meant when he said that. But I'm not sure. I believe that I mentioned what Jay had said to me to a few people who all gave me different explanations for what they believed he meant. Was it John Wayne who said that apologizing is a sign of weakness (in one of his movies).

I remember one time when I was a security guard for the Gillette Company in Andover, Massachusetts. Three of us were in the security room. Ray Walker, who was another guard, Al Lawn, our second shift supervisor and me. We all got along pretty good. Ray asked me about something. It wasn't a big thing, it was a little to medium thing that I had screwed up. I gave Ray and Al about a five minute explanation on why it had happened and why it wasn't my fault. They looked at me, looked at each other and Al said to Ray, "I think it would have been a lot easier if Dave had just said that he screwed up."

I got that message. I understood that one. It sunk in and it has stayed in. I later said to Al, "Al, you made a DP the other day about admitting a screw up instead of trying to explain it away." He said, "DP?" I said, "Decent Point."

My counselor at the state hospital arranged for me to go to a rehab in Ashburnham, Massachusetts. Naukeg Hospital, a nice place. Rumor had it that Jackie Gleason was there one time. He probably paid a lot of money to go there. Medicare health benefits paid for most of my twenty-one days there. I had been on Mass Health medical benefits at one time. They would have paid for all of it. Mass Health ended up disqualifying me for their medical benefits. They said that my social security disability insurance benefit was too high.

I received a bill from Naukeg for the balance of what Medicare did not pay. It was a lot of money. It took me awhile to pay it off, a little bit at a time. Naukeg did not look like a rehab. It looked more like a bed and breakfast. It was the nicest rehab that I have ever been in.

Even though Naukeg Rehabilitation Hospital was a pleasant place to go to for rehab, it was twenty-one difficult days. Back in rehab, again. When will this vicious cycle ever end? Will it ever end? Did it almost end? Did I really try to kill myself on November 8th, 2001?

Right now, January 10th, 2006, I would like to be able to say to you that, no, I didn't really try to kill myself. I did what I did to get MB's attention. I wanted her to feel sorry for me. I was looking for sympathy. Isn't it true that the majority of people who want to kill themselves succeed in doing so? Wouldn't I have chosen a time to jump out of my window when no one else was in my apartment? Wouldn't I have chosen a different way to kill myself?

Right now, January 10th, 2006, I don't know for sure if I really was trying to kill myself. I do know that right now, I am glad that I am here. I am glad that MB was there in my apartment on November 8th. Whether or not it was a real suicide attempt, or just an extreme cry for help, I think that I would have gone out that window. Maybe on the way down I would have said, ooops ... I'm not trying to be funny. You should try thinking with my brain, or what's left of it.

While at Naukeg, I made some calls to the Aurora Project. Larry A., the Director of the project (I'm not sure why they call it a 'Project') was happy to hear my voice. He had been my director at the Aurora, but, he had also been my friend. We became friends there. He told me that he had heard the rumors about my relapsing. He said that he didn't want to believe it, but he'd been in this business long enough to know that there were an awful lot of sad stories out there. More sad stories than nice stories. Thirty-five more sad stories than nice stories.

Can I give you any facts, quote any sources regarding the statement that I just made? No, I don't know anyone who can. I can only tell you what has been told to me in many detoxes, rehabs and programs. I didn't always hear that only one out of thirty-six addicts makes it. I think one time I heard it was one out of twenty-nine. But, I did hear a few times that only one out of thirty-six addicts makes it. I don't know how anyone can come up with exact data on how many make it and how many don't. It's impossible. I never received a survey or a questionnaire from any detox, rehab, or program that I went to. Not once. Whether any of those places tried to mail me a questionnaire or survey form or not, I don't know. I was transient, like a lot of other addicts. If I got booted from the place where I was living, I didn't always go to my local post office to register my new address.

I wasn't always on social security, where I would have needed an address in order for them to send me my check. If I started to accumulate some straight time, I suppose then, I would get around to registering my new address. I can say this. I spent a total of forty-two months in the Aurora Project. I was there two times for sixteen months and twenty-six months (approximately). I'm going to guess that about 300 addicts came and left the Aurora Project during my forty-two months there. You could stay there up to five years, if you wanted. Or, at least you could when I was a client there.

The PIP Homeless Shelter operated the Aurora Project at that time. The PIP Homeless Shelter has since been bought by SMOC (South Middlesex Opportunity Council), headquartered out of Framingham, Massachusetts. I don't know what SMOC's length of stay rules are. I don't know that anyone from the PIP Homeless Shelter ever did the paperwork on all the Aurora Project residents that went there from day one (I heard that the Aurora Project opened around 1992 or 1993) to figure out an average length of stay. I would guess that the average length of stay is about eight months. Out of those approximately 300 clients, or residents, some are dead, some I don't know what happened to, some are in jail, some are bouncing in and out of detoxes and programs; not giving up on themselves. A lot of them are drinking and/or drugging. I can count about twelve of us who are straight today that I know.

AA stresses one day at a time, but they give out yearly medallions for yearly lengths of recovery, or I should say sobriety. One day at a time, but we all know that it is how many consecutive days we put together that is what will turn our lives around. One day at a time, but do that every day. Anybody can drink and drug. It takes guts not to. And, the grace of God, and your hard work. And a lot of support from a lot of people. No one makes it in this crazy world on their own, no one. We all need help.

Larry asked me when I was getting out of Naukeg. I told him on December 6th. He told me that there would be an apartment waiting for me at the Aurora Project when I left Naukeg. One of the unusual benefits of the Aurora Project is that every client/resident gets his/her own studio apartment. The apartments have a full bathroom and a kitchenette, range, oven, sink, refrigerator. The living room area is fully carpeted. They are nice studio apartments on the fifth and sixth floors of the Aurora Apartments building in Worcester, Massachusetts. The building heating system is outstanding, top notch and the heat is included in the rent.

The Aurora Apartments building is six stories high. It is located near the PIP Homeless Shelter, on South Main Street. There are approximately eighty-five studio apartments all together that were all renovated not too many years ago. They are modern, nice units that are managed and maintained by a good staff. Steve Barry, the property manager, not only does an outstanding job of managing the building, but also appropriates the spending of a lot money to keep the property up to date. The parking lot is in the rear of the building. The concrete retaining wall between the end of the parking lot and the sidewalk was showing signs of wear and tear and maybe even leaning slightly. That would be an expensive project that could have been put off for a few more years.

Steve hired a masonry outfit to come in and take down the concrete wall and the wrought iron fence on top of the wall. They built a new, decorative concrete block wall with two curved corners at the end of the driveway and each layer of block is slightly back of the layer underneath it. They widened the driveway and lessened the angle on it and resurfaced it. They put a new fence on top of the wall. It's one of the nicest walls that I have ever seen. I could not even guess how much it cost. When maintenance things have to be done, Steve has them done. He doesn't hesitate. One of his maintenance men, Scott, is one of the hardest working guys that I have ever known. An awful nice man, too, who has a religious background.

My friend, Mike G., lives in Ashburnham. We were in the Aurora Project together my first time there. I called Mike a couple of times from Naukeg. He came to Naukeg to take me out for a couple of hours one time. When I told him that Larry was taking me back into the Aurora Project, Mike said, "What time should I pick you up to take you to Worcester?" I said, "You don't have to do that, Mike. Naukeg will provide transportation for me." Mike said, "They probably won't let you smoke cigarettes in their vehicle." I said, "Can you pick me up at 9:30 am?" Ashburnham to Worcester is about a forty minute drive.

We had been close friends at the Aurora Project. Mike is a good guy, a sports nut like myself who played ball when he was younger. He has a good sense of humor. Anytime that I goofed around with Mike, pulled something on him, I could always count on him getting me back. I use to love it. We had a lot of fun together. Mike also relapsed after leaving the Aurora. He came back into the Aurora Project this past July. He looks good. He has been doing great, one day at a time, for about six months worth of one day at a times.

If a person is not receiving any money from social security or Massachusetts Transitional Assistance (formerly Public Welfare), then she/he does not have to pay any rent to the Aurora Project. I was charged approximately thirty per cent of my disability check for rent. Everyone in the Aurora Project has to do community service at the PIP Homeless Shelter, whether you pay rent or not. The Aurora Project is not a half way house. It is a transitional living program, or 'project'. Most half way house programs have a maximum stay of six months. I don't know of any other programs, projects or half way houses that give their clients their own private studio apartment, and not have to pay rent for them if they don't have any income.

I have heard about other programs in Florida, California and Arizona that charge a lot of money to their clients for their private apartments. Working programs. You go to work everyday, just like most everyone else. And, you come home from work to a sober and drug free environment, with rules that you must follow. The Aurora Project is not a work program. After four months there (this was the rule when I was there, and rules tend to change all the time), a client could ask the director if he/she could get a job. It was up to the director. Most clients don't work while at the Aurora. The fact that the Aurora Project does not charge an indigent resident for his/her own studio apartment, I think, is an extraordinary thing. And the rent that the Aurora Project charged those of us who had an income was about half the market value, maybe slightly more than half. The heat was included in the rent and they paid our electric bills.

The Aurora Apartments Company rents the entire fifth and sixth floors to the Aurora Project. They are private floors for the Aurora Project clients and staff only. Those floors are off limits to the public residents of the Aurora Apartments building who live on floors one thru four. You need a special elevator key to get to the fifth and sixth floors. The Aurora Apartments building is a secured building; keyed entrance. The two stairway exit doors on either end of floors two thru six, open from the inside only, for safety and security reasons. Same thing with the front stairway exit door on the first floor, which is in the building lobby. The rear stairway exit door on the first floor opens from both sides for emergency reasons.

I don't know too much about who pays the rent for the indigent clients in the Aurora Project. Or, who pays the balance of the fair market value rent for those of us who did pay. The City of Worcester? The Commonwealth of Massachusetts? The Federal Government? The PIP Homeless Shelter? It's none of my business. But, I am curious, or I am grateful to someone, some outfit. Someone paid part of my rent for forty-two months. Someone paid my electric bills for forty-two months. I am grateful to someone else, besides the Aurora Project and the Aurora Apartments building.

Mike dropped me off at the Aurora building sometime in the late morning. I had all my belongings in one gym bag. I told the manager of my apartment building on Pleasant Street to donate my furniture, hand tools, stereo, TV, and anything else in my apartment to the Salvation Army. That's always the way it was with me. Whenever I got kicked out of a place or left a place on my own because I was going away for treatment, I would leave everything there, and not come back for it. How could I? I didn't own a vehicle. I would fill my gym bag with a few things. I was transient. I traveled light. I was use to always starting over.

I buzzed suite 507, Larry's office. He buzzed me into the building. I sat down on one of the sofas in the building lobby to wait for one of the residents to come down and get me. I love that lobby. I love that building. It felt good to be there.

Steve, the building manager, was working in his office. He looked up at me occasionally through his window. I did not make eye contact with him. I had dropped about twenty pounds since leaving the Aurora almost a year ago, maybe twenty-five pounds. I went from 165 lbs. to about 140 lbs. I left on December 28th, 2000, I believe. I'm back on December 6th, 2001, and not looking too good. Steve probably wasn't even sure if it was me.

One of the guys who I knew came down to get me. He said, "Hi" and then asked me the usual question, "Did it get any better out there?" I wasn't in any kind of a joking around mood. Otherwise, I probably would have said something like, as a matter of fact, it did. Would you be interested in looking at the photos I have from Hawaii? I just shook my head from side to side. He said, "You're in the right place."

I walked into Larry's office. Larry is a big, solid, good looking black man. He looks like he use to play middle linebacker in the NFL. He said, "Dave, you couldn't play for a pee wee football team right now." I said, "Yup" and sat down in the chair beside his desk. And I added, "But I'll tell you something Larry (I now decided to joke around because I was always in a good mood when I was with Larry), if it wasn't for guys like me who relapse all the time, you wouldn't have a job." He smiled a little bit, and then said, "Think about what you are going to do different this time." He handed me a set of keys (building key, apartment key, mailbox key and elevator key) and said, "603." I said, "If the Patriots make it to the Super Bowl, I don't care who their opponent is, I'll take the Pats and I'll give you 2 to 1 odds." He said, "Get out of here. You've got twenty minutes to make it to the noontime meeting."

The Aurora Project was a nice program but it was not an easy program. Two recovery meetings a day, seven days a week. That's a lot of freaking meetings. One good thing was that the PIP Homeless Shelter (as far as I know, it is still being called the PIP Homeless Shelter, after SMOC bought it) had a lot of recovery meetings in their fourth floor meeting hall. That's where we did the majority of our meetings. The PIP Homeless Shelter was a three minute walk from our building.

According to Alcoholics Anonymous, an AA meeting is an AA meeting no matter where it is and no matter who is there. That is idealistic. It is not true. Some things that I've heard about Pip Homeless Shelter meetings are, "The Pip Shelter meetings are the unhealthiest meetings that I have ever gone to in my life", and, "I wouldn't go to a PIP Shelter meeting if you paid me or if it was the last AA meeting in the world." Some things that I've heard from the podium at a PIP Homeless Shelter meeting are, "You know something people. A lot of folks talk about how they don't like coming to the PIP Shelter for AA meetings. Well, I love coming here for meetings. I would rather come to a PIP Shelter AA meeting than go anywhere else for an AA meeting." Another thing that I heard from the PIP Homeless Shelter podium one time was, "You people here at this PIP Shelter AA meeting are my kind of people. I would rather be here with you this morning (it was a Sunday morning AA meeting) than at any other AA meeting anywhere else, anywhere else. I love you people."

The last comment was made by a guy who came to the PIP Homeless Shelter on an AA commitment. An AA commitment is when one AA group goes to another AA group to put on the meeting. To share their experiences, strengths and hopes with those at the meeting. If an AA group is 'booked' or scheduled to put on a commitment, and for some reason they don't show up, then, the home group has a pick up meeting. Someone from the home group will chair or facilitate the meeting and usually call people from that group to speak, sometimes asking the person ahead of time if he/she would like to speak and sometimes not.

You can leave and enter the PIP Shelter's fourth floor meeting hall via an elevator or by a set of stairs leading from one of the side walls of the hall. I go to the bathroom usually a couple of times during any meeting and almost always at the end of every meeting. At the end of this meeting, I went to the bathroom. The elevator can only hold so many people at one time, I believe its capacity is suppose to be eight people. The certificate on the elevator wall gives a weight limit, but, since there is no scale outside the elevator for each of us to weigh ourselves, record the weights and add them up before we get on the elevator, we usually just go by how many of us we can jam in there at one time. Most folks will wait for the elevator. Most of the time I take the stairs. I went out the side door and on the stairs probably two floors below me, I heard a familiar voice saying that he would never come back to this dump again. It was the guy who told us from the podium that we were his kind of people.

I know that the popular thing for me to say would be that the PIP Homeless Shelter AA meetings are no different than any other AA meetings. But, that would not be true. They are different. If I had a choice of being able to go to a PIP Homeless Shelter AA meeting or an AA meeting in the town of Braintree, Massachusetts, I'd go to the AA meeting in the town of Braintree, Massachusetts, and so would most other folks, whether they would admit it or not. For those of you knucklebrains who are criticizing me right now for my opinion on PIP Homeless Shelter AA meetings, good. Not medium, but good. It gets you away from bitching about someone or something else. Your wives or husbands or kids are probably thanking me right now. And, enjoy your next meeting at the PIP Homeless Shelter.

The behavior of certain characters who show up on a regular basis at the PIP Homeless Shelter recovery meetings is not a reflection on the PIP Homeless Shelter. They rent out their meeting hall to AA and NA groups. They can't control the behavior of the folks who show up at the meetings. The PIP Homeless Shelter is an outstanding outfit. They do a world of good for the down and out, the less fortunate. There is a guy who works at the PIP Homeless Shelter named George, a recovering addict who has about twenty years of recovery under his belt. He use to live at the shelter. Now, he is in charge of Shelter Services, making sure that everyone who comes their for a meal is fed and has a place to sleep. And he does a lot of other things there, too. I can't think of too many people who I have met in my life who work as hard as George. He is always doing something. He is a way better than medium guy.

AA has an open door policy for their meetings. They do not turn anyone away from a meeting. I have seen people thrown out of meetings for acting up. It doesn't happen too often. It seems to me that some folks can get away with a lot of acting up before they get tossed from a meeting. And they know it. They are fully aware of how much they can get away with. I was walking down the sidewalk on South Main Street in Worcester one time when I ran across Robin, who asked me the usual questions. "Dave, you got a cigarette? You got a few bucks or any loose change that I can have to get a half pint of vodka?"

I gave her a cigarette and no money. Robin likes to drop in at recovery meetings to act up and draw attention to herself. When she enters the hall, she usually goes and sits down on some guys lap. She will talk to the guy as if she and him were the only two people in the hall. Sometimes, when people tell her to quiet down, she will tell them to go f___ themselves. Most of the time she ignores them and continues talking. I have found that it's almost impossible to get her off of my lap without knocking her on the floor. Out of all the meetings that Robin has disrupted, I have only seen her tossed out once.

I lit her cigarette and she said, "Are you going to the 9:30 am meeting?" I said, "Not if you're going to be there." She laughed and said, "Can you believe the shit that they let me get away with at those stupid meetings?"

No, I can't believe it. When I go to meetings I sit attentively and I listen to the speakers, most of the time. I behave myself appropriately. I do not act up. I bet if I did act up, they would waste no time in tossing me out. I believe that if all folks were tossed from meetings as soon as they started acting up, the next time those folks went to a recovery meeting they would think twice before acting up. What is it that AA says? The policy that I have experienced at meetings and their philosophy is, what if someone who is active (drinking and/or drugging) and misbehaving a little bit, and gets booted and then never returns to another recovery meeting?

Well, what if someone who is not acting up, is behaving him or herself, is sitting in a meeting where some clown is acting up? What if that person decides to never return to a recovery meeting again because of the knucklebrain who was acting up?

Maybe it's because of the particular recovery meetings that I have had to go to these past several years, that I don't care much for meetings. And maybe not. AA says that a meeting is a meeting. And AA is mostly right. Thank God that the AA meetings and the NA meetings are always there for me whenever I relapse and come crawling back to the halls, wherever they happen to be. AA is a good outfit. NA is a medium outfit.

I stayed in the Aurora Project my second time for approximately twenty-six months. I arrived on December 6th, 2001, and I left on January 27th, 2004. My first seventeen months there I did not know on a day to day basis whether I was going to stay straight or bail out and get high. It was the hardest seventeen months that I have ever experienced in recovery. It was mostly the grace of God that kept me there because I didn't have much energy to be able to work hard. I just didn't. I was like a zombie a lot of the time. I did what I was required to do by the program, not much else.

Besides doing community service at the PIP Homeless Shelter, and sweeping the South Main Street sidewalks around the Aurora building and the PIP Homeless Shelter, we also had our house chores to do. One of those house chores was vacuuming the fifth and sixth floor hallways. I can remember on my first morning there, December 7th, I heard the vacuum cleaner running out in the hallway around 7 am. I believe that if someone knocked on my door and told me that I had to come out and do the vacuuming that morning or else leave the program, I would have had to leave the program. As I was lying on my bed listening to someone vacuuming the hallway, I remember thinking about how much of a gigantic feat that was. I don't think that I would have been physically capable of doing it.

I started to gain my strength back and put on some weight. But, I was still zombie-like, and I was obsessing for a drink and a drug almost all of the time. I couldn't stop thinking about it. It was awful.

I had a decision to make. My self-esteem was about zero. My self-hatred was about 100 per cent. I could not stop obsessing for a drink and a drug.

On Monday through Friday's we had an 8:15 am meeting in the building community room on the first floor, off the lobby. We had a smaller, program community room on the sixth floor. Someone would open the meeting with a reading from the Hazeldon twenty-four hour book. Then, we would go around the room, each resident briefly sharing her/his goal and schedule for the day. The whole meeting lasted about ten minutes. I had seventeen months of recovery under my belt, but, I was ready to do something wrong ... or right ...

My schedule wasn't as busy after seventeen months as it was when I first came back to the Aurora Project. For the first four months back in the program I had to go to two meetings a day, seven days a week. After four months, I could take a weekend day off, per approval of the director. If I was doing what I was suppose to be doing. If I was attending our meetings, our three community suppers, our Saturday morning community breakfast followed by a three step meeting, the first three steps only of AA's twelve steps. I also had to do my community service and go to our 8:30 am-Monday through Friday start off the day meeting. And, our once a week house meeting or bitch session, and whatever else we were suppose to do. If I did all that, then there was no problem getting a weekend day off which cut my weekly AA and/or NA meeting total down to twelve.

After one year in the program, I could take a day off during the week as well as my weekend day off and I only had to go to an evening AA and/or NA meeting the other five days cutting my weekly AA and/or NA meeting total down to five. From fourteen AA and/or NA meetings a week down to five AA and/or NA meetings a week. Not bad. I never heard anyone complain about the decrease in AA and/or NA meetings.

Besides the things that I mentioned, there were other things that we had to do as well to stay a part of the Aurora Project. There was a cyclathon every year at a park in Worcester. Some top name bicycle racers from the U.S.A. and a few international bicycle racers would participate. The Aurora Project was in charge of part of it. We would load up a couple of the PIP Homeless Shelter vans. First, we had to remove the bench seats in the vans. After removing the bench seats we loaded them up with tents, folding tables, folding chairs, cases of soda, hot dogs, hamburgers, condiments, hot dog rolls and hamburger buns, snacks and other foods, a large industrial size gas grille, informational pamphlets and other things.

We set it all up for the race, manned and womanned our stations, and we broke it all down after the race was over. One year, the bicycle race was on a cold, drizzly, November day. I hated that day; still do. I shivered from 8 am until around 4 or 5 in the afternoon.

Whenever the PIP Homeless Shelter made a run to the food bank on Route 9 on the Worcester/Shrewsbury line, they would call the Aurora Project for a few guys. I got the call to drive the PIP Homeless Shelter cargo van to the food bank more than my share of times because I had my driver's license. At least with the cargo van we didn't have to remove the bench seats. The majority of Aurora residents did not have a driver's license. At least that's what they said when they were asked.

I remember seeing a resident driving a car one time after he had graduated from the Aurora Project. The next time I saw him at a meeting, I said to him, "I didn't know that you had your license?" He said, "I've had it all my life. I've never lost it." I said, "How come you didn't raise your hand that time at the morning meeting when Larry asked for a show of hands of people who had their licenses?" He said, "And then have to do all the shit that you had to do. What are you, nuts?"

Have you ever tried loading a cargo van from front to back, floor to ceiling, on your knees with cases of food? Boy, does that suck. Oh ya, we had to unload it too …

Often times, when the PIP Homeless Shelter's fourth floor meeting hall had to be decorated for whatever the season, the Aurora Project got the call. There is a sober cafe on the fourth floor of the PIP Homeless Shelter called the Justice cafe. The Aurora Project is in charge of running it. And restocking it. They have a pool table, some sofas, tables and chairs. It's a nice place to relax in a sober environment. The bar sells coffee, soda, juice, bottled water and snacks. You can still smoke cigarettes in there, as far as I know. Have you ever noticed how many of us alcoholics and drug addicts smoke cigarettes?

The first week that I was back at the Aurora for my second trip, I was volunteered to help restock the Justice Cafe. We had just finished having our morning meeting. The Justice Cafe committee called for their own meeting right after the morning house meeting. About five or six ladies and guys sat together around one of the building community room tables.

I got up from a table and instead of heading upstairs to my apartment, I went and sat down on one of the comfortable chairs in the building community room, next to the window. I wanted to rest before I went upstairs. I didn't pay too much attention to their meeting, until, I heard someone say, "Who is going to drive the cargo van to BJ's now that Jeff has relapsed? Does anyone have a license?" Kevin said, "Dave does." They all looked at me. I looked at all of them. And I said, "I didn't fart."

I knew that I should have gone upstairs after the morning house meeting. If only I had had the energy. I think that driving the cargo van to BJ's to get supplies for the Justice Cafe was about the only extra thing that I did during my first seventeen months back at the Aurora Project. It took all the energy that I had to do that.

The Aurora Project had fifteen residents/clients on the sixth floor and fourteen on the fifth floor of the Aurora Apartments building. One of the studio apartments on the sixth floor was the program's community room. One of the studio apartments on the fifth floor was Larry's (Director) office and another studio apartment on the fifth floor was Bob C.'s apartment (House Manager). Bob C. was the House Manager both times that I was there at the Aurora Project. Bob was there for about five years.

Bob is a good guy and he was an excellent house manager. He has retired from that job. That is one job that you couldn't pay me enough money to do. There are way too many headaches involved with that job. There are way too many addicts in programs who are always trying to cut corners, not do what they are suppose to do, get over on or get away with whatever they can.

After Bob retired, he moved into the Odd Fellows Loft Apartments building. They are next to the Santiago's Market building which is next to the Aurora Apartments building. The Odd Fellows Loft Apartments building is owned and operated by the same outfit that runs the Aurora Apartments-Community Builders. They bought the building a few years ago and completely renovated it.

It is beautiful, on the inside. The outside is medium. I have been in Bob's place several times. We are good friends. He has a spiral stair case leading to his bedroom loft. All brand spanking new fancy kitchen appliances, island kitchen counter, hardwood floors, modern bathroom, a high ceiling and lots of space. Those apartments have got to be some of the nicest apartments in the City of Worcester.

This part of Worcester is still considered by some to be a somewhat, depressed area to live in. The Community Builders Company has done more than its share to help improve our image.

Kevin and I restocked the Justice Cafe for the next eight months. We would take the PIP Homeless Shelter's cargo van and go to BJ's Wholesale Club in Auburn, Massachusetts, with the PIP Homeless Shelter's BJ's membership card. We would load up the cargo van with cases of soda, bottled water and snacks. We would bring it back to the PIP Homeless Shelter. If we were unloading at the rear door, one guy stayed in the van while the other guy went inside to get the four wheeler flatbed. One of us, on our knees, would hand the stuff to the other one who would stack it up on the flatbed. We would wheel it into the rear door, through the drop-in center where all the dining tables are and where the residents hung out, if they were allowed to.

Sometimes they could hang around the drop-in center all day long and sometimes they couldn't. It depended on the weather and the shelter's policy on that particular day.

Once through the drop-in center, we would push the flatbed onto the elevator, ride up to the fourth floor and into the Justice Cafe. We would do this two or three times until the cargo van was empty. If we off loaded at the front door of the shelter, on South Main Street, we would go from the cargo van through the front door of the shelter to the elevator that was located right inside the front door. It was a lot easier. But the problem with off loading at the front door of the PIP Homeless Shelter was that there wasn't always a parking spot available.

Main Street is a busy street. Double parking on Main Street is dangerous and it is not allowed. The one time that I did double park there, Kevin and I came out to the cargo van for our second trip. There was a Worcester Police vehicle in back of the cargo van. The Officer said to me, "I understand that it is a lot easier for you guys to off load at this door. But, I'm telling you for your own safety, and your vehicles safety and the safety of folks in other vehicles who might run into your van. It is not a good idea to double park here." I thanked him and moved the van to the rear door.

I just woke up. It's 4 PM, 1-14-06. No, I didn't just wake up from going to sleep last night. Last night, I fell asleep around 7 PM and I woke up at 3 am. I got on my computer and wrote three pages for my book, a lot of writing for me at one time. I lied down on my couch around 2 PM and I fell asleep. An hour before that, I had one of my all time favorite meals. Three hot dogs in hot dog rolls, mustard, hot dog relish, chopped onions and pepperoncini's on the side. A meal fit for a king or queen. I love it, always have.

For about two or three years in a row, when we were in our late teens, early twenties, I watched every Monday Night Football game at Steve Burke's (Plank) house. Steve, his brother, Big Al and I watched the games in Steve and Big Al's bedroom. Steve would make six hot dogs at half time. Three for him and three for me. Big Al use to eat turkey sandwiches. French's yellow mustard was our favorite mustard at that time. Monday nights was one of my favorite nights during the football season, if not my favorite.

I saw Steve for the first time in nineteen years a couple of weeks ago. The last time I saw him was at his father's wake, in 1986. He drove from Cape Cod to visit me at my place in Worcester. He took me out for Chinese food and then we watched the New England Patriots last 2005 regular season game against the Miami Dolphins at my place. We both got a huge kick out of Doug Flutie's drop kick for an extra point near the end of the game.

People are still talking about that and will be for quite awhile. It was the first time that had happened in the NFL since 1941. It might have been Doug Flutie's last play as a professional football player. I don't think that Doug is going to play next year, but you never know. I think he is forty-two. He had a long professional football career. And a good one.

Steve asked me if I still liked hot dogs. I told him that I will always love hot dogs and I told him about the additions: Cain's Hot Dog Relish, Cain's Sweet Relish, Gray Poupon's Dijon Mustard or Gulden's Hot & Spicy Brown Mustard, any one of the four, not all four at the same time, with chopped onions and B & G Pepperoncini's. He told me that he was still a straight hot dog and French's Yellow Mustard man. But, he said that he has experimented with different brands of hot dogs over the years. In fact, he told me that he recently tried a new brand of hot dogs. He said that he wasn't sure if he liked them or not, yet. It was great seeing Steve again. He looked good. He's one of the all-time great guys.

Speaking of the guys, the eight ball. Since we reconnected about two years ago, I've seen all of them except J. C. Nickel (John Cumming). I did see John's photo on my computer. Tyracks (Tom Rowan) sent photos to my computer of some of the guys and ladies at a recent get together. I believe that the photos were taken at Poopsie's Restaurant in Marshfield, Massachusetts. John looked the same as he looked in junior high school, high school and just before he left for his first year of college at the University of Houston. That was the last time that I saw him.

Others in the photos were Don O'Leary (Duck) and his wife Patti (Jones), Gerry Cook (Gig), Rick Kennedy (Kennard) and his girlfriend Florrie, Carolyn Royce, who I saw this past summer and Pat O'Connor who I haven't seen in over thirty years. Pat has lost a lot of weight, she looks good. Good for you, Pat. I've been using my very first brand new computer for about a month now. I blew up the computer with those photos on it.

And, of course, Tyracks, or Big T, or T, was in the photo's. I don't know, Tom. It looks to me like you've put on a few pounds. I think that I'm going to have to start calling you, 'Bigger T' from now on.

I see Rick frequently these days. We got in several games of chess in 2005. He still wins the bulk of our games, about 99.99 per cent of them. But I don't feel too badly about that. Not too many folks can beat him in chess. We have a way better than medium time whenever we get together. I hadn't been to a BC football game in way too many years. Rick has treated me to three BC games in the last two years. I hadn't been to a Boston Red Sox game in way too long. I've gone to a half dozen Sox games over the past two years, on Rick. He is a quality guy, always has been and always will be.

A few months ago I went to Rick's place in Jamaica Plain. I took a bus from Worcester to South Station in Boston. Then I walked to the Orange Line in Downtown Crossing, and I took the Orange Line subway train to the Green Street stop in Jamaica Plain. It's about a seven minute walk from the Green Street stop to Rick's place. From Rick's place, we drove to Randolph, Massachusetts, to meet up with Gerry (Gig) and Rich ('The Arm') for pizza and drinks.

I saw Gerry in June of 2004, but I hadn't seen Rich in about thirty years. He didn't look much different than he looked thirty years ago. He looked great, as did Gerry. Gerry and Rich are not ones for e-mailing a lot. But that doesn't stop me from e-mailing them. I remember Rich making a comment in one of his few group e-mails one time. He said that he had received sixty-three e-mails during the past week, and sixty of them were from me. Gerry and Rich are also quality guys as are all the guys in the eight ball. I took a vacation from being a decent guy. I'm starting to get back on track, with a lot of help from friends.

In June of 2004, the first time that I saw Gerry in about thirty years, I also saw his wife, Patty (Tom's wife Terry's sister) and met his son, Kevin and his daughter, Molly.

Don and his wife Patti were there. They looked great. I spent some time talking to Patti. She is a sweetheart. Rick's girlfriend, Florrie, was also there. It was the first time that I met her. Another sweetheart as is Gerry's wife, Patty. We sat on Gerry and Patty's backyard deck most of the evening before moving it inside. It was a beautiful spring evening. Tom treated us to Lynwood's pizza, the best pizza in the world.

Tom has been living in Colorado for the last twenty-four years. He forgot about that when he left Gerry's house in Braintree, Massachusetts, to go and get the Lynwood's pizza in Randolph, Massachusetts, the next town over. He came back five minutes later and said, "How do I get to Lynwood's?" When he came back from Lynwood's, it looked like he was carrying the Leaning Tower of Pizzas. He must have had ten pizzas in his arms. Lynwood's does not box their pizzas. They use two cardboard plates and then they wrap them in brown paper bags. You can carry a lot more of them that way. When the pizza chef came out of the kitchen and handed Tom ten pizzas, he said, "Do you think you ordered enough pizzas?" Tom said, "No, this is my first run. I'll be back in an hour."

Tom and I had arranged ahead of time to spend that Saturday evening at the Holiday Inn in Randolph, Massachusetts, on Tom. Rick and Florrie were heading down the Cape and Don and Patti were heading home to Pembroke, Massachusetts. I think we left Gerry and Patty's house around 10 PM. We got to the Holiday Inn, checked in at the front desk and got our room keys. They were right across the hall from each other. We were tired and decided to call it a night. I had made a cardboard sign the previous day that I had in my travel bag. I wrote on it in black marks-a-lot "Do Not Disturb I Am Having Sex". I waited about fifteen minutes after Tom and I had said good night and then I took out my sign and my roll of duct tape. I ripped off a piece of duct tape, doubled it over and stuck it on the back of my sign. I quietly opened my room door, tip toed across the hall carpet and stuck the sign on Tom's room door.

I got up early the next morning, around 6 am. I wasn't suppose to smoke cigarettes in my room. So I washed up quickly and went outside for my fill of smokes. As I entered the hallway, I didn't see my sign on Tom's door. I slowly turned around to look at my door, and sure enough, there was my sign … on my door … I have to get up pretty early in the morning to try to pull something over on Tom.

During Tom's business trips across the country, he has been close to Worcester, Massachusetts, a couple of times in the past two years. He has driven out of his way to come and see me. He came here to see me about a month ago. He took me out to dinner at Friendly's. He wanted to take me somewhere more expensive. I wanted to go to Friendly's. I love their food, especially their cheeseburger platters. The time before that, he took me to Bickford's for breakfast. Again, he wanted to go somewhere a little more expensive. I like Bickford's. I wish that I wasn't so poor. One of these days, I'd like to be able to pick up the tab.

I wrote almost six pages today, an awful lot of writing for me in one day. It's almost time to watch the N. E. Patriots beat the Denver Broncos in tonights playoff game. Tom and his family have been living in Denver for the past twenty-four years. But, once a N. E. Patriots fan, always a N. E. Patriots fan. I know that Tom is rooting for the Patriots tonight.

Well, you can't win them all. Good 2005-6 season New England. Congratulations

Denver! Good luck in the rest of your playoff games.

There is a high turnover rate at the Aurora Project. There is a large population in the City of Worcester. About 175,000 people. I was a resident at the North Cottage half way House in Norton, Massachusetts, in 1994. Our capacity was fifty male residents. I stayed there for the maximum time, six months. During that six months, maybe one or two guys would bail out every couple of weeks, due to relapsing or another reason before their time was finished. I was a resident at the Pathway Halfway House in Gardner, Massachusetts, in 1998. Our capacity was twenty male residents. The maximum time there was six months. I stayed the whole six months. We might lose one guy every two or three weeks.

The capacity at the Aurora Project is twenty-nine male and/or female residents. The maximum length of time you can stay there is five years. During the entrance interview, the director asks each candidate for a commitment of at least two years. It may be different now that SMOC has taken over. Every candidate says, sure, I can give you two years. They have to say that in order to be considered for acceptance. But hardly anyone lasts for two years. My friend, Nelly, interviewed for a spot and was accepted. She brought her bag into her new apartment. She sat down in a chair and began to read the Aurora Project's Rules & Regulations.

She got up from her chair after reading for about five minutes. She grabbed her bag, dropped her apartment keys off at the director's office and took the elevator down to the third floor. I moved to the third floor of the Aurora Apartments building after graduating from the Aurora Project my second time. Nelly knocked on my door. When I opened my door, the first thing that she said was, "You have got to be shitting me!" I said, "Come in darling, and tell me all about it."

So she did. She told me that there was no way she was going to do all the crap the Aurora Project wanted her to do. I said, "Nelly, how bad do you want it? How bad do you want to stay away from that first one?" She said, "Not that bad!" She ended up going back to jail a month or so later, for prostitution. She got out of jail a couple of months ago. My friend, Jenny, who was in jail with Nelly, said that Nelly went right from MCI Framingham, to a half way house in Boston. I hope that she is still doing good, one day at a time.

Because of the high turnover at the Aurora Project, we, as Aurora Project residents, had more work to do. When a resident relapsed or got thrown out for another reason or left on her/his own before he/she had planned on leaving, someone had to pack up all their stuff and bring it over to the third floor of the PIP Homeless Shelter for storage. It is amazing how much stuff folks start to accumulate in a very short period of time when they have their own apartment to put that stuff in.

We can get free clothing at the PIP Homeless Shelter's clothing room and also at the Salvation Army's clothing room which is a two minute walk from the Aurora building. The Salvation Army also has a clothing store and furniture store located in a different part of the city, on the bus line. Their prices are good. The Emmanuel Baptist church, about a ten minute walk from the Aurora building, sells a lot of different used items at a decent price. There are other discount stores as well in this area.

I can't say that every person who went to the Aurora Project did his/her share when it came to doing the extra stuff. They didn't. But, some of us did. There were times during those first seventeen months of my second trip back to the Aurora Project when Larry asked me to do something 'extra', and I wasn't sure if I was going to be able to do it or not. I always said yes (I think), and sometimes I prayed. "Lord, give me the strength and the motivation to do this."

The one nice thing about participating in all the things at the Aurora Project that we had to participate in, and all the extra things that we were asked to do, was, it got my mind off of obsessing for a drink and a drug. I would be so busy complaining to myself or to someone else about what I was doing that I wouldn't have time to think about a drink and a drug. I think the Salvation Army calls that 'Work Therapy'. After I was finished working or participating in something, I would go right back to obsessing, during those first seventeen months.

I know that I went off track, again. I've gone off track a lot in the course of writing this book. I'm not a professional writer. I have never written a book before. My publisher offers editing services. They are expensive, for me. I cannot afford them. The way that I have written this book is the way that it will be published. Mistakes and all. I could have taken the advice of the few of the AA long timers who said to me, don't even attempt to write a book until you've got at least five years of recovery under your belt. But I didn't. And I'm still glad that I didn't listen to them.

I know that there are a lot of mistakes in this book. But, I'm pretty sure that I have been getting my messages across. I set a goal to write this book. I accomplished that goal. I finished writing this book. I'm revising it now. I wrote this book to the best of my ability. That's the important thing. I gave it my best shot.

That decision that I had to make was to either drink and drug, or sign up at the YMCA. After the morning house meeting one day, I went upstairs to my apartment. I changed into my work out clothes and put a lot of money in one of my pockets. I walked out the front door of the Aurora building. I turned right and walked past Santiago's Market, past the Odd Fellows Loft Apartments building (it was being renovated at that time), past the Santiago's Market parking lot. I continued walking past a vacant lot that is now a used car dealership, past a vacant store that is now a small furniture store and past a beauty salon on the corner of Main and Wellington streets.

I stopped there at the corner. I lit a cigarette. I looked straight ahead in the direction of the YMCA, maybe 200 yards ahead and on the right. I looked to my right, down Wellington Street in the direction of the Brother's Two barroom, about forty yards ahead and set back off of the street, on the right. I smoked my cigarette. A life or death decision. Anytime anyone is thinking about relapsing, it is a life or death decision. We do not know if we are going to make it back. I finished my cigarette and I lit up another.

I had plenty of money in my pocket. Three or four beers and then an eight ball of crack, or … go to the gym to sign up and work out. I decided to sign up at the Y. I had already been a member at this branch before, the Central Branch of the YMCA-Worcester. I had signed up before sometime during my first trip to the Aurora Project.

When you walk through the front door of the Central Branch of the YMCA in Worcester, you are entering a different world. The YMCA is a tremendous outfit. My good friend, John, was working behind the front desk. He is a hell of a nice guy. He has been working there for the last nine years. He has a son named David, around twenty years old who he has talked to me about a couple of times. He loves his son and is proud of him. I hope David feels the same way about his father.

The YMCA kept me from relapsing on that day. I worked out for the next sixty-five consecutive weeks, M-W-F and a half work out on Saturday mornings. I missed under five scheduled workouts over that period of time. It was the first week in May of 2003 when I signed up. I stopped going to the gym sometime in August of 2004. During that period of time, my appearance had changed a little bit. I had bulked up a bit. Nothing like I would shoot for when I was younger. Just enough to start to feel good about myself. At my age, it's not important how much weight I'm working out with. What is important is showing up on a regular basis, staying dedicated. Or, like one of my older pals at the gym use to say, "I'm here and I'm moving. If you see me stop moving, don't bother calling 911. It won't do any good."

He was eighty-eight years old at that time. Chet would get on my case about cigarettes once in awhile. He never smoked in his life. Besides telling Chet that I was too busy working on other stuff to concern myself with quitting cigarettes, I would also say, "Chet, my man. What is better out of the following three equations: going to the gym and not smoking cigarettes; going to the gym and smoking cigarettes; or, not going to the gym and smoking cigarettes?" Chet said, "Going to the gym and not smoking cigarettes, you knucklebrain." I said, "That's correct. Now, which equation is the worst?" He said, "Not going to the gym and smoking cigarettes. What do you think, that I'm stupid?" I said, "I think that you are very smart for never having smoked cigarettes in your life." He said, "You're damn right, kid." I said, "Now, the middle equation is the medium way to go and I'm a medium type of a guy." He shook his head and laughed a little bit saying something about me being a unique character ... or a strange character ... one or the other.

One morning, in the middle of December, 2003, I was sitting on my couch in my apartment in the Aurora Project, drinking my cup of coffee and smoking a cigarette. I had accumulated a little over two years in the Aurora Project and a little over twenty-five months of recovery under my belt. It was time for me to make other arrangements. It was time for me to move on.

I would like to share one more quick story with you before I wrap up my book. I decided to stay in the Aurora Apartments building, the public part, floors one through four. I like this building very much. I like the studio apartments in this building very much. There are a lot of good people who live in this building. I believe that this area of Worcester (South Main Street) is improving. Every day this area is getting to be a better area to live in, I believe.

I went down to the building manager's office to talk to Steve about renting an apartment on one of the public floors. He said that he would have an apartment for me by the first of February, about six weeks from the time that I spoke to him. Steve requires the first months rent and a security deposit ahead of time. I paid him the money and was anxious about getting my own apartment and anxious about getting out of the program. On January 27th, 2004, Steve gave me the keys to my new apartment, number 305 on the third floor. It was beautiful, a perfect studio apartment for me. All the apartments are a little bit different from each other. I loved it.

My rental lease clearly stated that I wasn't allowed to attach shelves to my walls. But, me being me ... that didn't stop me. I had finished putting up five shelves. Two small shelves for my stereo speakers, up high and in the corners. One shelf for my stereo. One shelf for my microwave oven and one very small shelf for my electric can opener that I bolted to that shelf and hung underneath it. I used the top of that shelf to store my parakeet food. Five down and one to go. My last shelf was a two shelf unit with the bottom shelf sitting on feet on the carpet and the shelf above it sitting on shelving brackets. I almost chose to skip the brackets and go with side walls to support the top shelf. The holes in the bottom of the brackets lined up right in front of the water supply line that fed hot water to my neighbor, Gary's bathroom.

I have hung a lot of shelving in the past and I have never, not once, had a problem. I don't locate studs like some people do. You don't have to. With plastic plugs and sheet metal screws you can locate a hole anywhere you want to. As long as you have cleared the hole first. The way to do that is simple. I tap a small Phillips head screwdriver through the drywall, just through the drywall, no further. Then, I insert my long, thin screwdriver or anything long and thin, through the hole. If there is any plumbing, wiring or anything else in there, I will feel it and then I will locate my hole somewhere else. I did that for the first five shelves, as I have always done in the past. To this day, why I didn't do that for my last shelving unit, I have no idea. All I can say is, ooops ...

I marked out my bracket holes for the first bracket. I was sitting on my butt, working low. Instead of grabbing my small Phillips head screwdriver and hammer next, I grabbed my drill. I drilled into the drywall and into the hot water line. Copper is soft, it doesn't take long to drill through it. I don't even remember feeling the hit, when I hit the line. I pulled my drill bit out and a strong, steady stream of hot water came with it hitting me right in my crotch. Talk about a hot crotch. I had my sweat pants on and it took no time at all for that hot water to penetrate my sweats and underwear.

I was fortunate that Steve and Scott were around, because sometimes, things come up and they are not always available. They were able to shut off the line before I flooded out everyone below me. There was still plenty of water in my place. A pressure line pushes out an awful lot of water in a short period of time. I dumped all the tools out of my five gallon tool bucket and tried to catch as much of the water as I could in the bucket. But, then I'd have to run to the bathroom with it to dump out the water. I also had to call Steve on my phone. I was in panic mode. I couldn't believe what was happening, what I had done.

When Steve walked into my apartment, I could barely see him and he could barely see me. My apartment was filled with steam. My parakeets were going crazy chirping away faster than I thought was possible for parakeets to chirp. They didn't know what the hell was going on. Steve said, "Is that you, Dave?" I said, "Ya, Steve, it's me." He said, "Scott is killing the line right now." And then he said, "This is not good, Dave ... this is not good ..." I said, "I know, Steve ... I know ..." It wasn't a good time for me to try to say something funny.

I thank God that Steve didn't toss me out. He could have. I paid for the damages and the repair work, and I know that Steve undercharged me for those things. He knows that I'm poor. He could have charged me a lot more money than he did. Scott was able to save my carpet with his industrial wet/dry vacuum.

That alone would have cost me about four hundred dollars for a new carpet and installation.

Scott helped me to bring my furniture out into the hallway so that he could dry vac my carpet. Scott cut out about a three inch section of the copper pipe that I drilled through. He held it up to me and said, "Look, Dave. The hole you drilled is perfectly centered in the pipe." I smiled, but, I felt like crying.

A few days after that incident, I was talking to Steve in his office. I had agreed to retire my drill and I told Steve that I wouldn't do anything else in my apartment without getting his permission first. He didn't make me take down the other shelves, because, they were already up. As I was leaving his office I almost said, "By the way, Steve. I'm not going to charge you for washing your carpet ..." But, I thought twice about it.

More than one long timer in AA told me not to attempt writing a book until I had at least five years of recovery under my belt, and ten years would be better. I'm glad that I didn't listen to them. Writing this book has been a lot of hard work for me, but I enjoyed doing it. I feel a sense of accomplishment. I hope you non-addicts enjoyed reading it, maybe learned something. I hope you recovering addicts enjoyed reading it. Maybe I said something that will make you think twice about relapsing, if that has been on your mind. Maybe not. I hope any active addicts who might have read this book (I never read a book when I was active) will make a life or death decision to stop being active, one day at a time, but for the grace of God, and your hard work.

If you dislike most AA meetings, as I do (not for lack of trying; I guess-timated on my calculator that I have gone to about 2,000 AA and NA meetings, mostly AA, since 1981), try to figure out something else that will help you to stay away from that first one. It doesn't matter what it is. As long as you're not hurting anyone including yourself.

We are all different. We all like to do different things. Find a hobby that you like, to keep yourself busy. Go to shopping malls and walk around. Walk around your city or town. Join the gym or go to ball games. Go to an airport and watch the planes take off and land. Tons of things that you can do as long as you, nobody else, *you* enjoy doing them.

AA and NA are not for everyone. If you enjoy going to AA and/or NA meetings or feel that you have to go to stay away from that first one, then do what you have to do. AA is a good outfit. NA is a medium outfit. My opinions. Whatever it takes to stay away from that first one. It's not easy, but, it's worth it. YOU ARE WORTH IT!!! Don't ever let anyone tell you different. Everyone makes mistakes. Some of us have made more mistakes than others. So what. Don't miss out on an opportunity to have a good life.

David C., a well known long timer from the Snug Harbor AA group in the Germantown section of Quincy, Massachusetts, said to me one time around 1982, "You know something kid, about twenty years from now you are going to wish that you didn't play with this fellowship. You are getting away with bouncing in and out of here right now because you are young. You're not ready for recovery. You need it, but you're not ready for it. You're too young and you're too smart to get sober right now. You're too smart for your own good (I'm average intelligent). I hope in twenty years you get yourself sober. If you are still alive."

David C. was right. He was telling me the truth, and he meant well. He is a good man. One of the reasons that I bounced in and out of AA for so long was because I use to over analyze everything. I did not know how to keep things simple. There were other reasons as well, but that was one of the reasons.

My second favorite saying in AA is "Keep It Simple." My first is "Live And Let Live" or, mind your own business.

Some of us have to drink every drink that we drink and do every drug that we do, before it is 'our time' to get straight. I have heard a few people with good recovery time under their belts say from an AA podium that after she/he went to their first AA meeting, they never drank again. Cheeesch ... I wish I could say that. I've never heard any speaker say that from the podium at an NA meeting. That doesn't mean that it hasn't happened. It just means that I've never heard it.

I'm not sure how you feel about me now, Shelley, if you have read this book. I hope that we can sit down and talk ... soon ...

Today is January 16, 2006. Happy Martin Luther King Jr., Day.

978-0-595-40769-9
0-595-40769-2

Printed in the United States
220956BV00002B/29/A

9 780595 407699